CliffsNotes®
Parent's
Crash Course

ELEMENTARY SCHOOL
MATH

CliffsNotes®
Parent's
Crash Course

ELEMENTARY SCHOOL
MATH

David Alan Herzog

WILEY

Wiley Publishing, Inc.

CliffsNotes® Parent's Crash Course Elementary School Math

Published by:
Wiley Publishing, Inc.
111 River Street
Hoboken, NJ 07030-5774
www.wiley.com

The publisher and the author make no representations or warranties with respect to the accuracy or completeness of the contents of this work and specifically disclaim all warranties, including without limitation warranties of fitness for a particular purpose. No warranty may be created or extended by sales or promotional materials. The advice and strategies contained herein may not be suitable for every situation. This work is sold with the understanding that the publisher is not engaged in rendering legal, accounting, or other professional services. If professional assistance is required, the services of a competent professional person should be sought. Neither the publisher nor the author shall be liable for damages arising here from. The fact that an organization or Website is referred to in this work as a citation and/or a potential source of further information does not mean that the author or the publisher endorses the information the organization or Website may provide or recommendations it may make. Further, readers should be aware that Internet Websites listed in this work may have changed or disappeared between when this work was written and when it is read.

For general information on our other products and services or to obtain technical support please contact our Customer Care Department within the U.S. at (800) 762-2974, outside the U.S. at (317) 572-3993 or fax (317) 572-4002.

Wiley also publishes its books in a variety of electronic formats. Some content that appears in print may not be available in electronic books. For more information about Wiley products, please visit our web site at www.wiley.com.

Library of Congress Cataloging-in-Publication Data:
Herzog, David Alan.
  CliffsNotes parents' crash course elementary school math / David A. Herzog.
    p. cm.
  ISBN-13: 978-0-7645-9836-4 (pbk.)
  ISBN-10: 0-7645-9836-8
1. Mathematics--Study and teaching (Elementary).   I. Title: Eelmentary school math. II. Title
  QA135.6.H47 2006
  510--dc22

                                    2005018890

Printed in the United States of America

10 9 8 7 6 5 4

Book design by Elizabeth Brooks
Cover design by Jose Almaguer
Book production by Wiley Publishing, Inc. Composition Services

This book is dedicated to my sister Lois who has successfully undergone surgeries for a brain tumor, several melanomas, breast cancer twice, and thyroid cancer, and keeps on plugging along as an inspiration for all of us.

It is also dedicated to Uncles Ian and Dylan, Alex and Jakob Cherry, Reese, Myles, Kira, and Rocio Herzog, Hailee Foster, Gino Nicholas, Sebastian, and Francesco Bubba, all their parents, and Grandma Birdie.

Acknowledgment

The late Robert B. Davis, professor at Webster College and Syracuse University, was director of the Madison Project in the 1960s and 1970s, a program named for the Madison School in Webster Grove, Missouri, primarily funded by the National Science Foundation, and seeking to improve the teaching of school mathematics.

Bob, as he was known to almost everyone who was acquainted with him, was a quiet, dedicated man, who worked tirelessly to help math teachers to make their subject more user-friendly to their pupils. He was widely responsible for familiarizing the rest of us with the work of Jean Piaget, and to the U.K.'s Nuffield project. Through a series of freely lent films of himself and other selected teachers working innovatively in the classroom, I and others gained a clearer understanding of how math can be taught as a subject our students could enjoy learning.

I was honored to have been taken under his wing in the early seventies, as an associate of the Madison Project, while participating in one of his workshops at Syracuse University, and I shall be ever grateful for his influence on my subsequent successes as an educator.

Table of Contents

Introduction: Combining and Uncombining

Often parents are called upon to help their school-aged children with their homework, and just as often the parents have been removed from the subject matter for so long that they need to refamiliarize themselves with the basics of the material. That's what the *Parent's Crash Course* series is about.

This particular book is intended to help you, as parents, refresh your understanding of and familiarity with elementary school mathematics. Elementary math teachers approach the subject in several different ways, depending upon the way they were trained to teach it and their personal educational philosophies. Although we can't hope to cover all of those philosophies and techniques in the scope of this one volume, we'll try to stick to the underlying subject matter, so that you'll have the information that you need which you can then plug into the particular teaching approach being used at your child's school.

The concept of number is probably the first topic that needs to be dealt with, but we'll take that up second. Before that we need to take an overview of arithmetic—the primary operations of mathematics. There are two and only two types of operations in arithmetic. First is the type of operation that combines numbers, or puts them together. Second is the type of operation that uncombines numbers, or takes them apart.

When it comes to combining numbers, we can use two sub operations. The first is addition, wherein numbers are combined by a method that can be as simple as tallying. You have two sheep; you make two marks. You get three more sheep; make three more marks. How many sheep do you have altogether? Well, to find out, count up the marks. This is known as placing sheep and marks in one-to-one correspondence. This probably was the earliest form of numeration and counting used by the first shepherds.

> Primitive tribes used to have separate sets of counters for tallying flat things and round things. By the time numbers tallied got much larger than five, the idea of four marks and a slash to mark the complete five came into favor. After all, this is not much different than counting on one's fingers, and grouping the amounts into fives, just like the number of fingers on each hand. Try not to lose sight of the fact that the main reason we count in a system based on the number 10 is because we have two hands, and a total of 10 fingers on them.

Of course, our system of numbers has made the process in some ways more complicated, and in some ways easier. The second combining operation is multiplication. Multiplying is really a shortcut for repeated adding of the same quantity, for example 3 + 3 + 3 + 3 can be represented by 4 × 3 (4 times 3). The results are the same, 12.

For uncombining, we have the operation of subtraction, denoted by the minus sign (–). If we started out with 16 goats and 4 of them were sold, we remove those sold goats from our flock: 16 – 4 = 12. Take away 4 goats from 16 and only 12 goats **remain.** (You'll find words appearing in **boldface** in each chapter are in the Terms You Should Know section at the beginning of each Part.) The other uncombining operation is division. Often students have difficulty understanding division because they don't get the whole story. Division is repeated subtraction of the same number. 16 – 4 – 4 – 4 – 4. Having reached 0, we now count up how many 4s we were able to subtract and discover that it was 4. That might be written as 16 ÷ 4, or 16 divided by 4. Division is also the undoing of multiplication. $16 \times \underline{\quad} = 4$ could also be written $16 \div 4 = \underline{\quad}$. In all cases, the quotient is 4.

One thing is very important to bear in mind when learning or helping one to learn mathematics: Math is, in the immortal word of *Star Trek*'s Mr. Spock, "logical." If what you have just read does not make sense to you, read it again. The odds are that you missed or misread something. If after thinking about and trying out what you've read, it still doesn't make sense, go online if you have access to the Internet. There are plenty of math-help sites out there. Otherwise, call a friend who might have a better knowledge of the subject matter and can explain it to you. After all, if you don't understand something, you're not going to be able to help your student to understand it. Hopefully, I've made things clear enough in this book that you'll understand what each topic is about, but never hesitate to question.

Now that we've gotten that out of the way, let's get down to the concept of whole numbers.

Part 1
Whole Numbers

Terms You Should Know

After each word in the Glossary, the lesson where it first appears is cited. Occasionally a second or third appearance is also given if there are additional major references, but not all appearances of each word are necessarily cited.

append (Lesson 12). Stick on to the end; Example: to multiply 43 by 100, append two zeroes to the 43. [$43 \times 100 = 4300$].

associative property (Lessons 2, 4). Applies to addition and multiplication only and says however you group the numbers for addition or multiplication, the answer is not affected.

cardinal numbers (Lesson 1). The numbers we count with; a.k.a. counting numbers or natural numbers.

commutative property for addition (Lesson 2). No matter which way you add two numbers, the answer is always the same. That may be abbreviated as $a + b = b + a = c$.

commutative property for multiplication (Lesson 4). No matter which way you multiply two numbers, the answer is always the same. That may be abbreviated as $a \times b = b \times a = c$.

composite number (Lesson 14). The name applied to a number with more than 2 factors.

counting numbers (Lesson 1). See cardinal numbers.

decade (Lesson 13). A group of ten things; another name for the tens place (in addition, of course, to being ten years).

difference (Lesson 3). The answer in a subtraction; see remainder.

dividend (Lesson 10). In a division, the number being divided into.

divisible (Lesson 14). Can be perfectly divided by another.

divisor (Lesson 5). The number being divided by in a division.

exchange (Lessons 2, 3). See "rename"; also used to refer to money or barter.

factor (Lessons 9, 12, 14). **1.** *n.* A number multiplied to form another. **2.** *v.t.* To divide a quantity out of another.

ladder division (Lesson 10). A form of division in which groups of the divisor are repeatedly subtracted and written on steps below the division bracket.

magnitude (Lesson 1). A fancy word for size.

minuend (Lesson 8). The top number in a place value subtraction, or the number being subtracted from.

multiplicand (Lesson 9). The number being multiplied; the top number in a place value multiplication.

multiplier (Lesson 9). The number being multiplied by; the bottom number in a place value multiplication.

natural numbers (Lesson 1). See cardinal numbers.

ordinal numbers (Lesson 1). The numbers that are used to show position, that is 1st, 2nd, 3rd, . . . 25th, and so on.

parameter (Lesson 13). Is a word with several different meanings, but it is used in this book to mean a boundary or limit.

prime number (Lesson 14). A number which has exactly two factors, itself and one.

product (Lesson 4). The answer in a multiplication.

quotient (Lesson 5). The answer in a division.

regroup (Lesson 6). See "rename."

remainder (Lesson 3). **1.** The answer in a subtraction; see difference. **2.** The leftover amount in a division; the part not divided.

rename (Lesson 6). **1.** In addition, regroup ten of one quantity for one of the group under the column heading to its immediate left. **2.** In subtraction, regroup one of a quantity for ten in the column to its immediate right; also called "exchange."

running total (Lesson 12). An arithmetic operation where subtotals are found using two numbers at a time, and then another number is added to, subtracted from, used to multiply, or divided into the prior total; (often done with a calculator).

Sieve of Eratosthenes (Lesson 14). A hundreds square 10 across and 10 high naming the first 100 natural numbers and used to find prime numbers.

subtrahend (Lesson 8). The amount being subtracted, or the bottom number in a place value subtraction.

sum (Lesson 2). The answer in an addition.

tolerance (Lesson 11). The allowable amount of variation from a preset standard.

trial dividend (Lesson 10). Created by rounding the first two digits of a division's dividend or partial dividend to the nearest 10 for use with the trial divisor.

trial divisor (Lesson 10). Created by rounding the divisor to the nearer 10, 100, or whatever and then using only the leftmost digit to estimate a partial quotient in conjunction with the partial dividend.

within tolerance (Lesson 11). Within acceptable limits; see "tolerance."

Order and Magnitude

Most people think of numbers as a way of counting things, such as the number of students in a class or the number of lemon seeds in a glass of iced tea. Counting certainly is one way to use numbers. The numbers we count with are known as **cardinal numbers.** They have other names too, such as **counting numbers** and **natural numbers.** Totally distinct from the cardinal numbers, but obviously related to them, are the **ordinal numbers.** These are the numbers that are used to show position, that is 1st, 2nd, 3rd, . . . 25th, and so on. Some elementary math teachers will dwell upon these distinctions, but others will not. It is, however, a distinction that you should make sure that your child knows.

A much more important distinction exists in the meaning of numbers that some children are not taught, but are left to stumble upon, if they ever do. Rather than spelling it out immediately, I'd like you to consider the following diagram.

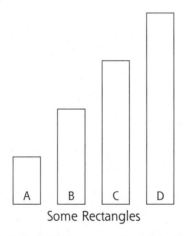

Some Rectangles

Suppose that we let the rectangle labeled "A" have a value of 1. Which rectangle would have a value of 2? You didn't have to think about that for very long, did you? If "A" has the value of 1, then the next one, "B" would be two. It's simple enough. Two comes after one; one comes before two.

Now, with that in mind, let's assign the value 1 to rectangle "B." Which rectangle would have the value 2? Hmm, this one may require a bit more thought. I'm certain that you're not considering rectangle "A" for a multitude of reasons, which I shall not yet share with you. How about rectangle "C?" C is next in line. Just as "B" followed "A", "C" follows "B." Well, that might or might not look good to you, but I'm afraid that "C" won't do. That's because there's more to the concept of numbers than just order or sequence. Two doesn't just come after one. Its **magnitude** is twice that of one. Which rectangle follows "B" and is twice as big as "B?" That would be rectangle "D." Therefore, if "B" is 1, "D" is 2.

Order and magnitude are the two essential properties of numbers. The reasons I was so sure you would not select "A" for 2 in the last mental exercise was that you would never move to the left to get a larger number, and you would never pick a smaller bar to represent a larger quantity. I know from many years of teaching experience that more than 50% of students will disregard relative magnitude and just go for the next larger in line, "C."

By the way, if "B" is 1 and "D" is 2, what are "A" and "C?" Take a moment and think about it. Since "A" is half the size of "B," it would stand for the number $\frac{1}{2}$. "C" is as big as "B" added to "A", and so would represent the number $1\frac{1}{2}$, but that's a topic for later concern.

Suppose that we assigned the value 1 to the rectangle "C." Suppose also that we added rectangles that grew at the same rate as the four pictured previously and were sequentially lettered. Which invisible lettered rectangle would have the value 2?

Did you think about it? It's going to be twice the size of "C". Just in case you need help, here's another figure. If you got the correct answer without need for the figure, good job.

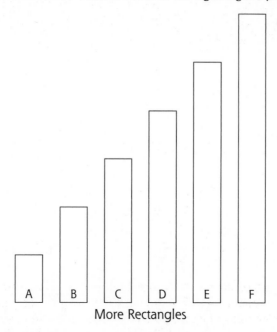

More Rectangles

The rectangle that's twice the height of "C" is "F," so when "C" has a value of 1, "F" has a value of 2. Remember, sequence *and* magnitude. Make sure that your child learns that. If you would like to know the values of "A," "B," "D," and "E," after you've thought about it, look at the footnote at the bottom of this page.*

---

*Answers: "A" = $\frac{1}{3}$ "B" = $\frac{2}{3}$ "D" = $1\frac{1}{3}$ and "E" = $1\frac{2}{3}$

Addition Facts

Addition (or adding) is the first and simplest combining operation. It is based upon counting and then naming the highest number counted. For example, if there were two sheep to your left and one sheep to your right, you might start on the right and count one and then turn left and continue two, three, hence 1 + 2 = 3. I'm sure you know that " + " is the plus sign indicating addition and " = " means "is equal to," but I don't want to take anything for granted.

It is essential that **addition facts** be committed to memory. By addition facts, I mean all **sums** (results of additions) totaling 10 or less. It is best to begin using counters of some type. Actually more than a single type is best. Pennies are readily available, as are pencils, matchsticks, nickels, paperclips, and so forth. Start your child out with 10 of any one of these, and let her show and tell you all combinations adding up to 10 or less, two at a time. Then do the same with a different counter. After four or five such exercises, move on to paper and pencil. There are 100 addition facts, and they follow this paragraph.

1. 1 + 0 = 1	**19.** 2 + 8 = 10	**37.** 5 + 2 = 7
2. 1 + 1 = 2	**20.** 3 + 0 = 3	**38.** 5 + 3 = 8
3. 1 + 2 = 3	**21.** 3 + 1 = 4	**39.** 5 + 4 = 9
4. 1 + 3 = 4	**22.** 3 + 2 = 5	**40.** 5 + 5 = 10
5. 1 + 4 = 5	**23.** 3 + 3 = 6	**41.** 6 + 0 = 6
6. 1 + 5 = 6	**24.** 3 + 4 = 7	**42.** 6 + 1 = 7
7. 1 + 6 = 7	**25.** 3 + 5 = 8	**43.** 6 + 2 = 8
8. 1 + 7 = 8	**26.** 3 + 6 = 9	**44.** 6 + 3 = 9
9. 1 + 8 = 9	**27.** 3 + 7 = 10	**45.** 6 + 4 = 10
10. 1 + 9 = 10	**28.** 4 + 0 = 4	**46.** 7 + 0 = 7
11. 2 + 0 = 2	**29.** 4 + 1 = 5	**47.** 7 + 1 = 8
12. 2 + 1 = 3	**30.** 4 + 2 = 6	**48.** 7 + 2 = 9
13. 2 + 2 = 4	**31.** 4 + 3 = 7	**49.** 7 + 3 = 10
14. 2 + 3 = 5	**32.** 4 + 4 = 8	**50.** 8 + 0 = 8
15. 2 + 4 = 6	**33.** 4 + 5 = 9	**51.** 8 + 1 = 9
16. 2 + 5 = 7	**34.** 4 + 6 = 10	**52.** 8 + 2 = 10
17. 2 + 6 = 8	**35.** 5 + 0 = 5	**53.** 9 + 0 = 9
18. 2 + 7 = 9	**36.** 5 + 1 = 6	**54.** 9 + 1 = 10

"What?" you're no doubt gasping. "I thought the book said 100."

Well, I kind of lied to you—twice. First of all, I said "I call addition facts sums to 10 and less." I do, but your child's teacher is probably going to call them sums to 20 or less. But don't get mad yet. I told you that you needed 100 addition facts, although, in fact, the 54 above make the ones we haven't yet gotten to much easier. If you learn the sums we've already done, you'll recognize which combinations make 10. That will make the rest much easier, for reasons you'll see later.

Before going on, I want to call your attention to the addition of "0". For reasons that should be apparent, "0" is known as the identity element for addition. Adding "0" to a number results in a sum that is identical to what you began with. All right. Let's finish the job we started.

55. $2 + 9 = ?$

Well, we know from having learned the preceding facts that $2 + 8 = 10$. 9 is 1 more than 8, so $2 + 9 = (2 + 8) + 1$. The parentheses are used for grouping purposes, tying together what we are going to add next. $(2 + 8) + 1 = 10 + 1 = 11$. Did you follow that? We group to 10 and then add on whatever's left over. Here's the next one.

56. $3 + 8 = ?$ Well, $2 + 8 = 10$, so $3 + 8 = (2 + 8) + 1 = 11$.

57. $3 + 9 = 2 + 10 = 12$

58. $4 + 7 = 1 + 10 = 11$

59. $4 + 8 = 2 + 10 = 12$

60. $4 + 9 = 3 + 10 = 13$

61. $5 + 6 = 1 + 10 = 11$

62. $5 + 7 = 2 + 10 = 12$

63. $5 + 8 = 3 + 10 = 13$

64. $5 + 9 = 4 + 10 = 14$

65. $6 + 5 = 1 + 10 = 11$

66. $6 + 6 = 2 + 10 = 12$

67. $6 + 7 = 3 + 10 = 13$

68. $6 + 8 = 4 + 10 = 14$

69. $6 + 9 = 5 + 10 = 15$

70. $7 + 4 = 1 + 10 = 11$

71. $7 + 5 = 2 + 10 = 12$

72. $7 + 6 = 3 + 10 = 13$

73. $7 + 7 = 4 + 10 = 14$

74. $7 + 8 = 5 + 10 = 15$

75. $7 + 9 = 6 + 10 = 16$

76. $8 + 3 = 1 + 10 = 11$

77. $8 + 4 = 2 + 10 = 12$

78. $8 + 5 = 3 + 10 = 13$

79. $8 + 6 = 4 + 10 = 14$

80. $8 + 7 = 5 + 10 = 15$

81. $8 + 8 = 6 + 10 = 16$

82. $8 + 9 = 7 + 10 = 17$

83. $9 + 2 = 1 + 10 = 11$

84. $9 + 3 = 2 + 10 = 12$

85. $9 + 4 = 3 + 10 = 13$

86. $9 + 5 = 4 + 10 = 14$

87. $9 + 6 = 5 + 10 = 15$

88. $9 + 7 = 6 + 10 = 16$

89. $9 + 8 = 7 + 10 = 17$

90. $9 + 9 = 8 + 10 = 18$

I think we can skip the $10 + 0$ through 9 that would round out the hundred, don't you?

You should know a couple of properties of addition. First is the **commutative property** that says no matter which way you add two numbers, the answer is always the same. That's usually abbreviated as $5 + 3 = 3 + 5 = 8$, or some such example.

Then there's the **associative property,** which is based upon addition (and all arithmetic operations) being **binary.** Binary is a fancy form of the word two. The point is, you can add only two numbers at a time. If you're going to add, say, $3 + 4 + 5$, you have to group them in pairs. You can group $(3 + 4) + 5$, meaning you'll add the $3 + 4$ first and then add 5 to the resulting 7, or you can group $3 + (4 + 5)$ and then add 3 to the resulting 9. Or, you could rewrite it as $(3 + 5) + 4$, and get $8 + 4$. The associative property says that however you group the numbers for addition, the answer is not affected. The preceding groups all total to 12. See? It all adds up!

Subtraction Facts

Subtraction (or taking away) is the first uncombining (or inverse) operation, and the simpler of the two. It is based upon counting backward and then naming the highest number counted. For example, if you had five chickens and you gave away two, you might start with the five and count five, less one is four, less another is three, hence 5 – 2 = 3. I'm sure you know that "–" is the minus sign indicating subtraction and " = " we've already encountered.

It is not at all essential that **subtraction facts** be committed to memory, since you can think of them as backward addition facts. Think about it: 8 – 3 = 5. That's really another way of saying 5 + 3 = 8. It's really more important to be able to relate subtraction facts to addition facts than to memorize them. Much as I hate to say it, it's possible to go through life using subtraction without ever learning the subtraction facts. You see it at the grocery store every day—if you go to a local non-Megamart. Buy a 35-cent pack of gum (if such a thing exists), and hand the cashier a dollar. He'll go "35 and 5, makes 40, and 10 makes 50, and 50 makes a dollar," and hand you 65 cents change. I call this "subtracting by adding up," or the "making change method."

I doubt that your kid's teacher is going to be placated by my musings here, so again, begin by using counters of some type. Start with a collection of 10 counters of one type and remove groups of varying numbers from that collection. Then do the same with a different counter. After many such exercises, move on to paper and pencil. Don't be shy about making flash cards on 3-×-5-inch index cards. The essential subtraction facts are listed here.

1. 1 – 0 = 0	**16.** 4 – 1 = 3	**31.** 7 – 1 = 6
2. 2 – 0 = 2	**17.** 4 – 2 = 2	**32.** 7 – 2 = 5
3. 3 – 0 = 3	**18.** 4 – 3 = 1	**33.** 7 – 3 = 4
4. 4 – 0 = 4	**19.** 4 – 4 = 0	**34.** 7 – 4 = 3
5. 5 – 0 = 5	**20.** 5 – 1 = 4	**35.** 7 – 5 = 2
6. 6 – 0 = 6	**21.** 5 – 2 = 3	**36.** 7 – 6 = 1
7. 7 – 0 = 7	**22.** 5 – 3 = 2	**37.** 7 – 7 = 0
8. 8 – 0 = 8	**23.** 5 – 4 = 1	**38.** 8 – 1 = 7
9. 9 – 0 = 9	**24.** 5 – 5 = 0	**39.** 8 – 2 = 6
10. 1 – 1 = 0	**25.** 6 – 1 = 5	**40.** 8 – 3 = 5
11. 2 – 1 = 1	**26.** 6 – 2 = 4	**41.** 8 – 4 = 4
12. 2 – 2 = 0	**27.** 6 – 3 = 3	**42.** 8 – 5 = 3
13. 3 – 1 = 2	**28.** 6 – 4 = 2	**43.** 8 – 6 = 2
14. 3 – 2 = 1	**29.** 6 – 5 = 1	**44.** 8 – 7 = 1
15. 3 – 3 = 0	**30.** 6 – 6 = 0	**45.** 8 – 8 = 0

46. 9 – 1 = 8
47. 9 – 2 = 7
48. 9 – 3 = 6
49. 9 – 4 = 5
50. 9 – 5 = 4
51. 9 – 6 = 3
52. 9 – 7 = 2

53. 9 – 8 = 1
54. 9 – 9 = 0
55. 10 – 1 = 9
56. 10 – 2 = 8
57. 10 – 3 = 7
58. 10 – 4 = 6
59. 10 – 5 = 5

60. 10 – 6 = 4
61. 10 – 7 = 3
62. 10 – 8 = 2
63. 10 – 9 = 1
64. 10 – 10 = 0

Just to break up the monotony, let me interject the hope that you've noticed that "0" is the identity element in subtraction as well as in addition. That is to say, subtracting 0 does not affect any number's value.

When larger numbers are subtracted, the place value property will kick in, and you'll never be required to subtract from anything greater than 9, but I'm getting ahead of myself. Just remember that it will be necessary to consider the sums that combine to make 10. That consideration will help to guide you when subtracting.

The answer to a subtraction is known as a **difference** or a **remainder.** Like addition, subtraction is binary. You'll recall that means you can operate with only two numbers at a time.

Unlike addition, order does matter. No commutative property exists for subtraction: 5 – 3 does not yield the same result as 3 – 5. There is also no associative property for subtraction.

One final thought on subtraction facts: Learn your subtraction facts, and you'll always make a difference (pun intended)!

LESSON 4

Multiplication Facts

As already noted in the Introduction, multiplication is a shortcut for repeated addition of the same number. You and/or your student may learn the multiplication facts by rote, or you can learn just some of them and use those to build others. For example, suppose that you need to know what 7×8 is, but you just happen to know that $5 \times 8 = 40$ and $2 \times 8 = 16$. Well, here's a thought for you. Build the multiplication facts you don't know by adding those that you do:

$$5 \times 8 = 40$$
$$+\underline{2 \times 8 = 16}$$
$$7 \times 8 = 56$$

There really are 100 multiplication facts. I wouldn't lie to you (unless it served a purpose, of course).

1. $1 \times 1 = 1$	**18.** $2 \times 8 = 16$	**35.** $4 \times 5 = 20$
2. $1 \times 2 = 2$	**19.** $2 \times 9 = 18$	**36.** $4 \times 6 = 24$
3. $1 \times 3 = 3$	**20.** $2 \times 10 = 20$	**37.** $4 \times 7 = 28$
4. $1 \times 4 = 4$	**21.** $3 \times 1 = 3$	**38.** $4 \times 8 = 32$
5. $1 \times 5 = 5$	**22.** $3 \times 2 = 6$	**39.** $4 \times 9 = 36$
6. $1 \times 6 = 6$	**23.** $3 \times 3 = 9$	**40.** $4 \times 10 = 40$
7. $1 \times 7 = 7$	**24.** $3 \times 4 = 12$	**41.** $5 \times 1 = 5$
8. $1 \times 8 = 8$	**25.** $3 \times 5 = 15$	**42.** $5 \times 2 = 10$
9. $1 \times 9 = 9$	**26.** $3 \times 6 = 18$	**43.** $5 \times 3 = 15$
10. $1 \times 10 = 10$	**27.** $3 \times 7 = 21$	**44.** $5 \times 4 = 20$
11. $2 \times 1 = 2$	**28.** $3 \times 8 = 24$	**45.** $5 \times 5 = 25$
12. $2 \times 2 = 4$	**29.** $3 \times 9 = 27$	**46.** $5 \times 6 = 30$
13. $2 \times 3 = 6$	**30.** $3 \times 10 = 30$	**47.** $5 \times 7 = 35$
14. $2 \times 4 = 8$	**31.** $4 \times 1 = 4$	**48.** $5 \times 8 = 40$
15. $2 \times 5 = 10$	**32.** $4 \times 2 = 8$	**49.** $5 \times 9 = 45$
16. $2 \times 6 = 12$	**33.** $4 \times 3 = 12$	**50.** $5 \times 10 = 50$
17. $2 \times 7 = 14$	**34.** $4 \times 4 = 16$	

Before going on, I want to call your attention to multiplication by or of "1". For reasons that should be apparent, "1" is known as the identity element for multiplication. Your multiplying "1" and another number results in a **product** (the name we give the answer in a multiplication) that is identical to what you began with. Also, multiplication by "0" results in a product of "0." All right. Let's finish the job we started.

Templates for multiplication flash cards may be found in the Appendix.

51. $6 \times 1 = 6$
52. $6 \times 2 = 12$
53. $6 \times 3 = 18$
54. $6 \times 4 = 24$
55. $6 \times 5 = 30$
56. $6 \times 6 = 36$
57. $6 \times 7 = 42$
58. $6 \times 8 = 48$
59. $6 \times 9 = 54$
60. $6 \times 10 = 60$
61. $7 \times 1 = 7$
62. $7 \times 2 = 14$
63. $7 \times 3 = 21$
64. $7 \times 4 = 28$
65. $7 \times 5 = 35$
66. $7 \times 6 = 42$
67. $7 \times 7 = 49$

68. $7 \times 8 = 56$
69. $7 \times 9 = 63$
70. $7 \times 10 = 70$
71. $8 \times 1 = 8$
72. $8 \times 2 = 16$
73. $8 \times 3 = 24$
74. $8 \times 4 = 32$
75. $8 \times 5 = 40$
76. $8 \times 6 = 48$
77. $8 \times 7 = 56$
78. $8 \times 8 = 64$
79. $8 \times 9 = 72$
80. $8 \times 10 = 80$
81. $9 \times 1 = 9$
82. $9 \times 2 = 18$
83. $9 \times 3 = 27$
84. $9 \times 4 = 36$

85. $9 \times 5 = 45$
86. $9 \times 6 = 54$
87. $9 \times 7 = 63$
88. $9 \times 8 = 72$
89. $9 \times 9 = 81$
90. $9 \times 10 = 90$
91. $10 \times 1 = 10$
92. $10 \times 2 = 20$
93. $10 \times 3 = 30$
94. $10 \times 4 = 40$
95. $10 \times 5 = 50$
96. $10 \times 6 = 60$
97. $10 \times 7 = 70$
98. $10 \times 8 = 80$
99. $10 \times 9 = 90$
100. $10 \times 10 = 100$

Multiplication is binary. It is only possible to multiply 2 numbers at a time.

The **commutative property for multiplication** says that no matter the order in which you multiply two numbers, the product is always the same. This is usually abbreviated as $5 \times 3 = 3 \times 5 = 15$, or some similar example.

Finally, there's the **associative property for multiplication.** This says if you're going to multiply $3 \times 4 \times 5$, since you have to group them in pairs, you can group $(3 \times 4) \times 5$, meaning you'll multiply the 3×4 first, and then multiply 5 by the resulting 12, or you can group $3 \times (4 \times 5)$ and then multiply 3 by the resulting 20. Or, you could rewrite it as $(3 \times 5) \times 4$ and get 15×4. The associative property says however you group the numbers for multiplication, the answer is not affected. The groups above all total to 60. So, as it says in the Bible, be fruitful and . . . Oh, I just can't do it!

Division Facts

We already commented in the Introduction that division is the most complicated operation, since it is both a shortcut for repeated subtraction of the same number and the undoing (or inverse) operation for multiplication.

$$12 - 3 - 3 - 3 - 3 = 12 \div 3 = 4$$

You and/or your student do not need to learn the division facts by rote, as long as you can relate them to the corresponding multiplication facts, since ultimately that is the relationship that is most critical.

There are 100 division facts, and that does not happen to be a coincidence. They are

1. $1 \div 1 = 1$	**8.** $8 \div 1 = 8$	**15.** $10 \div 2 = 5$
2. $2 \div 1 = 2$	**9.** $9 \div 1 = 9$	**16.** $12 \div 2 = 6$
3. $3 \div 1 = 3$	**10.** $10 \div 10 = 1$	**17.** $14 \div 2 = 7$
4. $4 \div 1 = 4$	**11.** $2 \div 2 = 1$	**18.** $16 \div 2 = 8$
5. $5 \div 1 = 5$	**12.** $4 \div 2 = 2$	**19.** $18 \div 2 = 9$
6. $6 \div 1 = 6$	**13.** $6 \div 2 = 3$	**20.** $20 \div 2 = 10$
7. $7 \div 1 = 7$	**14.** $8 \div 2 = 4$	

Note that since any odd numbers divided by 2 would result in answers that are not whole numbers, they are excluded from division facts for 2. You'll see similar patterns in the following set. You should also have noticed that 1 is the identity element for division. Anything divided by 1 is itself.

21. $3 \div 3 = 1$	**31.** $4 \div 4 = 1$	**41.** $5 \div 5 = 1$
22. $6 \div 3 = 2$	**32.** $8 \div 4 = 2$	**42.** $10 \div 5 = 2$
23. $9 \div 3 = 3$	**33.** $12 \div 4 = 3$	**43.** $15 \div 5 = 3$
24. $12 \div 3 = 4$	**34.** $16 \div 4 = 4$	**44.** $20 \div 5 = 4$
25. $15 \div 3 = 5$	**35.** $20 \div 4 = 5$	**45.** $25 \div 5 = 5$
26. $18 \div 3 = 6$	**36.** $24 \div 4 = 6$	**46.** $30 \div 5 = 6$
27. $21 \div 3 = 7$	**37.** $28 \div 4 = 7$	**47.** $35 \div 5 = 7$
28. $24 \div 3 = 8$	**38.** $32 \div 4 = 8$	**48.** $40 \div 5 = 8$
29. $27 \div 3 = 9$	**39.** $36 \div 4 = 9$	**49.** $45 \div 5 = 9$
30. $30 \div 3 = 10$	**40.** $40 \div 4 = 10$	**50.** $50 \div 5 = 10$

Templates for division flash cards may be found in the Appendix.

You might have noticed that there have not been any divisions by "0". That's because division by "0" results in a **quotient** (yes, that's the name for the answer in a division) that is undefined. Of course, you can divide "0" by anything and get a quotient of 0. Let's get back to the job at hand.

51. $6 \div 6 = 1$	68. $56 \div 7 = 8$	85. $45 \div 9 = 5$
52. $12 \div 6 = 2$	69. $63 \div 7 = 9$	86. $54 \div 9 = 6$
53. $18 \div 6 = 3$	70. $70 \div 7 = 10$	87. $63 \div 9 = 7$
54. $24 \div 6 = 4$	71. $8 \div 8 = 1$	88. $72 \div 9 = 8$
55. $30 \div 6 = 5$	72. $16 \div 8 = 2$	89. $81 \div 9 = 9$
56. $36 \div 6 = 6$	73. $24 \div 8 = 3$	90. $90 \div 9 = 10$
57. $42 \div 6 = 7$	74. $32 \div 8 = 4$	91. $10 \div 10 = 1$
58. $48 \div 6 = 8$	75. $40 \div 8 = 5$	92. $20 \div 10 = 2$
59. $54 \div 6 = 9$	76. $48 \div 8 = 6$	93. $30 \div 10 = 3$
60. $60 \div 6 = 10$	77. $56 \div 8 = 7$	94. $40 \div 10 = 4$
61. $7 \div 7 = 1$	78. $64 \div 8 = 8$	95. $50 \div 10 = 5$
62. $14 \div 7 = 2$	79. $72 \div 8 = 9$	96. $60 \div 10 = 6$
63. $21 \div 7 = 3$	80. $80 \div 8 = 10$	97. $70 \div 10 = 7$
64. $28 \div 7 = 4$	81. $9 \div 9 = 1$	98. $80 \div 10 = 8$
65. $35 \div 7 = 5$	82. $18 \div 9 = 2$	99. $90 \div 10 = 9$
66. $42 \div 7 = 6$	83. $27 \div 9 = 3$	100. $100 \div 10 = 10$
67. $49 \div 7 = 7$	84. $36 \div 9 = 4$	

Did you notice that these facts are the multiplication facts backward? Speaking of multiplication facts, there are some helpful hints you might or might not have noticed. Did you notice that every multiple of "5" ends in a "0" or a "5"?

Did it occur to you that every multiple of 9 has a first digit one lower than what 9 is being multiplied by? So, 6×9 is in the 50s, 7×9 is in the 60s, and so on. Additionally, the second digit is what you have to add to the first one to make 9: $5 + 4 = 9$, so 54; $6 + 3 = 9$, so 63; and so forth. You might also notice that in every multiple of 3, the digits add up to a multiple of 3. 12: $1 + 2 = 3$. 24: $2 + 4 = 6$, which is 2×3, and so on.

What makes it so easy to learn the 2 table is that it's the same as counting by 2s. (Of course, every other number's multiplication table is the same as counting by that number.)

Neither the commutative property nor the associative property is applicable to the operation of division. Just remember, in the immortal words of Groucho Marx, "Divide and conquer!"

Place Value

A **digit** is a finger or a toe. Interestingly, we have 10 of each. A digit is also a single-place numeral, such as 0, 1, 2, 3, 4, 5, 6, 7, 8, and 9. Count those, and you'll see that there are, not coincidentally, 10 of them. Although the 7 Roman numerals were fine for many hundreds of years, the 10 digits of the modern place value system—especially with the Arab invention of the zero—lets us get a lot more done with less effort. We are able to represent any number with just 10 digits with an economy that the Romans were unable to, because our system of numeration relies not only on the value of the digits, but on their positions within numerals, also known as their **places.**

Number is the idea of quantity, or the actual countable quantity itself. Numeral is the representation of number. If we count five people, that is the number five. We represent that number with the numeral, 5. In the **place value** system, a digit has value based not only upon its magnitude, but also upon its position or place within the numeral.

	hundreds (h)	tens (t)	units (u)
one			1
ten		1	
one hundred	1		

Places are arranged in periods, each of which contains three places, which are arranged from right to left as units (u), tens (t), and hundreds (h). To find the value of a place, read the digit in that place times the name of the place it's in. On the top line of the preceding table is 1 in the units place, or one. On the second line is 1 in the tens place or 1 ten, or as we more commonly call it, ten. Name the three quantities in the following table:

h	t	u
	3	
		4
6		

In this table we have first 3 tens, or 30, then 4 units, or 4, and finally, 6 hundreds, or six hundred. We have looked so far, at the ones period only. Just to the left of the ones period is the thousands period. Check this out.

Thousands			Ones		
h	t	u	h	t	u
	3				
		4			
6					

After we've moved beyond the ones period, it becomes necessary to say the name of the period after reading the column heading, so we have here 3 times 10 or thirty thousand on the first line, 4 thousand on the second line (remember, we don't say units), and 6 hundred thousand.

But there's not always just one digit on a line. Try reading these multiple digit entries:

Thousands			Ones		
h	t	u	h	t	u
	3	5		7	
2		4		6	1
5	2	6	9	3	

We read the first two digits of the top numeral the way we would if they had been in the ones period, but then we add the name of the period before continuing, so we have thirty-five thousand, seventy. Can you see why? Having read the thirty-five thousand in the second period, we continue reading what's in the units period. There were only three digits in that place value numeral. Let's go for four. The middle row's numeral is read two hundred four thousand, sixty-one. Notice that the name of the period is not used until all digits in that period have been read. We don't say two hundred thousand, four thousand, seventy. And, once more, we never say the name of the ones period. Are you ready for the big one? Okay, this last numeral is five hundred twenty-six thousand, nine hundred thirty.

Now let's add one more period. Left of the thousands is the millions period.

Millions			Thousands			Ones		
h	t	u	h	t	u	h	t	u
		4		7				9
	3	5	2	1	5	6	8	
9	2	8	4	3	7	1	6	5

Notice that just like the two periods we've been working with, adding the millions period means another h, t, and u place are added. Have you tried reading these numbers yet? If you haven't, I'll wait while you do.

By now, you should be getting good at this. Try to not be intimidated by the length of the numerals. As long as you're methodical in your approach, longer doesn't mean harder; it just means a few extra words. The first numeral is four million, seventy thousand, nine. Did you notice the commas in the last sentence? It is often customary to separate periods by commas when writing numerals larger than a thousand. More about that in a bit.

The second numeral starts in the ten millions place. It's 3 ten millions, read thirty million, but there's also a 5 in the units column in the millions period, so we read it thirty-five million, two hundred fifteen thousand, six hundred eighty. Finally, the numeral on the bottom line is read nine hundred twenty-eight million, four hundred thirty-seven thousand, one hundred sixty-five.

The next period to the left of the millions is the billions, but we're not going to go there—yet. Hopefully, you have absorbed the pattern of units-tens-hundreds, units-tens-hundreds, repeated as many times as needed, as it would be with billions if needed, trillions if needed, and so forth. The time has come to stop writing those column headings and find some other way of distinguishing one number from another in place value notation.

The problem with writing numbers without column headings is that there is no apparent way to know whether a 3 standing alone means three, thirty, three hundred, or, for that matter, three million. When writing the numerals in columns, we could look at the top of the column and read h, t, or u, and then read which period it was in, so there was no doubt as to what the value was. In order to serve the equivalent purpose, we introduce something called a place-holder. We use "0" as a place-holder, since it has no intrinsic value of its own but will hold any places where there is no other value indicated.

For purposes of writing place value numerals without column headings, we consider all numerals to be right justified. That is to say, the rightmost digit in any place value numeral is considered to be in the units column in the ones period:

Look at 3.   Three is in the units place in the ones period. This numeral is three.

Consider 30.   Zero is in the units place in the ones period. That forces three into the tens place. This numeral must have a value of thirty.

Think about the meaning of 300.   Zeroes occupy the units and tens places. That means that the 3 is in the hundreds place. 300 must be worth three hundred.

Let's look at the last three large numbers one more time.

Millions			Thousands			Ones		
h	t	u	h	t	u	h	t	u
		4		7				9
	3	5	2	1	5	6	8	
9	2	8	4	3	7	1	6	5

Without the column headings and using place-holders, the top numeral is 4,070,009. Notice the commas separating the different periods. Some books and some teachers use a comma for every numeral with more than three digits. In other words, three thousand would be written 3,000. Other books use commas with numerals greater than four digits in length. This book follows the second convention.

The second numeral written in **standard notation** is 35,215,680. The commas should help you to distinguish between periods, but it is now up to you to recall the names and orders of the periods, as well as whether a specific digit is an "h," a "t," or a "u".

The last of the three large numbers, in standard (also known as decimal, since it's based on 10 digits) notation is 928,437,165.

As a general rule, elementary school students are expected to be able to read numbers of as many as 12 digits. In the United States it's the billions period. (In the U.K., a million million is a billion. In the United States, it's a thousand million.)

Essential to understanding place value is the concept of renaming, or regrouping. If you consider counting with individual Popsicle sticks or another type of counter, it is possible to go as high as 9 units, but no higher. In order to add another 1, that 1 must be bundled together with the other 9 units and renamed as 1 group of 10 and 0 units. This is written as 10. Having that group of 10, units can be added to that one or more at a time up to and including 19, but at 9, the units column is full. Adding one more will require a renaming as 2 bundles of 10 and 0 units.

It is possible to continue in the same manner, regrouping 9 units + 1 unit as a bundle of 10 until both the units and the tens column are full. At that time there will be 9 tens and 9 units, or 99. Now, in order to add 1 more, exchange the 9 + 1 units for a bundle of 10, but there's no room for that in the tens place. You must take the 9 bundles of 10 along with the new bundle and exchange those 10 tens for a single bundle of one hundred, making a total of one hundred, no tens and no ones, or 100.

Since no place can ever hold a quantity greater than 9, you can see how the idea of renaming carries on from each column to the next as hundreds are renamed as thousands, thousands as ten thousands, ten thousands as hundred thousands, hundred thousands as millions, and so forth.

EXERCISES

Questions 1–7 refer to the following number: 38,409,056,217

1. What digit is in the ten billions place?
2. What digit is in the millions place?
3. What digit is in the ten thousands place?
4. What digit is in the tens place?
5. What digit is in the hundred millions place?
6. What digit is in the hundreds place?
7. What digit is in the billions place?

8. Write the number four million, eight hundred thousand, seventy-two.

9. Write the number three hundred twenty-nine thousand, five hundred sixty-three.

10. Write the number eighty billion, seventy-one thousand, four.

11. What is the meaning of 38,297?

12. What is the meaning of 321,459,068?

13. What is the meaning of 567,000,814,309?

ANSWERS

1. 3
2. 9
3. 5
4. 1
5. 4
6. 2
7. 8
8. 4,800,072
9. 329,563
10. 80,000,071,004
11. thirty-eight thousand, two hundred ninety-seven
12. three hundred twenty-one million, four hundred fifty-nine thousand, sixty-eight
13. five hundred sixty-seven billion, eight hundred fourteen thousand, three hundred nine

Place Value Addition

Let's assume that you have your addition facts down pat. There is never a need to add any two numbers that sum to more than 18. You might think that I'm making that up, but I'm really not. There might be occasions when you're adding multiple numbers and you find it convenient to add numbers that sum to more than 18, but you never need to. Remember, addition is binary. You can add only two numbers at a time. Well, the largest two digits you ever need to add are 9 + 9, which sums to 18.

Do you need to add 36 and 47? Okay, stack them; that is put one above the other.

$$\begin{array}{r} 36 \\ + 47 \\ \hline \end{array}$$

Now consider the digits in the units (or ones) column. Add them together:

$$\begin{array}{r} 36 \\ + 47 \\ \hline 13 \end{array}$$

But we don't want to put a sum into the tens column since we haven't added the tens yet, so we'll move that ten into the tens column as something still to be added:

$$\begin{array}{r} {}^{1}36 \\ + 47 \\ \hline 3 \end{array}$$

Now we add the 1 + 3 in the tens column to make 4 tens, and finally add those 4 tens to the 4 tens already there: 4 + 4 = 8:

$$\begin{array}{r} {}^{1}36 \\ + 47 \\ \hline 83 \end{array}$$

Now let's recap. To add 36 + 47 we put them into column addition form (stacked), added the ones and when the answer exceeded 10, we renamed the 10 ones as 1 ten. Then, finally, we added the tens. The largest sum we made in a single addition was 13, yet we found that the sum of 36 and 47 is 83. That's pretty cool, don't you think?

Let's try another one. How about adding 65 + 53?

First, stack them:

$$\begin{array}{r} 65 \\ + 53 \\ \hline \end{array}$$

We start adding in the ones column. 5 + 3 = 8, so . . .

$$
\begin{array}{r}
65 \\
+\ 53 \\
\hline
8
\end{array}
$$

That was easy enough. The sum of the ones is less than 10, so there's nothing in need of renaming. Now add the tens. 6 + 5 = 11. Let's show that:

$$
\begin{array}{r}
65 \\
+\ 53 \\
\hline
118
\end{array}
$$

Now 11 is greater than 9, so there's a "1" that falls into the hundreds column, but since there are no other hundreds to add, we can just leave it there. If there had been hundreds to be added, we would move it up top as a number to be added in the hundreds column. We found: 65 + 53 = 118.

Just to prove the point, let's consider the largest two-digit addition of two numbers that it's possible to have: 99 + 99 = __.

To start, put one above the other.

$$
\begin{array}{r}
99 \\
+99 \\
\hline
\end{array}
$$

Next, add the digits in the units column.

$$
\begin{array}{r}
99 \\
+99 \\
\hline
18
\end{array}
$$

They sum to 18, which is a ten and 8 ones, but we don't want to put a sum into the tens column since we haven't added the tens yet, so we'll move that ten to the top of the tens column as one ten still to be added:

$$
\begin{array}{r}
^199 \\
+99 \\
\hline
8
\end{array}
$$

Now we add the 1 + 9 in the tens column to make 10 tens, and finally add those 10 tens to the 9 tens already there: 10 + 9 = 19:

$$
\begin{array}{r}
^199 \\
+\ 99 \\
\hline
198
\end{array}
$$

Alternately, we could have stopped after we added the 1 to the 9, renaming the 10 tens as one hundred:

$$
\begin{array}{r}
^1199 \\
+\ ^099 \\
\hline
8
\end{array}
$$

Finally, add the 0 to the bottom 9 and bring down that 1 hundred:

$$\begin{array}{r} \overset{1}{1}99 \\ \overset{0}{+\ 99} \\ \hline 198 \end{array}$$

Addition is unique among the operations of arithmetic, in that while it is binary and you can add only two numbers at a time, an addition might contain several numbers to be added. Here's an example of that: $5 + 17 + 135 + 72 + 86 =$ __

We already noted in our discussion of place value that numerals are right justified when put into place value columns. That is just as true when aligning numbers in columns for addition. The preceding numbers get arranged as follows:

$$\begin{array}{r} 5 \\ 17 \\ 135 \\ 72 \\ \underline{86} \end{array} \qquad\qquad \begin{array}{r} 5\leftarrow \\ 17\leftarrow \\ 135 \\ 72 \\ \underline{86} \end{array}$$

In order to add, we start with the first two digits in the units column, 5 and 7. Add them together, and we get 12, which we write as a 2 in the ones column and rename the 10 ones as 1 ten.

$$\begin{array}{r} \overset{1}{5} \\ 17 \\ \overset{2}{135}\leftarrow \\ 72 \\ \underline{86} \end{array}$$

Next we move to the 2 and 5, which make 7; then the 7 and 2:

$$\begin{array}{r} \overset{1}{5} \\ 17 \\ \overset{2}{135} \\ \overset{7}{72}\leftarrow \\ \overset{9}{\underline{86}} \end{array}$$

Finally, in the units column, we add 9 to 6 and get 15, from which we write the 5 at the bottom of the column, while renaming the 10 ones as 1 ten, which we add to the already renamed ten at the top of the tens column.

$$\begin{array}{r} \overset{2}{5} \\ 17 \\ \overset{2}{13}5 \\ \overset{7}{72} \\ \overset{9}{86} \leftarrow \\ \hline 5 \end{array}$$

We can speed through the tens column by noting that 2 + 1 = 3, then 3 + 3 = 6, which brings us to 6 + 7:

$$\begin{array}{r} \overset{2}{5} \\ 17 \\ \overset{3\,2}{13}5 \\ \overset{\rightarrow\,6\,7}{\rightarrow\,72} \\ \overset{9}{86} \\ \hline 5 \end{array}$$

If you don't recognize at once that the sum is 13, you should realize that it makes 10 and 3, which is really the more important fact, since we'll write the 3 tens in the tens column and rename the 10 tens as 1 hundred:

$$\begin{array}{r} \overset{1\,2}{5} \\ 17 \\ \overset{3\,2}{13}5 \\ \overset{6\,7}{72} \\ \overset{\rightarrow\,3\,9}{\rightarrow\,86} \\ \hline 5 \end{array}$$

Finish off the tens column by adding 3 tens + 8 tens to get 11 tens, or 1 in the tens column and 10 tens to rename into the hundreds column, adding it to the 1 already at the top to make 2 renamed hundreds:

$$\begin{array}{r} \overset{2\,2}{5} \\ 17 \\ \overset{3\,2}{13}5 \\ \overset{6\,7}{72} \\ \overset{\rightarrow\,3\,9}{\rightarrow\,86} \\ \hline 15 \end{array}$$

Finally, 2 hundreds + 1 hundred makes 3 hundreds, which we write below the line, for a total sum of 315.

$$
\begin{array}{r}
^{\rightarrow\, 2\ 2}\ 5 \\
17 \\
^{3\ 2}\ \rightarrow 135 \\
^{6\ 7}\ 72 \\
^{3\ 9}\ 86 \\
\hline
315
\end{array}
$$

If any part of that did not make sense to you, go back and follow the pairs of arrows through each step. Hopefully, that will clear it up.

Now, all that was to show you that you can do column addition keeping the largest partial sum you will ever have to deal with at 18 or less. Although that is in the realm of the possible, you would have to devote more time than you're likely to be able to spare if you were given a page of additions like that. In reality, after having gained some proficiency with addition, you would be much more likely to solve the same addition in the following manner:

$$
\textbf{(a)}\quad
\begin{array}{r}
5 \\
17 \\
135 \\
72 \\
86 \\
\hline
\end{array}
\qquad
\textbf{(b)}\quad
\begin{array}{r}
^{2}\ 5 \\
17 \\
135 \\
72 \\
86 \\
\hline
5
\end{array}
\qquad
\textbf{(c)}\quad
\begin{array}{r}
^{2\ 2}\ 5 \\
17 \\
135 \\
72 \\
86 \\
\hline
15
\end{array}
\qquad
\textbf{(d)}\quad
\begin{array}{r}
^{2\ 2}\ 5 \\
17 \\
135 \\
72 \\
86 \\
\hline
315
\end{array}
$$

Starting with the ones column in (a), you would go "5 + 7 = 12, + 5 makes 17, + 2 makes 19, + 6 makes 25 [go to (b)] put down 5 and carry the 2." (*Carry* is an old-fashioned word that means rename as whatever the tens digit of what you added was in the next column to the left. That's how I learned it, and by gum I ain't gonna unlearn it. But I digress.)

Moving to the tens column in (b), you'll say to yourself or out loud, "2 + 1 makes 3, + another 3 makes 6, + 7 makes 13, + 8 makes 21 [go to (c)], put down 1 and rename 2 tens at the top of the hundreds column.

Finally, move to the hundreds and add 2 + 1 = 3, [go to (d)], and write the 3, and you're done. The sum is three hundred fifteen. Note, it's not three hundred "and" fifteen. If your student says "and" try to dissuade her. We save "and" for work involving fractions mixed with whole numbers—a subject for which we're not quite ready.

By the way, did you notice that there was no "+" sign in that addition? Since no other operation permits working with more than two numbers at a time, when you see three or more numbers stacked up, you should automatically recognize it as addition.

Let's try one more example before you do some practice exercises. Let's add 737 + 895 + 604. These stack easily:

$$
\begin{array}{r}
7\ 3\ 7 \\
\textbf{(a)} \quad 8\ 9\ 5 \\
6\ 0\ 4 \\ \hline
\end{array}
$$

These happen to all be three-digit numerals, so the columns line up well. Be sure to remember that when they don't line up so neatly, numerals must be right justified.

Since we're now on a new page, I'll redraw the column addition diagram:

(a)
$$
\begin{array}{r}
7\ 3\ 7 \\
8\ 9\ 5 \\
6\ 0\ 4 \\ \hline
\end{array}
$$

(b)
$$
\begin{array}{r}
^{1} \\
7\ 3\ 7 \\
8\ 9\ 5 \\
6\ 0\ 4 \\ \hline
6
\end{array}
$$

(c)
$$
\begin{array}{r}
^{1\ \ 1} \\
7\ 3\ 7 \\
8\ 9\ 5 \\
6\ 0\ 4 \\ \hline
3\ 6
\end{array}
$$

(d)
$$
\begin{array}{r}
^{2\ 1\ 1} \\
7\ 3\ 7 \\
8\ 9\ 5 \\
6\ 0\ 4 \\ \hline
2\ 2\ 3\ 6
\end{array}
$$

Starting with (a), you're going to add 7 + 5 to get 12, and if you must, write the partial sum, renaming the 10 ones as 1 ten. Or, continue and add 4 to the 12, writing the 6 below the line, while renaming as in (b).

Continuing with (b), we move to the tens column, adding 1 + 3 to make 4, 4 + 9 to make 13, and 13 + 0 is still 13 (thought you would never add a zero, didn't you?). Move on to (c) to write the three below the line and rename the 10 tens as 1 hundred.

Continuing with (c), move to the hundreds column. 1 + 7 makes 8, certainly no need to write that. 8 + 8 makes 16; your choice of whether to write before continuing or just keep it in your head, 16 + 6 (you can tell which way I went) makes 22. Since there are no more places to the left to be added, or for the sake of form, write the 2 and regroup the two hundreds. In either case you're covered in (d), where 2 thousands have been renamed at the top and then brought down, since there's nothing to add it to (literally).

EXERCISES

1. 27 + 54 + 67 + 95 + 76 = __
2. 85 + 69 + 94 + 35 = __
3. 28 + 9 + 47 + 6 + 93 = __
4. 687 + 49 + 86 + 394 + 7 = __
5. 81 + 539 + 62 + 94 + 188 = __

6. 534 + 671 + 483 + 32 + 8 = __
7. 95 + 612 + 837 + 86 + 456 = __
8. 437 + 69 + 320 + 4300 = __
9. 526 + 3157 + 694 + 14 = __
10. 6234 + 5893 + 475 + 872 = __

11.
```
    9 5
    4 8
  6 8 7
  9 0 8
```

12.
```
  7 6 4 9
    4 5 0
    8 4 7
  3 5 7 4
```

13.
```
    9 0 8
  8 5 6 4
    4 7 8
  6 8 5 3
```

14.
```
  9 5 7 6
  8 6 8 4
  7 9 8 7
  4 6 7 5
```

ANSWERS

1. 319
2. 283
3. 183
4. 1223
5. 964
6. 1728
7. 2086

8. 5126
9. 4391
10. 13,474
11. 1738
12. 12,520
13. 16,803
14. 30,922

Place Value Subtraction

The operation of subtraction is often known as "take away" by virtue of the fact that it is an undoing operation in which one is often heard to say "What do you get if you take away [some amount] from [a larger amount]?" The subtraction 58 – 26 = __ would be displayed in place value form as:

$$\begin{array}{r} 58 \\ -\ 26 \\ \hline \end{array}$$

The subtraction is accomplished by taking the bottom number away from the top number, moving from right to left, and writing down the **remainder.**

Take 6 from 8 and 2 remain:
$$\begin{array}{r} 58 \\ -\ 26 \\ \hline 2 \end{array}$$

Next, take 2 from 5 and 3 remain:
$$\begin{array}{r} 58 \\ -\ 26 \\ \hline 32 \end{array}$$

The remainder, 32, is also known as the **difference** between 58 and 26.

In a subtraction, the top number, or the number being subtracted from, is known as the **minuend.** The amount being subtracted, or the bottom number, is known as the **subtrahend.** Your student might or might not be required to know these terms, so don't compel him to. First find out whether his teacher requires it.

Let's try that with three digit numerals. Find the difference between 657 and 345.

First write the subtraction:
$$\begin{array}{r} 657 \\ -\ 345 \\ \hline \end{array}$$

How did we know which number was the minuend and which the subtrahend? For all math at the level of the audience for this book, the larger number in a subtraction is always on the top. Again, we'll start subtracting on the right. You might very well ask, "What difference does it make whether we start on the right or the left?"

Well, in the case of this particular subtraction it does not matter, but soon it is going to, so it's better to form good habits than to have to unlearn bad ones later.

Take 5 from 7:
$$\begin{array}{r} 657 \\ -\ 345 \\ \hline 2 \end{array}$$

Next, 4 tens from 5 tens:

$$
\begin{array}{r}
657 \\
-\ 345 \\
\hline
12
\end{array}
$$

Finally, 3 hundreds from 6 hundreds:

$$
\begin{array}{r}
657 \\
-\ 345 \\
\hline
312
\end{array}
$$

So the difference is 312. To check a subtraction to make sure that it is correct, add up from below the line. In the preceding subtraction, $2 + 5 = 7$, $1 + 4 = 5$, and $3 + 3 = 6$, so you know the difference is correct.

And now for something completely different, er, well, a little different. Consider this subtraction: $74 - 38 =$ __.

First write the subtraction:

$$
\begin{array}{r}
74 \\
-\ 38
\end{array}
$$

Now subtract 8 from 4. Huh? How do I subtract 8 from 4? The answer, of course, is without introducing the concept of negative numbers, I can't!

But don't despair; there's always renaming. In subtraction, we use renaming the opposite way of how we used it in addition. We're going to take 1 ten from the 7 tens and rename it as 10 ones:

$$
\begin{array}{r}
\overset{6}{7}{}^{1}4 \\
-\ 3\ 8
\end{array}
$$

Now we can subtract 8 from 14:

$$
\begin{array}{r}
\overset{6}{7}{}^{1}4 \\
-\ 3\ 8 \\
\hline
6
\end{array}
$$

Then on to the tens column:

$$
\begin{array}{r}
\overset{6}{7}{}^{1}4 \\
-\ 3\ 8 \\
\hline
3\ 6
\end{array}
$$

Now let's check that by adding up. Beginning below the line in the ones column, $6 + 8 = 14$. Rename the 10 ones as 1 ten and add it to the 3 below the line in the tens column, to make it a 4. Adding, we get $4 + 3 = 7$. Yep, it checks.

Do you see now why we work subtraction from right to left? Let's add a new wrinkle, by trying the following subtraction:

$$
\begin{array}{r}
756 \\
-\ 468
\end{array}
$$

Note that 8 cannot be subtracted from 6, so you're going to the tens column to get a ten to **exchange** for ten ones:

$$\begin{array}{r} 7\overset{4}{\cancel{5}}{}^{1}6 \\ -\ 4\ 6\ 8 \\ \hline \end{array}$$

Now you can take 8 from 16:

$$\begin{array}{r} 7\overset{4}{\cancel{5}}{}^{1}6 \\ -\ 4\ 6\ 8 \\ \hline 8 \end{array}$$

Uh oh! There's a similar problem in the tens column. Do you know what to do?

It's time to rename a hundred as 10 tens:

$$\begin{array}{r} \overset{6}{\cancel{7}}\overset{14}{\cancel{5}}{}^{1}6 \\ -\ 4\ 6\ 8 \\ \hline 8 \end{array}$$

Now you can take 6 from 14:

$$\begin{array}{r} \overset{6}{\cancel{7}}\overset{14}{\cancel{5}}{}^{1}6 \\ -\ 4\ 6\ 8 \\ \hline 8\ 8 \end{array}$$

And finally, subtract hundreds:

$$\begin{array}{r} \overset{6}{\cancel{7}}\overset{14}{\cancel{5}}{}^{1}6 \\ -\ 4\ 6\ 8 \\ \hline 2\ 8\ 8 \end{array}$$

I leave it to you to check the difference by adding up.

Do you think you've seen all there is to see about subtracting? Well, you haven't. Cast your eyes upon this beautiful subtraction:

$$\begin{array}{r} 804 \\ -\ 789 \\ \hline \end{array}$$

All right; in the units column we have 4 – 9, but you just saw how to deal with that. Whoa! There are no tens to rename as 10 ones. Now what? Well, the answer is go to the hundreds. After all, it's the only place where there is anything to rename. Start by exchanging 1 hundred for 10 tens:

1 hundred makes 10 tens:

$$\begin{array}{r} \overset{7}{\cancel{8}}{}^{1}0\ 4 \\ -\ 7\ 89 \\ \hline \end{array}$$

Now there are some tens to rename:

$$\begin{array}{r} \overset{7}{\cancel{8}}\,\overset{9}{\cancel{0}}{}^{1}4 \\ -\ 7\ 8\ 9 \end{array}$$

Now subtract the ones:

$$\begin{array}{r} \overset{7}{\cancel{8}}\,\overset{9}{\cancel{0}}{}^{1}4 \\ -\ 7\ 8\ 9 \\ \hline 5 \end{array}$$

And subtract the tens:

$$\begin{array}{r} \overset{7}{\cancel{8}}\,\overset{9}{\cancel{0}}{}^{1}4 \\ -\ 7\ 8\ 9 \\ \hline 1\ 5 \end{array}$$

The hundreds subtract to 0, which we never write as the left-most digit of a whole number representation. The difference is 15.

There's yet one more form of subtraction that we need to deal with in this lesson, but after the problem just worked, this probably won't be much of a problem for you.

$$\begin{array}{r} 6000 \\ -\ 2354 \end{array}$$

There are an awful lot of zeroes there before we reach the only place from which we can start to regroup, namely that 6 in the thousands place. So, start by exchanging 1 of those thousands for 10 hundreds.

$$\begin{array}{r} \overset{5}{\cancel{6}}{}^{1}000 \\ -\ 2354 \end{array}$$

Now that we have 10 hundreds, we need to rename one of them as 10 tens, in order to have something to subtract the 5 tens from:

$$\begin{array}{r} \overset{5}{\cancel{6}}\,\overset{9}{\cancel{0}}{}^{1}00 \\ -\ 2\ 3\ 5\ 4 \end{array}$$

Now that we have tens, we need to rename one of them in order to get some ones to subtract the 4 from:

$$\begin{array}{r} \overset{5}{\cancel{6}}\,\overset{9}{\cancel{0}}\,\overset{9}{\cancel{0}}{}^{1}0 \\ -\ 2\ 3\ 5\ 4 \end{array}$$

And there you have it. Every column is ready for its subtraction to be completed, so it's time to do it.

$$
\begin{array}{r}
\overset{5}{\cancel{6}}\,\overset{9}{\cancel{0}}\,\overset{9}{\cancel{0}}\,{}^{1}0 \\
-\ 2\ 3\ 5\ 4 \\
\hline
6
\end{array}
\qquad
\begin{array}{r}
\overset{5}{\cancel{6}}\,\overset{9}{\cancel{0}}\,\overset{9}{\cancel{0}}\,{}^{1}0 \\
-\ 2\ 3\ 5\ 4 \\
\hline
4\ 6
\end{array}
\qquad
\begin{array}{r}
\overset{5}{\cancel{6}}\,\overset{9}{\cancel{0}}\,\overset{9}{\cancel{0}}\,{}^{1}0 \\
-\ 2\ 3\ 5\ 4 \\
\hline
6\ 4\ 6
\end{array}
\qquad
\begin{array}{r}
\overset{5}{\cancel{6}}\,\overset{9}{\cancel{0}}\,\overset{9}{\cancel{0}}\,{}^{1}0 \\
-\ 2\ 3\ 5\ 4 \\
\hline
3\ 6\ 4\ 6
\end{array}
$$

      (a)   **(b)**   **(c)**   **(d)**

Starting on the right, in (a), 10 – 4 = 6; in the tens, (b), 9 – 5 = 4; in the hundreds place, (c), 9 – 3 = 6; finally, in the thousands, (d), 5 – 2 = 3. Now let's check that answer of 3646 by adding up. Starting on the extreme right, 6 + 4 = 10, put down 0 and rename 1 ten. 1 + 4 = 5; 5 + 5 = 10, put down 0 and rename 1 ten (really a hundred, but we're going to disregard that). 1 + 6 = 7 + 3 = 10, put down 0 and rename 1 into the next column. 1 + 3 = 4, to which we add the 2 to get the top number, 6.

Did you notice that it's a routine we are following? After awhile, it's no longer necessary to think in terms of hundreds, thousands, tens, or ones. What we are doing when subtracting is, if necessary, renaming 1 whatever as 10 in the next column to the right. When adding, if necessary, we are renaming 10 whatevers as 1 in the next column to the left. It is important that you understand what you are doing as it reflects operating within the laws of place value, but, having said that, with a little practice, it should become a routine in which the rationale for the mechanics of what you are doing is less important than the actual operating of the mechanism.

Here are some exercises to allow you to practice and develop those necessary routines. And remember, after you've mastered subtraction, you have a skill that nobody can take away.

EXERCISES

1. 87 – 69 = __

2. 78 – 48 = __

3. 817 – 694 = __

4. 572 – 469 = __

5. 368 – 247 = __

6. 534 – 349 = __

7. 344 – 96 = __

8. 634 – 561 = __

9. 354 – 265 = __

10. 836 – 678 = __

11. 737 – 356 = __

12. 807 – 653 = __

13.
$$
\begin{array}{r}
8007 \\
-\ 6354 \\
\hline
\end{array}
$$

14.
$$
\begin{array}{r}
7403 \\
-\ 4528 \\
\hline
\end{array}
$$

15.
$$
\begin{array}{r}
5060 \\
-\ 3421 \\
\hline
\end{array}
$$

16.
$$
\begin{array}{r}
5374 \\
-\ 4466 \\
\hline
\end{array}
$$

17.
$$
\begin{array}{r}
3005 \\
-\ 2968 \\
\hline
\end{array}
$$

18.
$$
\begin{array}{r}
6040 \\
-\ 3508 \\
\hline
\end{array}
$$

19.
$$
\begin{array}{r}
8000 \\
-\ 7265 \\
\hline
\end{array}
$$

20.
$$
\begin{array}{r}
7000 \\
-\ 4356 \\
\hline
\end{array}
$$

21.
$$
\begin{array}{r}
6000 \\
-\ 2857 \\
\hline
\end{array}
$$

ANSWERS

1. 18
2. 30
3. 123
4. 103
5. 121
6. 185
7. 248
8. 73
9. 89
10. 158
11. 381

12. 154
13. 1653
14. 2875
15. 1639
16. 908
17. 37
18. 2532
19. 735
20. 2644
21. 3143

Place Value Multiplication

Place value multiplication at first glance looks pretty much like place value subtraction or two-numeral addition, except for the times sign. It is a pretty good idea, however, to have a good command of the multiplication facts before embarking upon multiplying in place value format.

One-Digit by Two-Digit

The simplest form of place value multiplication is of the one-digit by 2-digit variety:

$$\begin{array}{r} 24 \\ \times\ 6 \\ \hline \end{array}$$

There are traditional names given to the parts of a multiplication. We already mentioned the name of the answer, product, in Lesson 3. The number being multiplied by (the 6 in the previous multiplication) is known as the **multiplier,** while the number being multiplied (the 24) is called the **multiplicand.** Your student's teacher might or might not use these names. The two numbers above the line are also collectively known as **factors.**

Like addition and subtraction, multiplication is performed from right to left, and for a reason. To solve the previous multiplication, first multiply the 4 by 6. The units digit of the product is written in the units column below the line, while the tens digit is renamed into the tens column, as shown here.

$$\begin{array}{r} \overset{2}{2}4 \\ \times\ 6 \\ \hline 4 \end{array}$$

Next, the 2 is multiplied by the 6 (the 2 that was there initially) to make 12, and the renamed number is added to the product to make 14. Since there are no additional numbers to be multiplied, the complete result of the foregoing is written below the line, like so:

$$\begin{array}{r} \overset{2}{2}4 \\ \times\ 6 \\ \hline 144 \end{array}$$

So the product of 6 and 24 is 144.

Try these on your own:

1. $\begin{array}{r} 35 \\ \times\ 7 \\ \hline \end{array}$

2. $\begin{array}{r} 69 \\ \times\ 5 \\ \hline \end{array}$

3.
$$
\begin{array}{r}
75 \\
\times\ 9 \\
\hline
\end{array}
$$

Here are the worked-out solutions, step by step:

1. (a)
$$
\begin{array}{r}
35 \\
\times\ 7 \\
\hline
\end{array}
$$
(b)
$$
\begin{array}{r}
^3\ \\
35 \\
\times\ 7 \\
\hline
5 \\
\end{array}
$$
(c)
$$
\begin{array}{r}
^3\ \\
35 \\
\times\ 7 \\
\hline
245 \\
\end{array}
$$

(a) states the multiplication. (b) $7 \times 5 = 35$, put down the 5 and rename 3 tens.
(c) $7 \times 3 = 21$ + the renamed 3 = 24. The product is 245.

2. (a)
$$
\begin{array}{r}
69 \\
\times\ 5 \\
\hline
\end{array}
$$
(b)
$$
\begin{array}{r}
^4\ \\
69 \\
\times\ 5 \\
\hline
5 \\
\end{array}
$$
(c)
$$
\begin{array}{r}
^4\ \\
69 \\
\times\ 5 \\
\hline
345 \\
\end{array}
$$

(a) states the multiplication. (b) $5 \times 9 = 45$, put down the 5 and rename 4 tens. (c) $5 \times 6 = 30$ + the renamed 4 = 34. The product is 345.

3. (a)
$$
\begin{array}{r}
75 \\
\times\ 9 \\
\hline
\end{array}
$$
(b)
$$
\begin{array}{r}
^4\ \\
75 \\
\times\ 9 \\
\hline
5 \\
\end{array}
$$
(c)
$$
\begin{array}{r}
^4\ \\
75 \\
\times\ 9 \\
\hline
675 \\
\end{array}
$$

(a) states the multiplication. (b) $9 \times 5 = 45$, put down the 5 and rename 4 tens. (c) $9 \times 7 = 63$ + the renamed 4 = 67. The product is 675.

Two-Digit by Two-Digit

Are you ready to get a bit more complex? Let's get to 2-d × 2-d (that's two-digit by two-digit). For openers, let's try 46×68.

$$
\begin{array}{r}
68 \\
\times\ 46 \\
\hline
\end{array}
$$

Remember, multiplication is commutative. If we'd put 68 on the bottom and 46 on the top, the product would still be the same. Once more, we begin on the right, multiplying 6×8.

$6 \times 8 = 48$, so write the 8 below the line and rename the 40 as 4 in the tens place.

$$
\begin{array}{r}
^4\ \\
68 \\
\times\ 46 \\
\hline
8 \\
\end{array}
$$

Next, multiply the 6 times the 6 to get 36, to which you'll add the renamed 4 tens to get a total of 40 tens, also known as 400. Since there are no more digits to the left, we simply write the total into the product:

$$
\begin{array}{r}
^4\ \\
68 \\
\times\ 46 \\
\hline
408 \\
\end{array}
$$

Next, we're going to multiply by the 4, but bear in mind that it is 4 tens. That means there will be no ones in the answer, since 40 times something is not going to produce any units. To account for this, place a 0 in the ones column beneath the 8:

$$
\begin{array}{r}
68 \\
\times\ 46 \\
\hline
408 \\
0
\end{array}
$$

You might have noticed that we cleared the renamed 4 from over the 6. That's because we could. Since you're using paper (I hope), you can just put a line through that 4, so that it doesn't get in your way with the multiplication by 40. Now we're going to multiply by 40, but since its proper place has already been assured by placing that 0, we can act as if we're simply multiplying by 4.

$4 \times 8 = 32$, so we place the 2 in the next available place and rename the 3 to the top of the next column:

$$
\begin{array}{r}
^{3} \\
68 \\
\times\ 46 \\
\hline
408 \\
20
\end{array}
$$

Now, we multiply 4×6 to get 24. Add the 3 to make 27. With no more digits to be multiplied, we can write the whole 27 (really 2700) in place, and add an addition line:

$$
\begin{array}{r}
^{3} \\
68 \\
\times\ 46 \\
\hline
408 \\
2720
\end{array}
$$

Next, add the two partial products together:

$$
\begin{array}{r}
^{3} \\
68 \\
\times\ 46 \\
\hline
408 \\
2720 \\
\hline
3128
\end{array}
$$

And you'll get the product three thousand, one hundred twenty-eight.

Two-Digit by Three-Digit

Let's move on to a multiplication involving a two-digit multiplier and a three-digit multiplicand, say 358×79:

$$
\begin{array}{r}
358 \\
\times\ 79
\end{array}
$$

As usual, begin multiplying on the right side, first multiplying 9×8. That product is 72, so:

$$
\begin{array}{r}
{\scriptstyle 7} \\
358 \\
\times \;\; 79 \\
\hline
2
\end{array}
$$

The 2 goes beneath the 9, while the 7 is renamed as 7 tens on top of the 5. Next, multiply 9×5 to get 45, to which we add the renamed 7, for a total of 52. Since there's another digit in the hundreds column, we write the 2 beneath the 7 and rename the 50 tens as 5 hundreds (that's the meaning of it, but in reality, we write the 2 and rename the 5 into the next column):

$$
\begin{array}{r}
{\scriptstyle 5\,7} \\
358 \\
\times \;\; 79 \\
\hline
22
\end{array}
$$

Next, complete the multiplication by 9, multiplying 9×3 to get 27, plus the renamed 5, which make 32. Since there are no more digits to the left, write the 32 beneath the line, (bearing in mind that it's 32 hundred).

$$
\begin{array}{r}
{\scriptstyle 5\,7} \\
358 \\
\times \;\; 79 \\
\hline
3222
\end{array}
$$

Before multiplying by 70, place a zero in the ones place (multiplying by 70 generates no ones).

$$
\begin{array}{r}
358 \\
\times \;\; 79 \\
\hline
3222 \\
0
\end{array}
$$

I've also cleared the renamed numbers, to make room for new ones. You might want to put a line through each of those on your worksheet to avoid confusion with your forthcoming renamings. Since placing the 0 forces all parts of the next multiplications into the proper places, we can act as if we're multiplying by 7. $7 \times 8 = 56$; put the 6 next to the 0 and rename the 5 into the next column:

$$
\begin{array}{r}
{\scriptstyle 5} \\
358 \\
\times \;\; 79 \\
\hline
3222 \\
60
\end{array}
$$

Next, $7 \times 5 = 35$, to which you'll add the renamed 5 to get 40. Put down the 0 next to the 6, and rename the 4 into the next column:

$$
\begin{array}{r}
{\scriptstyle 4\,5} \\
358 \\
\times \;\; 79 \\
\hline
3222 \\
060
\end{array}
$$

The last multiplication called for is 7×3, which makes 21, to which the renamed 4 is added. Since this is the last multiplication, the whole 25 may be written next to the 0 in the second partial product:

$$
\begin{array}{r}
\scriptstyle 4\ 5 \\
358 \\
\times\ \ 79 \\
\hline
3222 \\
25060 \\
\end{array}
$$

Finally, we add the two partial products together to get the final product:

$$
\begin{array}{r}
\scriptstyle 4\ 5 \\
358 \\
\times\ \ 79 \\
\hline
3222 \\
25060 \\
\hline
28,282 \\
\end{array}
$$

The final product is 28,282. Notice that since the product is 5 digits in length, a comma has been placed between the ones and thousands periods.

Three-Digit by Three-Digit

The most complex multiplication we'll do in this chapter is 3-d × 3-d, as in this one.

$$
\begin{array}{r}
576 \\
\times\ 648 \\
\end{array}
$$

I'll spare you the walk-through of the multiplication by 8. It looks like this:

$$
\begin{array}{r}
\scriptstyle 6\ 4 \\
576 \\
\times\ 648 \\
\hline
4608 \\
0 \\
\end{array}
$$

Feel free to go through it step by step, just to make sure that I didn't screw it up. I've also placed the "0" for the multiplication by 40. I'm going to spare you the step-by-step multiplication by 40, although, again, you are more than welcome to check it out. I've replaced the renaming numbers from the ones multiplication with the numbers from the tens multiplication.

$$
\begin{array}{r}
\scriptstyle 3\ 2 \\
576 \\
\times\ 648 \\
\hline
4608 \\
23040 \\
\end{array}
$$

What do you think comes next? Should there be a zero at the right end of the next line before multiplying by the 6? What is the smallest amount the answer to the next multiplication could possibly be?

$$
\begin{array}{r}
576 \\
\times\ 648 \\
\hline
4608 \\
23040 \\
00 \\
\end{array}
$$

That's right. There can be no ones or tens, since the next multiplication is by a figure in the hundreds column. Two zeroes are, therefore, called for to push the first partial product into the hundreds place. I've also removed the old renamed numbers to make room for the new ones.

$$
\begin{array}{r}
\overset{3}{576} \\
\times\ 648 \\
\hline
\textbf{(a)}\quad 4608 \\
23040 \\
600
\end{array}
\qquad
\begin{array}{r}
\overset{4\ 3}{576} \\
\times\ 648 \\
\hline
\textbf{(b)}\quad 4608 \\
23040 \\
5600
\end{array}
\qquad
\begin{array}{r}
\overset{4\ 3}{576} \\
\times\ 648 \\
\hline
\textbf{(c)}\quad 4608 \\
23040 \\
345600
\end{array}
$$

(a) $6 \times 6 = 36$; write the 6 and rename the 3. (b) $6 \times 7 = 42$ + the renamed 3 = 45; write the 5 next to the 6, and rename the 4 into the next column. (c) $6 \times 5 = 30$ + the renamed 4 = 34; since there are no more numbers to multiply, write it down next to the 5.

Now we're ready to add the partial products, which is done below. Feel free to check the addition. I never was very good at it.

$$
\begin{array}{r}
576 \\
\times\ 648 \\
\hline
4\,608 \\
23\,040 \\
345\,600 \\
\hline
373,248
\end{array}
$$

That comma separates the periods and makes that big numeral easier to read. Now you get to try some on your own. How lucky can you get!

EXERCISES

1. $\begin{array}{r}68\\ \times\ 35\end{array}$
6. $\begin{array}{r}348\\ \times\ 96\end{array}$
11. $\begin{array}{r}381\\ \times\ 567\end{array}$
16. $\begin{array}{r}693\\ \times\ 465\end{array}$

2. $\begin{array}{r}89\\ \times\ 64\end{array}$
7. $\begin{array}{r}657\\ \times\ 48\end{array}$
12. $\begin{array}{r}476\\ \times\ 598\end{array}$
17. $\begin{array}{r}830\\ \times\ 490\end{array}$

3. $\begin{array}{r}73\\ \times\ 87\end{array}$
8. $\begin{array}{r}782\\ \times\ 63\end{array}$
13. $\begin{array}{r}259\\ \times\ 436\end{array}$
18. $\begin{array}{r}387\\ \times\ 645\end{array}$

4. $\begin{array}{r}92\\ \times\ 59\end{array}$
9. $\begin{array}{r}854\\ \times\ 64\end{array}$
14. $\begin{array}{r}800\\ \times\ 706\end{array}$
19. $\begin{array}{r}897\\ \times\ 900\end{array}$

5. $\begin{array}{r}48\\ \times\ 76\end{array}$
10. $\begin{array}{r}509\\ \times\ 23\end{array}$
15. $\begin{array}{r}579\\ \times\ 687\end{array}$
20. $\begin{array}{r}749\\ \times\ 976\end{array}$

ANSWERS

1. 2380
6. 33,408
11. 216,027
16. 322,245

2. 5696
7. 31,536
12. 284,648
17. 406,700

3. 6351
8. 49,266
13. 112,924
18. 249,615

4. 5428
9. 54,656
14. 564,800
19. 807,300

5. 3648
10. 11,707
15. 397,773
20. 731,024

Place Value Division

Division is a bit different from everything we've done until now, first of all because it's done from left to right, and second because it can be handled by approaching it from the vantage point of either of the two related combining operations. Consider the following:

$$12\overline{)156}$$

The bracket indicates division, but unlike the other notation for division, $156 \div 12 =$ ___, which reads "156 divided by 12," this reads "12 divided into 156," in other words, the divisor comes first.

Considering division as a shortcut for repeated subtraction, we can ask, "How many 12s can be subtracted from 156?" There are certainly more than 2 of them, so let's start with 2:

$$
\begin{array}{r}
12\overline{)156} \\
\underline{24 \quad 2} \\
132
\end{array}
$$

Subtracting those 2 12s leaves 132 still to be divided out. Do you know that 10 12s make 120? They do, so I'm going to subtract that out.

$$
\begin{array}{r}
12\overline{)156} \\
\underline{24 \quad 2} \\
132 \\
\underline{120 \quad 10} \\
12
\end{array}
$$

Subtracting those 10 12s leaves 12 still to be uncombined. I know how many 12s there are in 12. (I'll bet you do, too):

$$
\begin{array}{r}
12\overline{)156} \\
\underline{24 \quad 2} \\
132 \\
\underline{120 \quad 10} \\
12 \\
\underline{12 \quad 1} \\
13
\end{array}
$$

By repeated subtraction, we have managed to find that 12 goes into 156 13 times. Some children repeat "goes into" so many times that they think another name for division is "the gazintas." Notice that with this form of division, called **ladder division** after the steps on which the partial quotients sit, is not especially structured. I could have, if I had not recognized 120 as being 10 12s, removed 5 12s and another 5 12s in an additional step, or 4 12s, 4 12s, and 2 12s, or 3 12s, 3 12s, 3 12s, and 1 12.

Far more structured than ladder division, but totally depending upon your knowledge of multiplication facts is what is known as **long division,** but can actually be much shorter than the ladder. Let's start with the same division:

$$12\overline{)156}$$

First ask yourself "Self, how many 12s are there in 15?" Hopefully, you conclude the answer is 1 and write that partial quotient above the ones digit of the "15." (Realize that it's actually one hundred fifty we're dividing by 12, and so the answer is going into the tens place, since there are 10 of them.)

$$12\overline{)\overset{1}{156}}$$

Next, multiply the 1 from the partial quotient times the divisor and write the product beneath the first 2 digits of the dividend:

$$\begin{array}{r} 1 \\ 12\overline{)156} \\ 12 \end{array}$$

Next, subtract to find the amount we still need to divide:

$$\begin{array}{r} 1 \\ 12\overline{)156} \\ \underline{12} \\ 3 \end{array}$$

And bring down the next digit. We've placed an "x" under it to show that it has been brought down. Although that might not seem much of a big deal in this division, it becomes a big deal in larger dividends:

$$\begin{array}{r} 1 \\ 12\overline{)156} \\ x \\ \underline{12} \\ 36 \end{array}$$

The new partial dividend is the 36, so ask yourself, "How many 12s are there in 36?" or "How many times 12 'gazinta' 36?"

$$\begin{array}{r} 13 \\ 12\overline{)156} \\ x \\ \underline{12} \\ 36 \end{array}$$

Hopefully, we've both reached the same conclusion. Now multiply 3 times 12, write the answer beneath the dividend, and subtract:

$$
\begin{array}{r}
13 \\
12\overline{)156} \\
x \\
12 \\
\hline
36 \\
36 \\
\hline
\end{array}
$$

Since the difference between the two numbers is nothing, we write "nothing" down. Do you see the repeating pattern of seven steps? It goes like this:

1. Divide.
2. Place the partial quotient.
3. Multiply the partial quotient just written by the divisor.
4. Write the product below the dividend.
5. Subtract.
6. Bring down the next digit (if there is one).
7. IF there are digits not yet dealt with in the dividend,

   THEN go to Step 1.

   ELSE Go to Ending.
8. Ending to be dealt with next!

A couple of safety checks are built into the 7-step method. First off, when the divisor is multiplied by the partial quotient (4), the result must be smaller than the number above it. If it's not, then the partial quotient is too large. When you subtract (5) the difference must be smaller than the divisor. If it is not, then the partial quotient was too small.

Remainders

The preceding division was a perfect one, in that the divisor times the quotient equals the dividend.

That usually won't be the case. That brings us to the question of remainders. "Remainders in division?" you ask; "I thought that was subtraction." Well, I've been telling you all along that division is a form of subtraction. Now, I'm going to prove it to you. Here's a relatively easy division:

$$9\overline{)85}$$

9 doesn't go into 8, since it's larger than 8, so we must divide the full 85 by the 9. If you know your 9s table, then you know:

$$
\begin{array}{r}
9 \\
9\overline{)85} \\
81 \\
\hline
4 \\
\end{array}
$$

We put in the partial quotient of 9, multiplied that times the divisor, and got 81, which we subtract from the divisor to get a remainder of 4. What do we do with it? There are no more digits in the dividend to "bring down." We didn't divide the 4; we arrived at it by subtraction, so the answer to this division is:

$$\begin{array}{r} 9r4 \\ 9\overline{)85} \\ \underline{81} \\ 4 \end{array}$$

That is read, "9 remainder 4." It's really a combination obtained by division and subtraction. The 9 was obtained by division; the 4 by subtraction. The quotient could have been written another way, as well. The remainder could have been put over the divisor to form the common fraction, $\frac{4}{9}$:

$$\begin{array}{r} 9\frac{4}{9} \\ 9\overline{)85} \\ \underline{81} \\ 4 \end{array}$$

Estimating Quotients

Suppose that you have a division like 8896 ÷ 27. It is obvious that you're not going to divide 27 into 8, so you will divide it into 88. It is not so obvious how many 27s there are in 88. To make it easier to estimate how many 27s there are in 88, it helps to create a **trial divisor** and a **trial dividend.** A trial divisor is created by rounding the divisor to the nearer 10 and then using only the tens digit. If the ones digit in a two-digit numeral is 5 or greater, round up to the next 10, so 27 would round up to 30. If the divisor had been 23, we would have rounded down to 20. The trial divisor for the preceding division would be 3 (the tens digit from rounding 27 up to 30). The trial dividend is created in the same way, in this case from rounding 88 to 90, and then using the 9. How many 3s are there in 9? Okay, then try 3 27s in 88:

$$\begin{array}{r} 3 \\ 27\overline{)8896} \\ \underline{81} \end{array}$$

That worked. The possibility exists that you might get a partial quotient a little too big or a little too small. If that happens, adjust your answer accordingly. Next, subtract and bring down:

$$\begin{array}{r} 3 \\ 27\overline{)8896} \\ x \\ \underline{81} \\ 79 \end{array}$$

Now the trial divisor is still 3, but the trial dividend is 8 (from rounding 79 to 80). 8 divided by 3 is 2 and change:

$$\begin{array}{r} 32 \\ 27\overline{)8896} \\ x \\ \underline{81} \\ 79 \end{array}$$

Next multiply and subtract:

$$
\begin{array}{r}
32 \\
27\overline{)8896} \\
\text{x} \\
81 \\
\overline{79} \\
54 \\
\overline{25}
\end{array}
$$

Since the difference is less than the divisor, the 2 partial quotient was correct. So, the final step is to bring down the 6:

$$
\begin{array}{r}
32 \\
27\overline{)8896} \\
\text{xx} \\
81 \\
\overline{79} \\
54 \\
\overline{256}
\end{array}
$$

The trial divisor, 3, goes into the trial dividend, 25, 8 times. Multiply 8×27 and you'll get 216, which is more than 27 too small, so the last digit of the quotient should be 9.

$$
\begin{array}{r}
329 \\
27\overline{)8896} \\
\text{xx} \\
81 \\
\overline{79} \\
54 \\
\overline{256} \\
243 \\
\overline{13}
\end{array}
$$

The quotient is 329, r(remainder)13, or $329\frac{13}{27}$.

EXERCISES

1. $16\overline{)285}$

2. $24\overline{)372}$

3. $35\overline{)280}$

4. $47\overline{)593}$

5. $43\overline{)649}$

6. $58\overline{)784}$

7. $69\overline{)852}$

8. $84\overline{)798}$

9. $37\overline{)1569}$

10. $54\overline{)2836}$

11. $37\overline{)2483}$

12. $46\overline{)3910}$

13. $64\overline{)3648}$

14. $24\overline{)4896}$

15. $73\overline{)6815}$

16. $62\overline{)7750}$

ANSWERS

1. 17, r13
2. 15, r12
3. 8
4. 12, r29
5. 15, r4
6. 13, r30
7. 12, r24
8. 9, r42

9. 42, r15
10. 52, r28
11. 67, r4
12. 85
13. 57
14. 204
15. 93r26
16. 125

Adding and Subtracting Larger Numbers

You might think that adding and subtracting larger numbers works the same way as adding and subtracting smaller numbers, and to a certain extent you're correct. When you magnify the numbers, however, you also magnify the possibility that you'll make an error. Because of that, it is helpful to estimate the sum or difference before actually performing the operation.

Estimating for Addition

Suppose that you have 50,285 persons attending a Mets game, 39,417 persons attending a Tigers game, 41,817 persons attending a Phillies game, and 47,283 persons attending a Cardinals game all on the same July evening. Without adding the totals, would it be reasonable for you to **estimate** that there are around 140,000 persons (give or take 5000) attending all four of those games? Think about it before answering. All ready? The answer is *absolutely not.* An estimate is an approximation, and it is often as good as, if not better than, an exact count. If the same food-service outfit provided refreshments for all four of those ballgames, they would need to know about how many hot dogs they would need to order from their frankfurter supplier in order to have enough on hand. Suppose that each attendee averages one hot dog apiece at each game, and our pretend food-service operator had used the preceding estimate; would they have ordered too few or too many hot dogs?

How can I be sure that the estimate of 140,000 was way off? Look at the first two figures: one was more than 50,000, and the second was nearly 40,000. That makes a sum of about 90,000. Now look at the Phillies and Cardinals figures: almost 42,000 and more than 47,000, for a total there of almost 90,000. That's 90,000 + 90,000, or a total of about 180,000. It's actually going to be a little less than 180,000; say 178,000. Now add the figures and see what you get:

$$
\begin{array}{ccccccccc}
& & ^{2} & & & ^{2\,2} & & & ^{1\ 2\,2} & & & ^{1\,1\ 2\,2} & & & ^{1\,1\ 2\,2} \\
& 50,285 & & & 50,285 & & & 50,285 & & & 50,285 & & & 50,285 \\
& 39,417 & & & 39,417 & & & 39,417 & & & 39,417 & & & 39,417 \\
\textbf{(a)}\ & 41,817 & \textbf{(b)}\ & 41,817 & \textbf{(c)}\ & 41,817 & \textbf{(d)}\ & 41,817 & \textbf{(e)}\ & 41,817 \\
& 47,283 & & & 47,283 & & & 47,283 & & & 47,283 & & & 47,283 \\
\hline
& 2 & & & 02 & & & 802 & & & 8\ 802 & & & 178,802 \\
\end{array}
$$

In (a), I've added the units column, gotten 22, and you know what to do with that. In (b), the tens have been added to get a column total of 20. The addition of the hundreds is shown in (c), totaling to 18. Next come the thousands, shown in (d), and I have deliberately not placed a comma, but your student's teacher might want one there. Finally, (e) shows the addition of the ten thousands, and the comma is placed.

Hey, I'm rather pleased with the closeness of my estimate. And I really did *not* do the addition in advance. An awful lot of people would have been disappointed if only 140,000 hot dogs had been distributed—sellers as well as fans. We have not yet discussed percent, but the error in the estimate of 178,000 was off by less than half a percentage point (see Lesson 33 for more on percentages). Most important: If after estimating 178,000, my sum had been 200,000 or 150,000, I would have suspected that I had done something wrong and would have gone back and checked my work. The easiest way to check an addition of this magnitude is with a calculator, and don't think I won't.

Yep! That's the sum.

Estimating for Subtraction

The notion of estimating the difference when subtracting larger numbers might scare you at first, but it is really much easier than doing the same for addition. After all, only two numbers are involved, no matter what their magnitudes. Suppose that 17,283,724 persons live in the state of New York, and of those, 7,938,953 live in New York City. From that, I estimate that about 10,456,271 live in the rest of New York State (the numbers are made up, so don't use them if you're ever on *Jeopardy*). How good an estimate is that? Don't read any further until you've had a chance to decide whether my estimate was a good one or a bad one.

Well, it's my objective to not play favorites so, just as in addition, my estimate was a lousy one. The first figure is almost 17,300,000, while the second is nearly 8,000,000. Just from those two figures, knock 5 "0s" off of each to get 173 vs. 80. That's a difference of 93. Now put the 5 "0s" back and estimate the difference as 9,300,000. Did you follow that? Removing the 5 "0s" from each made for an easier subtraction (use the maximum number of zeroes present in both numerals). Then by putting the 5 zeroes back, you can see the actual magnitude of the number with which you're dealing. Now let's see how close the new estimate is to the actual difference. Keep in mind the fact that the whole purpose of estimating the difference before subtracting is to recognize when your computed answer doesn't make sense, so the more accurate the estimate, the better:

$$
\textbf{(a)} \quad \begin{array}{r} 17,283,724 \\ -\ 7,938,953 \\ \hline 1 \end{array}
\qquad\qquad
\textbf{(b)} \quad \begin{array}{r} 17,283,\overset{6}{7}{}^{1}24 \\ -\ 7,938,953 \\ \hline 71 \end{array}
$$

Step (a) is easy enough, since 4 – 3 = 1. In step (b), we can't subtract 5 tens from 2 tens, so we go to the hundreds column and rename 1 of the 7 hundreds as 10 tens. That leaves 6 in the hundreds place and makes 12 tens. Now subtract: 12 – 5 = 7.

$$
\begin{array}{r}
\overset{2}{}\overset{16}{}\\
17,28\cancel{3},\cancel{7}{}^{1}24\\
\text{(c)}\quad -\ 7,938,953\\
\hline
771
\end{array}
$$

$$
\begin{array}{r}
\overset{7\,12}{}\overset{16}{}\\
17,28\cancel{3},\cancel{7}{}24\\
\text{(d)}\quad -\ 7,938,953\\
\hline
4\ 771
\end{array}
$$

Step (c) requires taking 9 from 6, which obviously can't be done, so it's necessary to rename the 3 in the thousands place. Then subtract: 16 – 9 = 7.

Let's not even worry about the names of the places any more. We can pretty much mechanically move from right to left one place at a time. (d) requires the impossible job of taking 8 from 2, so we go left one column to rename 1 from there as 10 in the column where we're subtracting, and adding it to the 2 to make 12. Then, we find that 12 – 8 = 4.

$$
\begin{array}{r}
\overset{7\,12}{}\overset{16}{}\\
17,2\cancel{8}\cancel{3},\cancel{7}{}^{1}24\\
\text{(e)}\quad -\ 7,938,953\\
\hline
44,771
\end{array}
$$

$$
\begin{array}{r}
\overset{6}{}\ \overset{7\,12}{}\overset{16}{}\\
1\cancel{7},{}^{1}2\cancel{8}\cancel{3},\cancel{7}{}^{1}24\\
\text{(f)}\quad -\ 7,938,953\\
\hline
344,771
\end{array}
$$

Step (e) is the easiest one we've had since (a). 7 – 3 = 4. Use this opportunity to place a comma between the ones and thousands periods. In (f) it'll take another renaming before 9 can be taken from 2. Moving to the left we'll rename that 7 as a 6 and regroup ten, which gets added to the 2 to make 12, Then subtract 9 from the 12: 12 – 9 = 3.

$$
\begin{array}{r}
\overset{6}{}\ \overset{7\,12}{}\overset{16}{}\\
1\cancel{7},{}^{1}2\cancel{8}\cancel{3},\cancel{7}{}^{1}24\\
\text{(g)}\quad -\ 7,938,953\\
\hline
9,344,771
\end{array}
$$

Finally, in (g), bundle that 1 together with the 6 in your head, so as to be able to subtract 7 from 16: 16 – 7 = 9, and, of course, place that comma for a difference of 9 million, 3 hundred 44 thousand, 7 hundred 71. Wow! That's some difference!

Now I have to look back a page to see what the estimate was: It was 9 million 3 hundred thousand. It was certainly in the ballpark. Again, you can check this difference by adding up.

By the way, that's the way to check an addition, too, but in addition you don't add the sum to what's above it. You just add up each column to see whether you get the same sum going up as you did going down. With one this size, however, I'd much rather check my addition on a calculator. For goodness sake, why do you think calculators were created?!

It checks.

Second Chances

Now that you've had one chance at estimating the results in an addition and a subtraction involving large numbers, I think you deserve a second chance, or more, at each.

Here are two additions to estimate to the nearest 1,000. (To round to thousands, drop everything to the right of thousands.)

1. $472,671 + 627,832 + 1,545,439 + 372,218$
2. $837,158 + 467,281 + 591,347 + 914,643$

To solve number one, round to thousands $473,000 + 628,000 + 1,545,000 + 372,000$. Next, get rid of 3 zeroes: $473 + 628 + 1545 + 372$. Next, separate the hundreds just with the hundreds: There are 4, 6, 15 and 3 hundreds. Conveniently, 4 hundred and 6 hundred make 10 hundred (yes, I know that's a thousand, but I only want to think in terms of hundreds right now). 15 hundred and 3 hundred make 18 hundred, which I'll add to the 10 to get a total of $10 + 18 = 28$ hundreds. Now look at the remaining parts, 73, 28, 45, and 72. $72 + 28 = 100$. That makes 30 hundreds. Take 27 from the 45 to add to the remaining 73 to make 30 hundreds. Finally, subtracting the 27 from the 45 left leaves 18 remaining. Let's recap: there are 30 hundreds and 18. That's written 3018. Finally, stick those three zeroes back on to get the excellent estimate of 3,018,000.

I'm now going to put the original numbers into my calculator, but you can feel perfectly free to add them on paper if you would like the practice. I got 3,018,060. That's within 1 thousand!

I have a confession to make. When I first did that solution, I was off by a hundred thousand. That was because I accidentally copied "1545" as "1646." It wasn't until my third time through it that I caught the error. The reason I'm confessing this is because there's a lesson to be learned. That lesson is *be careful!*

Now for number two: Round to thousands and strip three zeroes at the same time: $837 + 467 + 591 + 915$. (Remember, if the digit to the right of the one you're rounding to is 5 or greater, round up, so "9146" becomes "915.") Collect the hundreds: 8, 4, 5, 9 hundreds: $8 + 4 = 12 + 5 = 17 + 9 = 26$ hundreds. Remaining are $37 + 67 + 91 + 15$: $65 + 35 = 100$, so $37 + 67 = 4$ more than 100, or 104. 91 needs 9 more to be 100, which you'll take from the 15 making 106. $104 + 106 = 210$. Combine the 2 hundreds with the 26 hundreds you found before and get 28 hundred ten. That's written 2810. Now put back the 3 zeroes to make 2,810,000, and there's the estimate. How close is it? Do the addition and find out. Just between you, me, and the wall, I'll tell you that it's off the mark by only 429, but if you want to know what the answer is, you'll have to do the addition.

Here are two subtractions to estimate to the nearest 10,000. (To round to ten-thousands, drop everything to the right of ten-thousands.)

1. $875,734 - 457,372$
2. $2,785,632 - 1,586,729$

To do number 1, round to the ten thousands: That gives you $880,000 - 460,000$. Drop the 4 zeroes and subtract: $88 - 46 = 42$, so with the zeroes that's 420,000. That means the difference will be no less than 410,000 nor more than 430,000. If you want to try the subtraction before I tell you what the answer is, don't look past this point. Using my trusty scientific calculator, I get a difference of 418,362. That's certainly well **within tolerance.**

Rounding number 2 to the ten thousands, we get $2,790,000 - 1,590,000$. Drop the 4 zeroes and subtract: $279 - 159 = 120$. That makes the estimated quotient 1,200,000. That means the difference must be no smaller than 1,190,000 or larger than 1,210,000. As a teaser, I'll tell you that the actual difference is 1097 away from the estimated value, but if you want to know what it is, you'll have to do the subtraction.

EXERCISES

Estimate the answer to the nearest 10,000; then solve.

1.
$$
\begin{array}{r}
539,734 \\
2,347,586 \\
382,967 \\
81,263 \\
\hline
\end{array}
$$

2.
$$
\begin{array}{r}
1,725,619 \\
-286,574 \\
\hline
\end{array}
$$

3.
$$
\begin{array}{r}
4,317,503 \\
-634,871 \\
\hline
\end{array}
$$

4.
$$
\begin{array}{r}
6,459,738 \\
87,563 \\
453,891 \\
2,564,917 \\
\hline
\end{array}
$$

5.
$$
\begin{array}{r}
472,634 \\
-254,975 \\
\hline
\end{array}
$$

6.
$$
\begin{array}{r}
45,387 \\
263,546 \\
538,295 \\
67,809 \\
438,752 \\
\hline
\end{array}
$$

7.
$$
\begin{array}{r}
2,186,493 \\
-798,674 \\
\hline
\end{array}
$$

8.
$$
\begin{array}{r}
759,826 \\
97,870 \\
438,561 \\
583,452 \\
645,343 \\
\hline
\end{array}
$$

9.
$$
\begin{array}{r}
5,479,253 \\
6,587,580 \\
8,365,397 \\
4,843,674 \\
\hline
\end{array}
$$

Estimate the answer to the nearest 1,000; then solve.

10.
$$
\begin{array}{r}
815,328 \\
-697,499 \\
\hline
\end{array}
$$

11.
$$
\begin{array}{r}
327,486 \\
632,598 \\
217,843 \\
85,617 \\
56,409 \\
\hline
\end{array}
$$

12.
$$
\begin{array}{r}
243,536 \\
-94,618 \\
\hline
\end{array}
$$

13.
$$
\begin{array}{r}
2,507,642 \\
95,468 \\
635,703 \\
4,367,580 \\
857,458 \\
\hline
\end{array}
$$

14.
$$
\begin{array}{r}
567,433 \\
-426,532 \\
\hline
\end{array}
$$

15.
$$
\begin{array}{r}
138,495 \\
-97,628 \\
\hline
\end{array}
$$

16. 891,267 + 482,658 + 2,567,460 + 9847 + 821,369

17. 654,179 + 2,367,518 + 63,678 + 840

18. 7,589,326– 4,276,458

ANSWERS

1. 3,350,000; 3,351,550
2. 1,440,000; 1,439,045
3. 3,690,000; 3,682,632
4. 9,560,000; 9,566,109
5. 220,000; 217,659
6. 1,360,000; 1,353,789
7. 1,390,000; 1,387,819
8. 2,530,000; 2,525,052
9. 25,280,000; 25,275,904
10. 118,000; 117,829
11. 1,320,000; 1,319,953
12. 149,000; 148,918
13. 8,464,000; 8,463,851
14. 140,000; 140,901
15. 40,000; 40,867
16. 4,772,000; 4,772,601
17. 3,087,000; 3,086,215
18. 3,313,000; 3,312,868

Multiplying Larger Numbers

As with addition and subtraction, it is helpful to know about how big the answer is going to be in order to have a measuring stick against which to compare your worked out answer. When multiplying large numbers, the product tends to get large quickly, and you'll find the same thing is true of your estimates. Fortunately, a little trick to estimating products will make it easier than you might think. Check out the following.

Mental Multiplication

$$2 \times 10 = 20$$
$$20 \times 10 = 200$$
$$200 \times 10 = 2000$$
$$2 \times 40 = 80$$
$$20 \times 40 = 800$$
$$200 \times 40 = 8000$$

Do you see the pattern? To mentally multiply any number by 10, **append** a zero to the end of it (that means stick it on the end); to mentally multiply any number by 100, append two zeroes to the end of it. In general, to mentally multiply any number by a multiple of 10, multiply the non-zero parts together, and then append as many zeroes as there are in the multiple of 10:

Following that format, $300 \times 43 = 3 \times 43$ (which is 129), append "00" = 12,900.

Similarly, $4000 \times 21 = 4 \times 21$ (which is 84), append "000" = 84,000.

Estimating Large Products

Since you've made it to this point, I'll assume you understand the last section. When estimating large products, the same formula as before is followed, with one exception. Consider the following multiplication:

$$526$$
$$\times\ 385$$

You'll be multiplying hundreds times hundreds. $100 \times 100 = 10,000$. Again, you multiplied the non-zero portions together ($1 \times 1 = 1$), but this time you have zeroes from both factors. Each hundred contributes 2 zeroes, so you have 4 zeroes to append to the partial product, 1. That's the 10,000.

Suppose that you were multiplying 900 × 900. Following the same format, you'll multiply 9 × 9, and then append 4 zeroes (2 from each factor): 9 × 9 = 81; append 4 zeroes, and get 810,000.

If you wished to estimate the product to the nearest hundred thousand, start with hundreds times hundreds. You've already seen that the range could go as low as 10,000, but it's not going to unless the multiplication is 100 × 100.

Do you remember this multiplication? It first appeared on the last page.

$$526$$
$$\times 385$$

To estimate the product to the nearest 10,000, first multiply the hundreds together:

$$500 \times 300 = 15 \text{ and 4 zeroes, } = 150,000$$

Then multiply the tens in the bottom factor times the hundreds in the top:

$$80 \times 500 = 40 \text{ and 3 zeroes, } = 40,000$$

Then add them together: 150,000 + 40,000 = 190,000

That's it. The product should be in the neighborhood of 190,000. Now let's actually work it out.

$$\overset{1\ 3}{526}$$
$$\times 385$$
$$\overline{2630}$$

Starting with the ones, multiply: 5 × 6 = 30; write the 0 and rename the 3 tens; 5 × 2 = 10, + 3 = 13; write the 3 and rename the ten. (Note, after you have it down pat, you no longer have to concern yourself with the technical fact that it's really a hundred.) Next multiply 5 × 5 to get 25, + 1 = 26, which you can write below the line in its entirety.

$$\overset{2\ 4}{526}$$
$$\times 385$$
$$\overline{2630}$$
$$42080$$

We place a zero in the ones column, since there are no ones when multiplying by tens. Then we multiply 8 × 6 = 48; write the 8 below the 3 and rename the 4 tens above the 2. 8 × 2 = 16, + 4 = 20; write the 0 below the 6 and rename the 2 above the 5. Next multiply 8 × 5 to get 40, + 2 = 42, which you can write in its entirety.

$$\overset{1}{526}$$
$$\times 385$$
$$\overline{2630}$$
$$42080$$
$$157800$$

We place zeroes in the ones and tens places, since there will be no ones or tens when multiplying by hundreds. Then we multiply 3 × 6 = 18; write the 8 below the 0 and rename the ten above the 2. 3 × 2 = 6, + 1 = 7; write it below the 2. Next multiply 3 × 5 to get 15, which you write in its entirety.

$$\begin{array}{r} 526 \\ \times\ 385 \\ \hline 2630 \\ 42080 \\ 157\,800 \\ \hline 202,510 \end{array}$$

Finally, add the three partial products together (and insert a comma) to get a total product of 202,510. Is that within 10,000 of the original estimate?

The estimate was 190,000.   202,520 – 190,000 = 12,520.

Close, but no cigar! (No, I'm not encouraging smoking. It's just an expression I grew up with, which apparently originated in carnival contests in the 1800s and early 1900s, when a contestant had to hit a target to win a cigar. The intimation is "You were almost successful, but not quite." or "Even a near miss is still a miss.")

If you recall, the estimate was arrived at by multiplying the hundreds of one factor by the hundreds and tens of the other. Suppose that the top factor had been rounded to the nearest 10 (530) and multiplied by the ones digit of the other:

$$530 \times 5 = 2650$$

Adding that to the prior estimate gets: 190,000 + 2650 = 192,650, and that estimate wins the cigar by a margin of 140: (202,510 – 192,650 = 9860)

Let's try doing one more of these, estimating the product, and then multiplying a 4-digit numeral times a 3-digit one. I promise no more discussion of stogies:

$$\begin{array}{r} 654 \\ \times\ 8467 \end{array} \text{ becomes } \begin{array}{r} 8467 \\ \times\ 654 \end{array}$$

First, turn over the factors. Why would you want to multiply by four different numbers when you only need to multiply by three? Next, do the estimate, aiming for a number within 10,000 of the actual product. Although you could multiply each of the bottom factors by 8400, it's easier to do the mental multiplication by separating 8400 into 8000 and 400:

$$600 \times 8000 = 6 \times 8 \text{ and } \text{``00000''} = 4,800,000$$
$$600 \times 400 = 6 \times 4 \text{ and } \text{``0000''} = 240,000$$
$$50 \times 8000 = 5 \times 8 \text{ and } \text{``0000''} = 400,000$$
$$50 \times 400 = 5 \times 4 \text{ and } \text{``000''} = 20,000$$
$$4 \times 8000 = 4 \times 8 \text{ and } \text{``000''} = 32,000$$
$$4 \times 400 = 4 \times 4 \text{ and } \text{``00''} = 1600$$

Add up all but the top number and the bottom number first: 240 + 400 = 640, + 20 = 660, + 32 = 692,000. The last sentence is an example of keeping a **running total**. Take note of the fact that since all the numbers being added were thousands, we didn't bother to add the thousands, waiting until the last step to tack them on.

Now, add the 692 thousand to the 4800 thousand and get 5,492,000. Why didn't we add the final 1600? Because it contains no ten thousands, so it's not relevant. That means the product must be within 10,000 either side of 5,492,000, or within the gap 5,392,000 and 5,592,000. Let's see whether it is:

<table>
<tr><td align="right">**Ones:**</td><td>
<pre>
  1 2 2
  8467
× 654
───────
 33868
     0
</pre>
</td><td align="right">**Tens:**</td><td>
<pre>
    2 3 3
    8467
  × 654
  ───────
   33868
  423350
      00
</pre>
</td><td align="right">**Hundreds:**</td><td>
<pre>
      2 4 4
      8467
    × 654
    ───────
     33868
    423350
   5080200
</pre>
</td></tr>
</table>

Note that we first multiplied by the ones and placed the 0 for the tens. Then we multiplied by the tens and placed the two 0s for the hundreds. Finally, we multiplied by the hundreds.

<table>
<tr><td align="right">**Add:**</td><td>
<pre>
    8467
  × 654
  ───────
   33868
  423350
 5080200
 ───────
 5537418
</pre>
</td><td align="right">**Place commas:**</td><td>
<pre>
     8467
   × 654
   ─────────
    33 868
   423 350
 5 080 200
 ─────────
 5,537,418
</pre>
</td></tr>
</table>

Take note of the fact that the commas were not placed in the partial products but were placed only after the complete product was found.

The estimate was that the product must be within 10,000 either side of 5,492,000, or within the gap between 5,392,000 and 5,592,000. 5,537,418 is well within that range. Remember that an estimate is just that. It won't always necessarily be as close as you would like it to be, but that's a tradeoff you make in exchange for being able to make it using a minimum amount of time.

It might occur to you, and/or your student, that the answer in the previous product was arrived at by adding, so why is it referred to as a "product" rather than a "sum?" My answer is that first of all, we have never tried to hide the fact that multiplication is a form of addition. Having said that, however, each of the partial products was arrived at by multiplication. The final answer is a sum of partial products, and as such is a product. If, after that explanation, you're still not satisfied, remember that all mathematics is the product of natural and/or physical law, or of human invention.

EXERCISES

Estimate each product to the nearest 10,000. Then solve to find the product.

1. $357 \times 468 =$ ___

2. $563 \times 732 =$ ___

3. $249 \times 385 =$ ___

4. $938 \times 765 =$ ___

5.
<pre>
  897
× 678
</pre>

6.
<pre>
  389
× 342
</pre>

7.
<pre>
  986
× 569
</pre>

8.
<pre>
  638
× 460
</pre>

9.
<pre>
  756
× 385
</pre>

10.
<pre>
  447
× 398
</pre>

Estimate each product to the nearest 100,000. Then solve to find the product.

11. $8470 \times 231 =$ ___

12. $574 \times 6572 =$ ___

13. $6643 \times 846 =$ ___

14. $279 \times 5018 =$ ___

15. $\begin{array}{r} 2891 \\ \times\ 345 \\ \hline \end{array}$

16. $\begin{array}{r} 5834 \\ \times\ 627 \\ \hline \end{array}$

17. $\begin{array}{r} 874 \\ \times\ 2695 \\ \hline \end{array}$

18. $\begin{array}{r} 597 \\ \times\ 6438 \\ \hline \end{array}$

19. $\begin{array}{r} 204 \\ \times\ 7934 \\ \hline \end{array}$

20. $\begin{array}{r} 67345 \\ \times\ 489 \\ \hline \end{array}$

ANSWERS

1. 170,000; 167,076
2. 410,000; 412,116
3. 100,000; 95,865
4. 720,000; 717,570
5. 600,000; 608,166
6. 130,000; 133,038
7. 560,000; 561,034

8. 290,000; 293,480
9. 282,000; 291,060
10. 180,000; 177,906
11. 1,900,000; 1,956,570
12. 3,700,000; 3,772,328
13. 5,600,000; 5,619,978
14. 1,400,000; 1,400,022

15. 900,000; 997,395
16. 3,700,000; 3,657,918
17. 2,300,000; 2,355,430
18. 3,800,000; 3,843,486
19. 1,600,000; 1,618,536
20. 32,300,000; 32,931,705

I hope you knew to turn the factors in 17, 18, and 19 over before multiplying them. It would have made your life much easier.

Dividing Large Numbers

Since division is the undoing (or inverse) of multiplication, there are certain aspects of multiplication that reverse in division. I have to be careful of how far I can go with that subject at this time, since we have not yet dealt with decimal fractions, which would normally come into play here.

Mental Division

For the reason already mentioned, I'm going to confine the discussion of mental division to multiples of 10. When hundreds are divided by tens, tens result:

$$800 \div 10 = 80$$

$$800 \div 20 = 40$$

$$800 \div 40 = 20$$

$$800 \div 80 = 10$$

Do you see a pattern there? It's 8 divided by 1, 2, 4, and 8 with the zeroes from the 100 redistributed into tens and tens. In other words, if you multiply from right to left across the " = " (quotient times divisor) you'll get the dividend as the product. (Remember multiplying tens, or look back to mental multiplication in the last lesson.)

What do you suppose happens when you divide thousands by hundreds?

$$8000 \div 100 = 80$$

$$8000 \div 200 = 40$$

$$8000 \div 400 = 20$$

$$8000 \div 800 = 10$$

Count the zeroes on each side of the "divided by" sign. Do you see that there are three zeroes on each side? This time it's 8 divided by 1, 2, 4, and 8 with the zeroes from the 1000s redistributed into hundreds and tens. Check these out:

$$80,000 \div 100 = 800$$

$$80,000 \div 200 = 400$$

$$80,000 \div 400 = 200$$

$$80,000 \div 800 = 100$$

Here we've divided eight ten thousands (also known as 80 thousand) by hundreds. Did you notice that there are four zeroes on each side of the division sign? This time it's 8 divided by 1, 2, 4, and 8 with the zeroes from the 10,000s redistributed into hundreds and hundreds. The pattern should by now be clear. When dividing a multiple of ten by another, smaller one, the number of zeroes remains the same on both sides of the division. They are just redistributed between the divisor and the quotient.

Short Division

Let's digress, or, if you like, take a "short" break from the main theme of the current symposium. Short division may be the first form of division you ever learned. It certainly was the first that I ever learned. It is meant for division by a single-digit divisor. It works from left to right and is 1 step removed from mental division, but completely disregards place value. To divide 832 by 4, we would proceed like this:

$$\frac{2}{4\overline{)832}}$$

Ask yourself: "How many times does 4 go into 8?" The answer is 2 and none remaining, so write the 2 above the 8.

Next, ask yourself, "How many times does 4 go into 3?"

$$\frac{20}{4\overline{)83^32}}$$

The answer is none, so write the 0 above the 3 and regroup the 3 with the 2 to make 32. (Some teachers will not bother with the additional notation but ask the student to mentally group the 3 with the 2 to make 32.)

Next, ask yourself, "How many times does 4 go into 32?"

$$\frac{208}{4\overline{)83^32}}$$

The answer is 8 (since 8 × 4 = 32), so write the 8 above the 2, and you're done. It's not quite as simple as it looks, but you can get used to it after you know all the wrinkles, and it does work well.

Here's another example:

$$9\overline{)2357}$$

Ask yourself: "How many times does 9 go into 2?"

The answer, of course, is, "It doesn't," so regroup the 2 with the 3 to make 23. This you do in your head, since you can visualize the 23 by blocking out the rest of the numeral mentally or with your hand. No numeral will be written above the 2, since we're treating it as if it were the tens digit in a two-digit number.

Next, ask yourself, "How many times does 9 go into 23?"

$$\frac{2}{9\overline{)23^557}}$$

The largest number of 9s that can be crammed into 23 is 2, for a total of 18, which is 5 short of 23. Write the 2 over the 3 of the 23 you divided it into, and look what I've done with the remaining 5 (from 23 – 18 = 5). It has been attached to the 5 to make 55. (Don't worry about the 7. We'll pay that toll when we come to the bridge—or something like that.)

So, now ask yourself, "How many times does 9 go into 55?"

$$9\overline{)23\,^55\,^17}$$
$$\frac{2\;6}{\phantom{9\overline{)}}}$$

If you're up on your 9s, you know that 6 of them make 54. Guess what happens to the difference between 55 and 54. Oh, you must have peeked.

Finally, ask yourself "How many 9s in 17?"

$$9\overline{)23\,^55\,^17}$$
$$\frac{2\;6\;\;1r8}{\phantom{9\overline{)}}}$$

There is exactly one 8 in 17. Subtracting the 9 from 17 gives a remainder of 8, which is dutifully tacked on as an "r."

Estimating Large Quotients

$$265\overline{)5839}$$

Look at the divisor in the preceding division. It's closer to 300 than it is to 200, so for purposes of estimating the quotient, we'll round it up. Now look at the dividend. Round it up to 6000. *About what* would you expect the quotient to be? Well, we're dividing thousands (3 zeroes) by hundreds (2 zeroes), so we're going to get (3 zeroes – 2 zeroes = 1 zero) an answer that's in the 10s. 6 divided by 3 is 2, so the quotient should be somewhere around 2 tens, or 20. I'd feel comfortable with a quotient somewhere between 17 or 18 and 22 or 23. In fact, the quotient is 22, r9

Now estimate the quotient for this one:

$$423\overline{)12,395}$$

Did you actually estimate the quotient or are you waiting for me to do it? Okay. You've had enough time. You should have rounded 423 down to 400 and 12,395 down to 12,000. Once again, it's hundreds and thousands, so the answer should be in the **decades** (tens). 12 divided by 4 is 3, so I would estimate the quotient to be around 30; would you? It's actually 29, r128. Are you wondering why we called 12,000 in the thousands instead of in the ten-thousands? The "1" is in the ten thousands, but if we're bundling it with the "2" to make "12," it's 12 thousand, which, in point of fact has its left-most digit in the 10,000's place.

Let's do one more. Try estimating the quotient for this one:

$$567\overline{)352,457}$$

Are you finished? All right then, here goes. 567 rounds up to 600; 352,457 rounds down to 350,000. That's 2 zeroes versus 4 zeroes, so the estimate should have "00" (4 – 2 = 2). 35 divided by 6 is 5 and change. Actually, that change is much closer to 1 than to 0, since there are 6 "6s" in 36. For that reason, I would go with 600 as my rough estimated quotient. Now I'm going to take a look at the quantities I discarded, because they're pretty sizeable. I increased the divisor by about 30 when rounding up, and I decreased the dividend by almost 2,500. 30 goes into 2500

about 80 times, and if both had been rounded up or down I would either increase or decrease my estimate by 80, respectively. However, since one got bigger and one got smaller, I would split the difference and say the actual quotient might be 40 either side of 600—in other words, greater than 560 and less than 640. Does that sound reasonable? Let's see what actually happens:

(a) $\begin{array}{r} 6 \\ 567\overline{)352,457} \\ 3402 \\ \hline 122 \end{array}$ **(b)** $\begin{array}{r} 62 \\ 567\overline{)352,457} \\ 3402\downarrow \\ \hline 1225 \\ 1134 \\ \hline 91 \end{array}$ **(c)** $\begin{array}{r} 621 \\ 567\overline{)352,457} \\ 3402\downarrow\downarrow \\ \hline 1225\downarrow \\ 1134\downarrow \\ \hline 917 \\ 567 \\ \hline 350 \end{array}$

(a) Using 600 as a trial divisor, put it over the hundreds digit (you already estimated that your answer is going to be in the hundreds). Multiply 6×567, write the product below 3524, and subtract.

(b) Start by bringing down the 5, placing it next to the second 2 of 122, and turning that into 1225. Divide that 1225 by 600 and get 2. Place that 2 above the 5 in the dividend and multiply that 2 times the numerator to get 1134. Subtract the 1134 from the 1225 above it to get 91.

(c) Start by bringing down the 7 and placing it next to the 1 of 91 and turning that into 917. Divide that 917 by 600 and get 1. Place that 1 above the 7 in the dividend and multiply that 1 times the numerator to get 567. Subtract the 567 from the 915 above it to get 350, the remainder. The final quotient is 621, r 350.

You might recall that the estimated quotient was 600 ± 40, so this quotient certainly falls within those parameters.

EXERCISES

For 1–8, solve by short division.

1. $8\overline{)9645}$

2. $5\overline{)2769}$

3. $3\overline{)81,654}$

4. $7\overline{)144,956}$

5. $6\overline{)32,952}$

6. $9\overline{)573,481}$

7. $4\overline{)38,216}$

8. $8\overline{)329,766}$

For 9–20, estimate the quotient; then find it.

9. $241\overline{)6895}$

10. $384\overline{)9268}$

11. $857\overline{)17,586}$

12. $435\overline{)62,391}$

13. $308\overline{)81,736}$

14. $436\overline{)46,729}$

15. $684\overline{)19,435}$

16. $542\overline{)38,679}$

17. $365\overline{)148,362}$

18. $725\overline{)648,925}$

19. $234\overline{)657,532}$

20. $441\overline{)768,462}$

ANSWERS

1. 1205, r5
2. 553, r4
3. 27,208
4. 20,708
5. 5492
6. 63,720, r1
7. 9554
8. 41220, r6
9. 35*; 28, r147
10. 22; 24, r52

11. 20; 20, r446
12. 150; 143, r186
13. 270; 265, r116
14. 120; 107, r77
15. 30; 28, r283
16. 80; 71, r197
17. 400; 406, r172
18. 900; 895, r50
19. 3000; 2809, r226
20. 1900; 1742, r240

---

*This might seem like a strange estimate, but consider the trial divisor is 200 and the dividend is 7000. 70 ÷ 2 = 35.

Evens, Primes, and Divisibility

A few things might be helpful to you when dealing with whole numbers, and I thought that this might be a good place to bring them to your attention. Some things are easy to take for granted, such as everyone knows the difference between odd and even numbers. Just in case you're looking for an easy definition, even numbers are those that can be divided by 2 with no remainders. Odd ones are those that cannot be. Zero is an even number, since two goes into it exactly 0 times with no remainder. (Actually, zero divided by any number is zero.)

Prime Numbers

A **prime number** is defined as a number that has exactly two factors, itself and 1. The first prime number is 2, with factors of 1 and 2 and no others. Two is also the only even prime number, since every other even number must have 2 as a factor, as well as itself and 1. A number with more than 2 factors is known as a **composite number.**

Prime numbers show up very frequently among the first 20 natural numbers. The higher you count, however, the rarer they become. The easiest way to find the prime numbers in the first 100 is by using the ancient **Sieve of Eratosthenes.**

1	2	3	4	5	6	7	8	9	10
11	12	13	14	15	16	17	18	19	20
21	22	23	24	25	26	27	28	29	30
31	32	33	34	35	36	37	38	39	40
41	42	43	44	45	46	47	48	49	50
51	52	53	54	55	56	57	58	59	60
61	62	63	64	65	66	67	68	69	70
71	72	73	74	75	76	77	78	79	80
81	82	83	84	85	86	87	88	89	90
91	92	93	94	95	96	97	98	99	100

Make a copy of the preceding table and then start crossing out. Start with 1 and put a line through it. 1 does not meet the criteria for being prime. It has only one factor, itself. Next circle the 2; then cross out every multiple of 2.

1̸	②	3	4̸	5	6̸	7	8̸	9	1̸0̸
11	1̸2̸	13	1̸4̸	15	1̸6̸	17	1̸8̸	19	2̸0̸
21	2̸2̸	23	2̸4̸	25	2̸6̸	27	2̸8̸	29	3̸0̸
31	3̸2̸	33	3̸4̸	35	3̸6̸	37	3̸8̸	39	4̸0̸
41	4̸2̸	43	4̸4̸	45	4̸6̸	47	4̸8̸	49	5̸0̸
51	5̸2̸	53	5̸4̸	55	5̸6̸	57	5̸8̸	59	6̸0̸
61	6̸2̸	63	6̸4̸	65	6̸6̸	67	6̸8̸	69	7̸0̸
71	7̸2̸	73	7̸4̸	75	7̸6̸	77	7̸8̸	79	8̸0̸
81	8̸2̸	83	8̸4̸	85	8̸6̸	87	8̸8̸	89	9̸0̸
91	9̸2̸	93	9̸4̸	95	9̸6̸	97	9̸8̸	99	1̸0̸0̸

Well, that kind of narrowed the field in a hurry. To speed things up, I'm going to circle the 3, 5, and 7, since each of those has exactly two factors. Then I'm going to cross out every multiple of 3, 5, and 7 that's left in the chart. You might want to do that with the 3s first, then the 5s, and finally the 7s.

1̸	②	③	4̸	⑤	6̸	⑦	8̸	9̸	1̸0̸
⑪	1̸2̸	⑬	1̸4̸	1̸5̸	1̸6̸	⑰	1̸8̸	⑲	2̸0̸
2̸1̸	2̸2̸	㉓	2̸4̸	2̸5̸	2̸6̸	2̸7̸	2̸8̸	㉙	3̸0̸
㉛	3̸2̸	3̸3̸	3̸4̸	3̸5̸	3̸6̸	㊲	3̸8̸	3̸9̸	4̸0̸
㊶	4̸2̸	㊸	4̸4̸	4̸5̸	4̸6̸	㊼	4̸8̸	4̸9̸	5̸0̸
5̸1̸	5̸2̸	㊾	5̸4̸	5̸5̸	5̸6̸	5̸7̸	5̸8̸	㊾	6̸0̸
㊿	6̸2̸	6̸3̸	6̸4̸	6̸5̸	6̸6̸	6̸7̸	6̸8̸	6̸9̸	7̸0̸
71	7̸2̸	73	7̸4̸	7̸5̸	7̸6̸	7̸7̸	7̸8̸	79	8̸0̸
8̸1̸	8̸2̸	83	8̸4̸	8̸5̸	8̸6̸	8̸7̸	8̸8̸	89	9̸0̸
9̸1̸	9̸2̸	9̸3̸	9̸4̸	9̸5̸	9̸6̸	97	9̸8̸	9̸9̸	1̸0̸0̸

Whoa! "Why," you're asking yourself, "did he put all those other circles up on the chart?" Well, the answer is that after the multiples of 3, 5, and 7 have been eliminated, nothing but prime numbers remain on the chart. I suppose that's why Eratosthenes called it a "sieve." All the non-primes fall right through it. Of the first 100 natural numbers, 22 are prime, 77 are composite, and 1 is neither.

Divisibility Tests

Certain tests make it easier to tell whether a large number is **divisible** (can be perfectly divided) by another without having to actually divide.

1. Every whole number is divisible by 1, so that's not a number for which you need to test divisibility.

2. If a number is even, it is divisible by 2. A number is even if its ones digit is 2, 4, 6, 8, or 0.

3. A number is divisible by 3 if the sum of its digits is divisible by 3. For example, to test 18,291 for divisibility by 3, add $1 + 8 + 2 + 9 + 1 = 21$. If you don't recognize 21 as being divisible by 3, simply add its digits: $2 + 1 = 3$, so 18,291 is divisible by 3.

4. A number is divisible by 4 if its tens and ones digits form a number that is a multiple of 4. For instance, 217,5<u>24</u> is divisible by 4, because $6 \times 4 = 24$.

5. A number is divisible by 5 if its ones digit is a "5" or a "0."

6. A number is divisible by 6 if it is divisible by 3 *and* is even.

7. Fuhgeddaboudit! The tests for divisibility by 7 are not worth memorizing. Just divide.

8. If the number formed by the rightmost 3 digits is divisible by 8, then the whole number is divisible by 8. Of course, if you need a calculator to compute whether that 3-digit number is divisible by 8, then there's no point in using this method.

9. A number is divisible by 9 if adding the digits together repeatedly gets you to 9. This is the same as the 3s rule, only with 9s.

10. A number is divisible by 10 if its 1s digit is 0.

EXERCISES

1. Find the next 3 primes after 97.

Tell whether the following numbers are prime or composite:

2. 133

3. 627

4. 143

5. 286

6. 507

7. 307

8. 139

9. 301

10. 683

By which numbers between 2 and 10 are the following numbers divisible?

11. 1,567,982

12. 87,592,428

13. 789,465

14. 32,173,330

15. 8,673,256

16. 69,835,317

17. 379,831,732

18. 421,634,569

19. 834,953,826

20. 10,080

ANSWERS

1. 101, 103, 1072
2. prime
3. composite
4. composite
5. composite
6. composite
7. prime
8. prime
9. composite
10. prime

11. 2
12. 2, 3, 4, 6, 7, 8, 9
13. 3, 5
14. 2, 5, 10
15. 2, 4, 8
16. 3
17. 2, 4, 7
18. none
19. 2, 3, 6, 7
20. 2, 3, 4, 5, 6, 7, 8, 9, 10

Part 2
Fractions

Terms You Should Know

After each word in the Glossary, the lesson where it first appears is cited. Occasionally a second or third appearance is also given if there are additional major references, but not all appearances of each word are necessarily cited.

cancel (Lesson 22). To simplify a fraction by removing common factors from numerator and denominator across a multiplication sign or multiple multiplication signs; canceling.

common denominator (Lesson 18). A denominator in terms of which two fractions with different denominators are to be renamed and then added or subtracted; usually found by using LCD or GCF.

common fraction (Lesson 15). A fraction with a numerator and denominator, usually, but not always, having a value less than one.

common multiple (Lesson 18). A multiple that is shared by two or more numbers, for example, 12 is a common multiple of 2, 3, 4, 6, and 12.

decimal fraction (Lesson 27). The part of a number that's to the right of the decimal point.

decimal point (Lesson 27). The dot that marks the demarcation between whole numbers (to its left) and fractions (to its right).

denominator (Lesson 15). The bottom member of a common fraction.

equivalent fractions (Lesson 16). Two fractions that look different but have the same value; there is an infinite number of them for every fractional value.

fraction line (Lesson 15). The line that separates a common fraction's numerator from its denominator.

GCF (Lesson 17). Greatest common factor; the largest factor common to both the numerator and denominator of a fraction; factoring it out produces the fraction in simplest terms.

greatest common factor (Lesson 17). See GCF.

half (Lesson 15). One of two equal parts into which a whole object or group has been cut.

improper fraction (Lesson 15). An antiquated term, but still in use in some classrooms, used to refer to a fraction whose numerator is greater than its denominator, i.e. its value is greater than 1.

LCD (Lesson 18). See least common denominator.

LCM (Lesson 18). See least common multiple.

least common denominator (Lesson 18). The lowest denominator in terms of which two or more fractions with different denominators can be renamed for the purpose of addition or subtraction.

least common multiple (Lesson 18). Abbreviated LCM, it's the smallest multiple of two or more denominators in a fractional addition or subtraction.

lowest terms (Lesson 17). The simplest form in which a common fraction may be written; also simplest terms.

mixed number (Lesson 23). A number that is a combination of a whole number plus a fraction, e.g. $1\frac{1}{2}$.

numerator (Lesson 15). The top member of a common fraction.

percent (Lesson 32). Literally, per hundred; a way to represent fractions based upon 100 representing a whole thing, and utilizing the "%" sign.

percentage (Lesson 33). A specific percent of something.

prime factor tree (Lesson 17). A visual representation of a prime factorization, so called because it is triangularly shaped like a traditional pine tree.

prime factorization (Lesson 17). Breaking down a composite number into its prime number components.

proportion (Lesson 15). An equating of two ratios, e.g. 4:6 = 2:3 or $\frac{1}{2} = \frac{5}{10}$.

quarter (Lesson 15). An alternate name for one-fourth.

ratio (Lesson 15). A comparison involving 2 or more numbers; may be represented in colon form, e.g. 2:3, read "2 is to 3," or as a common fraction.

reciprocal (Lesson 21). The number by which you multiply another in order to get a product of one.

reciprocal operations (Lesson 21). Operations that undo one another, e.g. addition and subtraction; multiplication and division.

significant digit (Lesson 27). A digit having a value other than zero.

simplest terms (Lesson 17). See lowest terms; (also see terms).

terms (Lesson 17). The collective name given to the numerator and denominator of a fraction.

third (Lesson 15). One of three equal parts into which a whole object or group has been cut.

LESSON 15

Common Fractions

Common fractions aren't that common any more, primarily due to our heavy reliance on computers and calculators for fractional computation. In fact, the decimal fraction and percent (yes, that's a kind of fraction, too) get much more attention than the common fraction, yet this is where it all begins. The common fraction has three parts, the **numerator,** which goes on top; the **denominator,** which goes on the bottom; and the **fraction line,** which separates the two. The fraction is read from the top down. The following fractions are represented with their names beneath them:

$\frac{1}{4}$ $\frac{2}{5}$ $\frac{4}{6}$ $\frac{5}{8}$ $\frac{9}{10}$

one-fourth   two-fifths   four-sixths   five-eighths   nine-tenths

Fractions can be used in many ways and to represent many things.

Fraction as Part of a Whole

A fraction may represent a part of a whole. The darkened parts of each of the figures that follow illustrate what each of the five preceding fractions represents.

Name	Symbol	Meaning
one-fourth	$\frac{1}{4}$	

OR

Name	Symbol	Meaning		
two-fifths	$\frac{2}{5}$		OR	
four-sixths	$\frac{4}{6}$		OR	
five-eighths	$\frac{5}{8}$		OR	
nine-tenths	$\frac{9}{10}$		OR	

Do you see the pattern? When used to name parts of a whole, the denominator of a fraction names the number of equal parts into which the whole has been divided, and the numerator names the number of parts being considered.

Two fractions have special names that depart from the usual naming scheme. They are wholes that have been cut into two equal parts and wholes that have been cut into three equal parts: One part of the first is named one-**half;** one part of the second is named one-**third,** rather than the "one-twoth" and "one-threeth" that would follow the naming pattern of the other fractions. Additionally, fourths are sometimes referred to as **quarters**—most frequently when referring to parts of a dollar or a sporting event.

Fraction as Part of a Group

If we have 6 apples, 3 apples make up a group that is half the size of the entire group of apples. That's represented by the following picture. Also evident from that picture is something that we'll get into in the next lesson, but which we won't dwell on just yet.

$\frac{3}{6}$ or $\frac{1}{2}$

If a tray of fruit contains 6 apples and 4 oranges, then 10 pieces of fruit are on that tray. Six-tenths of the fruit are apples; four-tenths of the fruit are oranges.

apples = $\frac{6}{10}$ oranges = $\frac{4}{10}$

In the examples just given, fractions are used to describe parts of groups of objects.

Fractions may also be used to describe parts of groups of animals or people. A small flock of sheep contains 2 rams and 7 ewes. Two-ninths of the sheep are rams; seven-ninths of the sheep are ewes.

rams = $\frac{2}{9}$ ewes = $\frac{7}{9}$

Notice that the denominator of the fraction equals the total number of members of the group, and the numerator names the number of members that exhibit the specified criteria.

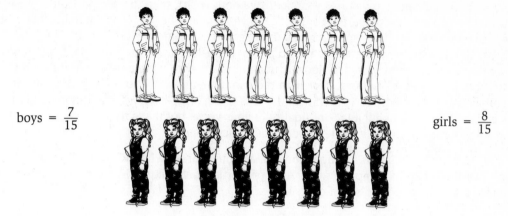

boys = $\frac{7}{15}$ girls = $\frac{8}{15}$

Suppose that 15 students showed up for cheerleading tryouts, and 7 of them were boys. Then eight-fifteenths of those trying out were girls, and seven-fifteenths were boys.

Fraction as a Whole

Did you ever order a piece of pie in a restaurant? Did you ask for an eighth of pie or a twelfth of pie? Of course not. You asked for "a piece of pie" or "a slice of pie," or even "a wedge of pie." What I'm getting at here, is that even though you knew that what you were eating or ordering was a fraction of the original pie, you treated it as a whole thing: a piece of pie.

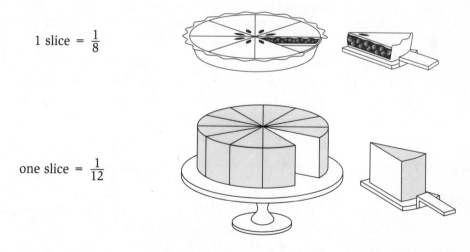

1 slice = $\frac{1}{8}$

one slice = $\frac{1}{12}$

You might even want to share the piece of cake or slice of pie with your dinner companion. You are unlikely to consider that you will each be eating one-sixteenth of a pie or one-twenty-fourth of a cake. You'll cut it in two, and you'll each have "a half a slice."

Fraction as a Comparison

If I were 45 years old and you were 23 years old (we both wish), then the comparison of your age to mine would be $\frac{23}{45}$, and the comparison of my age to yours would be $\frac{45}{23}$. Notice that *order counts!* This type of a comparison has a very special name. It is known as a **ratio.** If you were to just look at these ratios without knowing the context, you would probably mistake them for fractions. Well, that wouldn't be a mistake, because they *are* fractions. A fraction is a way to write a ratio; not the only way, but one way. A ratio is read: "The numerator is to the denominator . . . ," so the two ratios in the previous example would be read: "23 is to 45," and "45 is to 23," respectively. That might sound like you always end reading a ratio with a lack of finality in your voice, but that's because you're only reading half the story. Ratios are usually related to each other across an equal sign.

Such a relationship is known as a **proportion,** so, as noted earlier when we were discussing 3 apples as being half the group of 6 apples, $\frac{3}{6} = \frac{1}{2}$. As a proportion involving two ratios, that would be read "Three is to 6 as 1 is to 2," and so, of course, it is.

Fraction as a Division

Have you ever noticed that on a calculator, if you press the "÷" button, you get the "/" printed on your screen? Have you ever wondered what that's all about? On a computer keyboard, there is no "÷" button. When you want to divide, you have to press the "/" button. Why the "/" instead of the "÷"?

Well, in case you haven't figured it out by now—especially given the sub-heading above—"/" is the fraction line. I wouldn't swear to this, but I would conjecture that in ancient times (like the early twentieth century and before), printers couldn't or wouldn't print fractions the way we do in this book. They always wrote them in-line, so the fraction one-half would have been written "1/2." Well, consider what the value of the fraction 4/2 would be. 2/2 = 1 whole. 4/2 is twice as big as 2/2, so the fraction is worth two wholes, or 2. Now it may be true that 4 halves are 2, but it's just as true that 4 divided by 2 is equal to 2.

Is this one of those special, "oh sure, it works for four-halves phenomena," or will it work for anything else? Well, why don't you try reasoning out the values of the following, and see what conclusions you draw:

1. $\frac{6}{3}$ 3. $\frac{20}{5}$ 5. $\frac{24}{8}$

2. $\frac{12}{2}$ 4. $\frac{36}{4}$

ANSWERS

1. Three-thirds make one, so twice as many, or six-thirds make 2; $6 \div 3 = 2$.

2. Two-halves make one, so 6 times as many (12) make 6; $12 \div 2 = 6$.

3. Five-fifths make one, so 4 times as many (20) make 4; $20 \div 5 = 4$.

4. Four-fourths make one, so 9 times as many (36) make 9; $36 \div 4 = 9$.

5. Eight-eighths make one, so 3 times as many (24) make 3; $24 \div 8 = 3$.

The conclusion seems clear enough. A fraction is actually one more way of writing a division.

Proper versus Improper

Historically, and old-fashionedly, a **proper fraction** was one in which the magnitude of the numerator was less than that of the denominator. An **improper fraction** was one with a numerator of greater magnitude than the denominator. Some teachers may still be using that terminology, so you need to be aware of what it means. As far as I'm concerned, however, the only time a fraction would be improper is if it stayed out past midnight and didn't phone home.

EXERCISES

Write the fraction that best answers the question.

1. A sack contains 9 apples, 12 pears, and 8 oranges. What part of the fruit is oranges?
2. A parking lot contains 15 equally sized parking spaces. What part of the lot does 4 spaces take up?
3. John earns $300 per week; Mary earns $500 per week. Represent Mary's weekly earnings in comparison to John's.

Questions 4–7 refer to a square of paper that is ruled into 25 squares of equal size. 7 of those squares are blackened.

4. Write the fraction of the squares that are blackened.
5. Write the fraction of the squares that are not blackened.
6. Write the fraction that compares the squares that are blackened to those that are not blackened.
7. Write the fraction that compares the squares that are not blackened to those that are blackened.

For Questions 8–12, write the whole number equivalent of each.

8. $\frac{45}{9}$ 10. $\frac{48}{12}$ 12. $\frac{63}{7}$

9. $\frac{56}{8}$ 11. $\frac{64}{8}$

ANSWERS

1. $\frac{8}{29}$ 5. $\frac{18}{25}$ 9. 7

                                          10. 4

2. $\frac{4}{15}$ 6. $\frac{7}{18}$ 11. 8

3. $\frac{500}{300}$ or $\frac{5}{3}$ 7. $\frac{18}{7}$ 12. 9

4. $\frac{7}{25}$ 8. 5

Equivalent Fractions

In the last lesson you saw (almost by accident) that a fraction could have more than one name. In case you don't recall, the example was 3 out of 6 apples being written as the fraction $\frac{3}{6}$ or $\frac{1}{2}$.

Common Equivalent Fractions

We could actually have called this section "Common Equivalent Common Fractions," because that is what's being discussed. It is a fact that every fraction can be written in an infinite number of ways. In other words, there is no end to the number of ways in which one can express a single fraction. Before we get into that, take a look at some equivalent fractions you're likely to come across again and again. Here are a few of the more commonly used equivalent fractions:

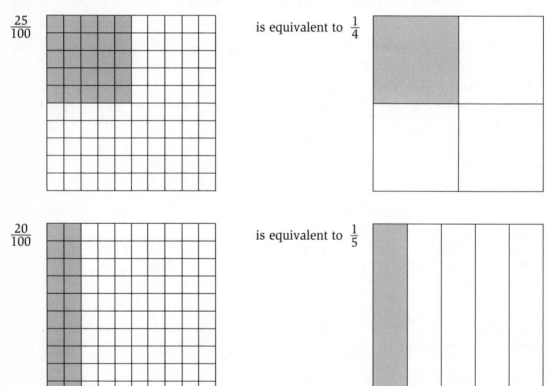

$\frac{25}{100}$ is equivalent to $\frac{1}{4}$

$\frac{20}{100}$ is equivalent to $\frac{1}{5}$

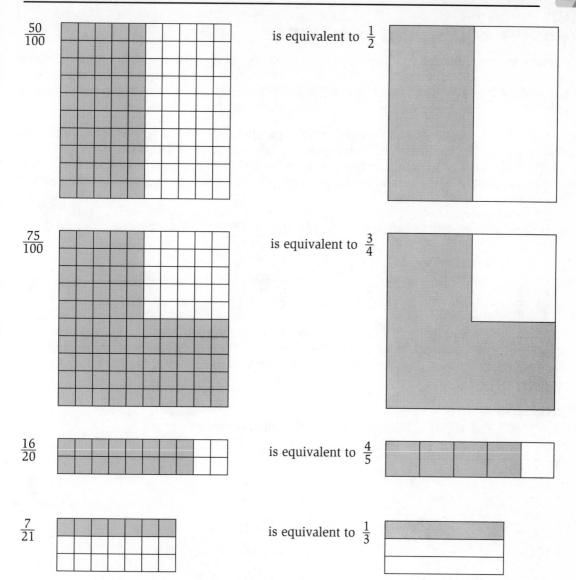

The equivalent fractions in the preceding were not picked at random. With the possible exception of the next to last fraction, you'll be seeing them repeatedly when we look at decimal fractions and percents.

Creating Equivalent Fractions

As noted earlier, every fraction can be written in an infinite number of ways. If you're wondering how that can be true, consider the fraction $\frac{2}{2}$. Since we've already seen that a fraction can be considered to be a division, and $2 \div 2 = 1$, then $\frac{2}{2} = 1$. Indeed, $\frac{2}{2}, \frac{3}{3}, \frac{4}{4}, \frac{5}{5}$, and any other of an endless string of possible fractions that have the same numerator and denominator are equal to 1.

You may recall that 1 is the *identity element* for multiplication. That is to say, you can multiply any number (whole or fraction) by 1 without changing its value. Do you see where this is going? Let's take the fractional number one-half and multiply it by 1 several different times. By the way, to multiply two fractions (which is still a few lessons away), you multiply the numerators together and the denominators together.

Okay. Enough dilly-dallying. Here are four multiplications of one-half by 1:

$$\frac{2}{2} \times \frac{1}{2} = \frac{2}{4} \qquad \frac{3}{3} \times \frac{1}{2} = \frac{3}{6}$$

$$\frac{4}{4} \times \frac{1}{2} = \frac{4}{8} \qquad \frac{5}{5} \times \frac{1}{2} = \frac{5}{10}$$

I hope you're not surprised by my talking about 1 and then bringing in the other forms that 1 can take. That's what mathematics is all about: getting the shoe to fit. There is no limit to what we can multiply one-half by, and so there is no limit to how many equivalent fractions there can be with a value of one-half.

EXERCISES

Write three of the lowest six equivalent fractions for each of the following:

1. $\frac{2}{3}$

2. $\frac{3}{5}$

3. $\frac{3}{4}$

4. $\frac{1}{6}$

5. $\frac{5}{6}$

6. $\frac{3}{8}$

7. $\frac{5}{8}$

8. $\frac{7}{12}$

9. $\frac{4}{7}$

10. $\frac{11}{16}$

ANSWERS

Following are the first six equivalent fractions for each of the preceding exercises. Of course, you needed to come up with only three of the six to be correct, so I must have needed the exercise.

1. $\frac{4}{6}, \frac{6}{9}, \frac{8}{12}, \frac{10}{15}, \frac{12}{18}, \frac{14}{21}$

2. $\frac{6}{10}, \frac{9}{15}, \frac{12}{20}, \frac{15}{25}, \frac{18}{30}, \frac{21}{35}$

3. $\frac{6}{8}, \frac{9}{12}, \frac{12}{16}, \frac{15}{20}, \frac{18}{24}, \frac{21}{28}$

4. $\frac{2}{12}, \frac{3}{18}, \frac{4}{24}, \frac{5}{30}, \frac{6}{36}, \frac{7}{42}$

5. $\frac{10}{12}, \frac{15}{18}, \frac{20}{24}, \frac{25}{30}, \frac{30}{36}, \frac{35}{42}$

6. $\frac{6}{16}, \frac{9}{24}, \frac{12}{32}, \frac{15}{40}, \frac{18}{48}, \frac{21}{56}$

7. $\frac{10}{16}, \frac{15}{24}, \frac{20}{32}, \frac{25}{40}, \frac{30}{48}, \frac{35}{56}$

8. $\frac{14}{24}, \frac{21}{36}, \frac{28}{48}, \frac{35}{60}, \frac{42}{72}, \frac{49}{84}$

9. $\frac{8}{14}, \frac{12}{21}, \frac{16}{28}, \frac{20}{35}, \frac{24}{42}, \frac{28}{49}$

10. $\frac{22}{32}, \frac{33}{48}, \frac{44}{64}, \frac{55}{80}, \frac{66}{96}, \frac{77}{112}$

Expressing Fractions in Lowest Terms

The numerator and denominator are collectively referred to as the **terms** of a fraction. In the last lesson you saw that there are an infinite number of ways to write any fraction. There is, however, only one form of any common fraction that is expressed in **lowest terms,** also known as **simplest terms.** When doing fractional arithmetic (which we'll begin in the next lesson), it is customary and good form to express all answers in lowest terms. Ten-twentieths, fifty-hundredths, and four-eighths are three different names for the same fraction. Expressed in lowest terms, that fraction is one-half.

GCF (Greatest Common Factor)

Consider the fraction $\frac{16}{48}$. Its terms are 16 and 48. They contain many of the same factors—numbers that are multiplied together. The diagram that follows shows the **prime factorization** (breaking down a composite number into its prime number components; see Lesson 14 for an explanation of prime numbers) of both terms. Although not the most elegant of prime factorizations, it is rather like a seasonal conifer, hence the diagram itself is known as a "**prime factor tree.**"

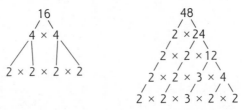

Check out the 16 first in the prime factor tree. Most students would instantly recognize that 16 is 4×4, and so the second line on the left shows that. Every student will recognize that each 4 is made up of 2×2, and so the third line. Now on to the 48. This is the less elegant of the two factorizations by far. I would recognize something other than what I used in the diagram, but the typical student would say to herself, "I know that 48 is even, so 2 must be a factor," hence the line that follows, 2×24. The 2 is brought down to the next line, and the 24 is factored into 2 and 12. Everything is multiplied together on every line. The 12 is next broken into 3×4, and finally the 4 is broken down. Notice that the bottom line of both trees contains nothing but prime numbers multiplied together.

Now is the time to do some noticing. The bottom line of 16's tree contains four 2s. 48's tree's bottom line also contains four 2s, and a 3. What does this mean? Well, it means that the greatest factor common to both trees is four 2s: $2 \times 2 \times 2 \times 2 = 16$. 16 is the **greatest common factor,** which mathematicians in their notorious

The result of the prime factorization of 16 and 48 holds a lesson that you might use as a caution for your student: Before you go doing a prime factorization on the terms of a fraction, try dividing the larger factor by the smaller one. It could save you a ton of time.

laziness abbreviate **GCF**. By removing (factoring out by division) the GCF from both terms of a fraction, you can guarantee that the fraction will be in lowest terms. $16 \div 16 = 1$; $48 \div 16 = 3$, and $\frac{16}{48}$ in lowest terms is $\frac{1}{3}$.

Reducing

Expressing a fraction in lowest terms used to be called "reducing" fractions. That is probably the most damaging term ever used in arithmetic, since it was totally undescriptive of what was taking place. Your child's teacher may (heaven forbid) use the term *reducing*, and if that's the case you'll have to step in, stopping just short of villifying the teacher, and explain to your student that when simplifying fractions, the size of the terms in which the fraction is expressed are reduced in order to simplify it. The value of the fraction remains totally unchanged.

I'll do one more prime factor tree for you and show you how to use it to find the GCF before turning you loose on some exercises. I'll find the GCF for $\frac{90}{120}$. The factorization is in the following diagram.

$$
\begin{array}{cc}
90 & 120 \\
/\ \backslash & /\ \backslash \\
2 \times 45 & 3 \times 40 \\
/\ /\ \backslash & /\ /\ \backslash \\
2 \times 5 \times 9 & 3 \times 5 \times 8 \\
/\ /\ /\ \backslash & /\ /\ /\ \backslash \\
2 \times 5 \times 3 \times 3 & 3 \times 5 \times 2 \times 2 \times 2
\end{array}
$$

Looking at the bottom lines of both factor trees, each has a 2, a 3, and a 5. That means the greatest common factor is $2 \times 3 \times 5$, which equals 30. To put the fraction into lowest terms, divide both the numerator and denominator by 30:

$$\frac{90 \div 30}{120 \div 30} = \frac{3}{4}$$

As a New York cab driver once said when asked how to get to Carnegie Hall: "Practice, practice, practice!"

EXERCISES

Find the GCF for each of the following pairs of numbers

1. 72, 63
2. 98, 49
3. 66, 99
4. 120, 150
5. 96, 128

6. 60, 100
7. 72, 96
8. 140, 175
9. 96, 224
10. 46, 69

Express each of the following fractions in lowest terms.

11. $\frac{34}{51}$

12. $\frac{25}{30}$

13. $\frac{36}{48}$

14. $\frac{49}{56}$

15. $\frac{44}{121}$

16. $\frac{38}{57}$

17. $\frac{45}{81}$

18. $\frac{54}{72}$

19. $\frac{156}{169}$

20. $\frac{75}{80}$

ANSWERS

1. 9

2. 49

3. 33

4. 30

5. 32

6. 20

7. 24

8. 35

9. 32

10. 23

11. $\frac{2}{3}$

12. $\frac{5}{6}$

13. $\frac{3}{4}$

14. $\frac{7}{8}$

15. $\frac{4}{11}$

16. $\frac{2}{3}$

17. $\frac{5}{9}$

18. $\frac{3}{4}$

19. $\frac{12}{13}$

20. $\frac{15}{16}$

Adding Fractions

As with whole numbers, fractions can be added, subtracted, multiplied, and divided, but specific rules govern each of these operations. For you to be able to add fractions, their denominators must be alike. Only the numerators are added. The following diagrams demonstrate the operation.

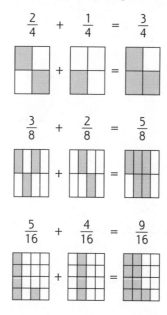

$$\frac{2}{4} \quad + \quad \frac{1}{4} \quad = \quad \frac{3}{4}$$

$$\frac{3}{8} \quad + \quad \frac{2}{8} \quad = \quad \frac{5}{8}$$

$$\frac{5}{16} \quad + \quad \frac{4}{16} \quad = \quad \frac{9}{16}$$

Should an answer be in other than lowest terms, it is customary to change it so that it is expressed in lowest terms.

Common Multiples

As noted, for you to be able to add fractions they must have the same denominators. Now neither you nor I am naive enough to believe that we're never going to come across fractions with different denominators in need of being added. That means that there must be some mechanism by which to add two fractions with different denominators, and so, of course, there is. We have to force them to have the same denominator. Actually, that's what all that equivalent fraction stuff from two lessons back was leading up to. We need to come up with a way to find fractions equivalent to the ones we need to add that have the same denominator. Actually, we call the new denominator, that we must create, the **common denominator.**

Say you want to add: $\frac{1}{4} + \frac{1}{3}$

Look at the denominators of those fractions, 3 and 4. Next, make a list of multiples of those numbers:

Multiples of 3: 3, 6, 9, **12**, 15, 18, 21, **24**, 27, 30, 33, **36**, . . .

Multiples of 4: 4, 8, **12**, 16, 20, **24**, 28, 32, **36**, 40, 44, . . .

Those multiples in bold type are **common multiples** of 3 and 4. Any one of those could be used as a common denominator for new fractions. Let's use 36ths.

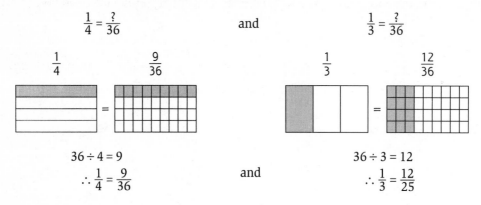

$$\frac{1}{4} = \frac{?}{36} \qquad \text{and} \qquad \frac{1}{3} = \frac{?}{36}$$

$$36 \div 4 = 9 \qquad\qquad 36 \div 3 = 12$$
$$\therefore \frac{1}{4} = \frac{9}{36} \qquad\qquad \therefore \frac{1}{3} = \frac{12}{25}$$

The three-dot pyramid means "therefore."

An alternative to working it out (as in the figures) is to divide the common denominator by the original denominator. This yields the number of parts of the new whole represented by the old fraction. Before you write that quotient in the numerator, multiply it by the old numerator. That process won't make any difference this time, but it will in later problems.

Now add: $\frac{9}{36} + \frac{12}{36} = \frac{21}{36}$

That simplifies to $\frac{7}{12}$.

You also could have solved that addition using 24ths, and if you want to try it, be my guest. If you get something other than $\frac{7}{12}$, go over your work again. In any case, that solution was more cumbersome than it had to be. Instead of working with any multiples of the denominators in question, it's simplest to work with the **least common multiple,** or **LCM.** In this case, 12.

Working with twelfths, $\frac{1}{4} = \frac{3}{12}$; $\frac{1}{3} = \frac{4}{12}$

$$\frac{3}{12} + \frac{4}{12} = \frac{7}{12}$$

$$\therefore \frac{1}{4} + \frac{1}{3} = \frac{7}{12}$$

Before moving on, try a few more LCMs just to help fix the technique in your mind.

Find the LCMs for the following pairs of numbers:

1. 4, 8
2. 5, 11
3. 8, 12
4. 9, 12

5. 4, 6
6. 12, 20
7. 8, 14
8. 6, 15

ANSWERS

1. 8
2. 55
3. 24
4. 36

5. 12
6. 60
7. 56
8. 30

They don't all turn out the way you think they will, do they? By using the LCM, we are able to find the **least common denominator** (abbreviated **LCD**) that will allow two fractions with unequal denominators to be added together. But the LCD is useful only some of the time.

Factor Trees Return

Try finding the least common denominator for this fractional addition:

$$\frac{7}{36} + \frac{21}{54} = \underline{\quad}$$

Well, you could start laying out two rows of multiples of 36 and 54, and in this case, you might get lucky, but I know that with most numbers of this magnitude and larger, I would be furrowing my brow in short order. You can always find a common denominator by multiplying the two denominators together, but it won't be the LCD. Instead, let's return to our old friend from the last lesson, the prime factor tree:

I took a couple of shortcuts to get to the bottom lines in a hurry. Both lines of primes contain two factors of 3s and one 2. The LCD is not going to need that 18 from both denominators, so get rid of one of them.

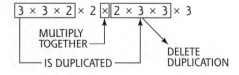

MULTIPLY: $3 \times 3 \times 2 \times 2 \times 3 = 108$

Now rename the fractions in terms of our common denominator, 108ths:

$108 \div 36 = 3; 3 \times 7 = 21;$ so $\frac{7}{36} = \frac{21}{108}$.

Remember, after dividing the new denominator by the old, multiply the quotient by the old numerator.

Then: $108 \div 54 = 2; 2 \times 21 = 42;$ so $\frac{21}{54} = \frac{42}{108}$.

Finally, $\frac{21}{108} + \frac{42}{108} = \frac{63}{108} = \frac{7}{12}$.

The sum was put into lowest terms by factoring a nine out of both terms.

Let's try one more of those:

How about: $\frac{12}{27} + \frac{24}{45} = $ _____

Use prime factor trees to get $3 \times 3 \times 3$ for 27 and $3 \times 3 \times 5$ for 45. There's a duplication of 3×3 in the prime factorizations, so drop one of those, and multiply $27 \times 5 = 135$.

Next, convert both fractions to 135ths: $135 \div 27 = 5; 5 \times 12 = 60;$ so $\frac{12}{27} = \frac{60}{135}$.

Remember, after dividing the new denominator by the old, multiply the quotient by the old numerator.

$135 \div 45 = 3; 3 \times 24 = 72;$ so $\frac{24}{45} = \frac{72}{135}$.

Finally, $\frac{60}{135} + \frac{72}{135} = \frac{44}{45}$.

The sum was put into lowest terms by factoring a 3 out of both terms.

Do you have the idea well chewed on now? Let's do some exercises and help digest it.

EXERCISES
Solve the following. Express answers in lowest terms.

1. $\frac{5}{16} + \frac{7}{16} = $ _____

2. $\frac{7}{12} + \frac{9}{24} = $ _____

3. $\frac{5}{8} + \frac{7}{32} = $ _____

4. $\frac{3}{20} + \frac{4}{5} = $ _____

5. $\frac{4}{7} + \frac{3}{10} = $ _____

6. $\frac{5}{14} + \frac{9}{35} = $ _____

7. $\frac{1}{4} + \frac{5}{6} = $ _____

8. $\frac{3}{8} + \frac{5}{12} = $ _____

9. $\frac{11}{24} + \frac{15}{36} = $ _____

10. $\frac{21}{54} + \frac{18}{45} = $ _____

11. $\frac{25}{42} + \frac{13}{36} = $ _____

12. $\frac{5}{18} + \frac{7}{24} = $ _____

13. $\frac{8}{21} + \frac{12}{35} = $ _____

14. $\frac{40}{64} + \frac{30}{96} = $ _____

15. $\frac{9}{36} + \frac{8}{48} = $ _____

16. $\frac{25}{72} + \frac{35}{96} = $ _____

ANSWERS

1. $\frac{3}{4}$

2. $\frac{23}{24}$

3. $\frac{27}{32}$

4. $\frac{19}{20}$

5. $\frac{61}{70}$

6. $\frac{43}{70}$

7. $\frac{13}{12}$ or $1\frac{1}{12}$

8. $\frac{19}{24}$

9. $\frac{7}{8}$

10. $\frac{71}{90}$

11. $\frac{241}{252}$

12. $\frac{41}{72}$

13. $\frac{76}{105}$

14. $\frac{15}{16}$

15. $\frac{5}{12}$

16. $\frac{205}{288}$

Subtracting Fractions

Subtracting fractions works essentially the same way as adding fractions. The only difference (no pun intended) is that you take the numerator of the second fraction away from the numerator of the first fraction. As with adding fractions, both denominators must be the same before subtraction can take place. So,

$$\frac{3}{4} - \frac{2}{4} = \frac{1}{4}$$

$$\frac{7}{8} - \frac{3}{8} = \frac{4}{8} = \frac{1}{2}$$

$$\frac{11}{16} - \frac{7}{16} = \frac{4}{16} = \frac{1}{4}$$

There are three fraction subtractions modeled for you here. But, the fun doesn't start until you get to having to find common denominators. Check out the following subtraction:

$$\frac{3}{4} - \frac{2}{3} = ???$$

Of course, you already know the following equivalent renamings:

$$\frac{3}{4} = \frac{9}{12} \qquad \frac{2}{3} = \frac{8}{12}$$

So, now it's possible to subtract:

$$\frac{9}{12} - \frac{8}{12} = \frac{1}{12}$$

You'll need to use all the forms of finding equivalent fractions that you've learned in order to solve the following exercises. Now go ahead and make a difference (many, in fact).

EXERCISES

Solve the following. Express answers in lowest terms.

1. $\frac{11}{16} - \frac{5}{16} =$ _____

2. $\frac{7}{12} - \frac{9}{24} =$ _____

3. $\frac{5}{8} - \frac{7}{32} =$ _____

4. $\frac{4}{5} - \frac{3}{20} =$ _____

5. $\frac{5}{7} - \frac{3}{10} =$ _____

6. $\frac{9}{14} - \frac{9}{35} =$ _____

7. $\frac{5}{6} - \frac{1}{4} =$ _____

8. $\frac{7}{8} - \frac{5}{12} =$ _____

9. $\frac{18}{24} - \frac{15}{36} =$ _____

10. $\frac{29}{54} - \frac{18}{45} =$ _____

11. $\frac{25}{42} - \frac{11}{36} =$ _____

12. $\frac{13}{18} - \frac{9}{24} =$ _____

13. $\frac{16}{21} - \frac{17}{35} =$ _____

14. $\frac{40}{64} - \frac{30}{96} =$ _____

15. $\frac{10}{36} - \frac{8}{48} =$ _____

16. $\frac{35}{72} - \frac{35}{96} =$ _____

ANSWERS

1. $\frac{3}{8}$

2. $\frac{5}{24}$

3. $\frac{13}{32}$

4. $\frac{13}{20}$

5. $\frac{29}{70}$

6. $\frac{27}{70}$

7. $\frac{7}{12}$

8. $\frac{11}{24}$

9. $\frac{1}{3}$

10. $\frac{37}{270}$

11. $\frac{73}{252}$

12. $\frac{25}{72}$

13. $\frac{29}{105}$

14. $\frac{5}{16}$

15. $\frac{1}{9}$

16. $\frac{35}{288}$

Multiplying Fractions

To understand the language of multiplication of fractions, you need to understand that the words "of" and "times" are interchangeable. For instance, 3 of 4 = 12, just as surely as 3 × 4 = 12. When you see 3 of 4, that means that you are being asked to consider 3 groups, each of which contains 4 things, as in the following figure.

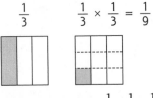

3 of 4

When fractions are being multiplied, you are taking a part of a part. Half of a half is a fourth.

$\frac{1}{2}$ $\frac{1}{2}$ of $\frac{1}{2}$ = $\frac{1}{4}$

Half of a half, or $\frac{1}{2} \times \frac{1}{2} = \frac{1}{4}$

That's why fractional multiplication is so different from whole number multiplication. With the latter, you expect the product to be larger than the factors. When multiplying fractions, however, the product is smaller than either of the factors. What do you suppose the product of one-third and one-third is? That product is illustrated here:

$\frac{1}{3}$ $\frac{1}{3} \times \frac{1}{3} = \frac{1}{9}$

Third of a third, or $\frac{1}{3} \times \frac{1}{3} = \frac{1}{9}$

Remember the association between "of" and multiplication. It will serve you and your student well when he reaches elementary algebra. Any time the word "of" appears in an algebraic word problem, it is an indication that the quantities in question are to be multiplied.

By now, you have probably figured out all that you need to know about multiplying fractions, but I think one more illustration is in order. Following is an illustration of two-thirds of two-thirds.

$$\frac{2}{3} \qquad \frac{2}{3} \times \frac{2}{3} = \frac{4}{9}$$

Two thirds of two thirds, or $\frac{2}{3} \times \frac{2}{3} = \frac{4}{9}$

There you have it. To multiply two fractions together, multiply the numerators together, and multiply the denominators together. Also, make sure that the product is expressed in lowest terms.

EXERCISES

Solve the following. Express in lowest terms.

1. $\frac{2}{3} \times \frac{3}{4} =$ _____

2. $\frac{3}{5} \times \frac{2}{3} =$ _____

3. $\frac{4}{6} \times \frac{3}{8} =$ _____

4. $\frac{4}{5} \times \frac{3}{8} =$ _____

5. $\frac{3}{4} \times \frac{7}{8} =$ _____

6. $\frac{5}{6} \times \frac{7}{12} =$ _____

7. $\frac{11}{12} \times \frac{5}{6} =$ _____

8. $\frac{1}{9} \times \frac{1}{8} =$ _____

9. $\frac{5}{9} \times \frac{6}{10} =$ _____

10. $\frac{12}{15} \times \frac{6}{9} =$ _____

11. $\frac{5}{7} \times \frac{3}{4} =$ _____

12. $\frac{7}{9} \times \frac{3}{14} =$ _____

13. $\frac{8}{15} \times \frac{10}{12} =$ _____

14. $\frac{15}{16} \times \frac{1}{2} =$ _____

15. $\frac{2}{3} \times \frac{15}{16} =$ _____

16. $\frac{15}{24} \times \frac{12}{30} =$ _____

ANSWERS

1. $\frac{1}{2}$

2. $\frac{2}{5}$

3. $\frac{1}{4}$

4. $\frac{3}{10}$

5. $\frac{21}{32}$

6. $\frac{35}{72}$

7. $\frac{35}{72}$

8. $\frac{1}{72}$

9. $\frac{1}{3}$

10. $\frac{8}{15}$

11. $\frac{15}{28}$

12. $\frac{1}{6}$

13. $\frac{4}{9}$

14. $\frac{15}{32}$

15. $\frac{5}{8}$

16. $\frac{1}{4}$

Dividing Fractions

The techniques used for dividing fractions will probably seem the strangest of all to you—especially if you have any recollection of the way you probably learned to do it when you first studied elementary math. The old saw was, if you recall, "invert and multiply." Since multiplication of fractions less than one results in a product smaller than the factors, it stands to reason that the quotient in a division of fractions less than one will be larger than the numbers being divided. We'll check that out in a little bit.

Reciprocals

Division of fractions relies upon the fact that multiplication and division are **reciprocal** (or inverse) **operations.** That is to say, they undo each other. A **reciprocal** is the number by which you multiply another in order to get a product of one. The reciprocal of $\frac{1}{2}$ is 2, because $2 \times \frac{1}{2} = \frac{2}{1} \times \frac{1}{2} = 1$. What do you suppose are the reciprocals of $\frac{1}{3}, \frac{1}{4}, \frac{1}{5}, \frac{1}{100}$, and $\frac{1}{256}$?

The answers to the just posed group of reciprocals are 3, 4, 5, 100, and 256, respectively. Pretty easy, huh? Now contemplate this one: What are the reciprocals of $\frac{2}{3}, \frac{3}{4}, \frac{4}{5}$, and $\frac{7}{8}$? Feel free to take a minute or two to think about it. Are you sure you've thought it over? Okay, the answers, respectively, are $\frac{3}{2}, \frac{4}{3}, \frac{5}{4}$ and $\frac{8}{7}$. Do you see the pattern?

Each of the original fractions has been turned upside down to get its reciprocal. Multiply each original fraction by its corresponding reciprocal, and you will get a product with the same numerator and denominator, or, in other words, one.

Reciprocal Multiplication

To effect division of common fractions (remember that subject? It's the name of this chapter!), we turn division into multiplication, multiplying by the reciprocal of the divisor. Consider this:

$$\frac{1}{2} \quad \div \quad \frac{1}{4} \qquad = \qquad \frac{1}{2} \quad \times \quad \frac{4}{1}$$

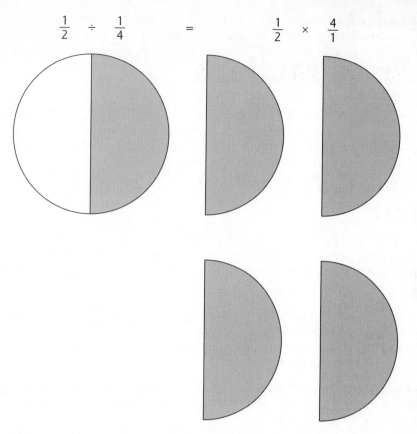

That makes a larger quantity of halves, just like we had predicted before, since you now have to multiply the numerators together and the denominators together:

$$\frac{1}{2} \times \frac{4}{1} = 2$$

$$\frac{1}{2} \quad \div \quad \frac{1}{4} \qquad = \qquad \frac{4}{2} \quad = \quad 2$$

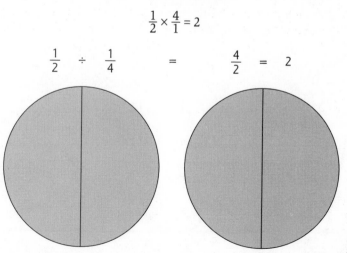

Think about it: How many fourths are in one half? We just found the answer, of course. It's two.

And there you have the essential recipe for division of common fractions. You might even summarize the formula as "invert and multiply." Hey, where have I heard that before?! Just bear in mind that it's the divisor that must be inverted (another way of saying substituted for by its reciprocal), when you change the division to multiplication.

Suppose that we had done that the other way around, dividing one-fourth by one-half? How many halves are there in one-fourth? You can ponder that while I'm working out the solution:

$$\frac{1}{4} \div \frac{1}{2} = \frac{1}{4} \times \frac{2}{1} = \frac{2}{4} = \frac{1}{2}$$

I inverted the one-half and changed it to multiplication. Then I multiplied and got two-fourths, which simplifies to one-half. Half of one-half makes one-fourth. It makes sense, doesn't it? If two-fourths make one-half, then when one-fourth is divided by half, only a half of it would fit.

Are you wondering whether the same technique would work for whole numbers? Check this out:

$$5\overline{)30} = 30 \div 5$$

In other words, the divisor is the 5. Then, $30 \div 5 = 30 \times \frac{1}{5}$

To make that work, we have to stick a 1 under the 30; then we can multiply the terms together:

$$\frac{30}{1} \times \frac{1}{5} = \frac{30}{5} = 6$$

Well, I don't know about you, but it seems to me that it worked. It kind of makes you wonder why they ever invented division in the first place—until you begin thinking about larger numbers, that is.

EXERCISES
Solve the following. Express in lowest terms.

1. $\frac{3}{4} \div \frac{5}{6} =$ _____

2. $\frac{5}{8} \div \frac{2}{3} =$ _____

3. $\frac{2}{3} \div \frac{5}{8} =$ _____

4. $\frac{9}{16} \div \frac{3}{8} =$ _____

5. $\frac{18}{32} \div \frac{7}{8} =$ _____

6. $\frac{16}{25} \div \frac{14}{20} =$ _____

7. $\frac{24}{25} \div \frac{3}{5} =$ _____

8. $\frac{3}{4} \div \frac{3}{4} =$ _____

9. $\frac{15}{42} \div \frac{25}{56} =$ _____

10. $\frac{14}{35} \div \frac{6}{18} =$ _____

11. $\frac{9}{27} \div \frac{7}{21} =$ _____

12. $\frac{11}{19} \div \frac{7}{9} =$ _____

13. $\frac{36}{42} \div \frac{25}{40} =$ _____

14. $\frac{54}{63} \div \frac{36}{42} =$ _____

15. $\frac{36}{45} \div \frac{24}{25} =$ _____

ANSWERS

1. $\frac{9}{10}$

2. $\frac{15}{16}$

3. $\frac{16}{15}$ or $1\frac{1}{16}$

4. $\frac{3}{2}$ or $1\frac{1}{2}$

5. $\frac{9}{14}$

6. $\frac{32}{35}$

7. $\frac{8}{5}$ or $1\frac{3}{5}$

8. 1

9. $\frac{4}{5}$

10. $\frac{42}{35} = 1\frac{1}{5}$

11. 1

12. $\frac{99}{133}$

13. $\frac{48}{35}$ or $1\frac{13}{35}$

14. 1

15. $\frac{5}{6}$

Canceling

In the last two lessons, I solved the exercises in a lot less time than you did, and I'm not just guessing that. It happened because I knew a trick that you didn't. It's a trick that you, too, will know before this lesson's over, but we need to lead up to it, so be patient for a few minutes longer.

I'm sure you recollect how we are able to simplify fractions by finding a common factor in the numerator and denominator. Recollect? It's a skill that you've been using in day-to-day work with common fractions:

Simplifying fractions: $\dfrac{\cancel{6}^{3}}{\cancel{8}^{4}} = \dfrac{3}{4}$ $\qquad \dfrac{\cancel{12}^{1}}{\cancel{36}^{3}} = \dfrac{1}{3}$

In the first example, 2 was factored out of both numerator and denominator. In the second, 12 was factored out of both.

Multiplying Fractions

Now consider what happens when two fractions are multiplied together:

$$\frac{3}{4} \times \frac{4}{6} = \frac{\cancel{12}^{1}}{\cancel{24}^{2}} = \frac{1}{2}$$

The numerators are multiplied together; the denominators are multiplied together; and finally the GCF is divided out of both terms so that the fraction is left expressed in lowest terms.

But if that's the procedure, we could just as well have made the multiplication into a single fraction:

$$\frac{3}{4} \times \frac{4}{6} = \frac{3 \times 4}{4 \times 6}$$

Looking at the combined fraction (the one on the right), I see common factors that I can divide out on both top and bottom. There are two 4s, which cancel to become 1s ($4 \div 4 = 1$):

$$\frac{3 \times \cancel{4}^{1}}{\cancel{4}_{1} \times 6}$$

And 3 and 6 are both divisible by 3, so I'll factor that out:

$$\frac{{}^{1}\cancel{3} \times \cancel{4}^{1}}{\cancel{4}_{1} \times \cancel{6}_{2}}$$

Finally, I'm going to multiply what I have left:

$$\frac{\overset{1}{\cancel{3}} \times \overset{1}{\cancel{4}}}{\underset{1}{\cancel{4}} \times \underset{2}{\cancel{6}}} = \frac{1}{2}$$

Well, what do you know about that? I got the same result and didn't have to simplify the answer—in fact, I never will if I always factor out all common factors. Now that may look like a lot of work to you, but that's because I did each step separately. Normally, it would all be done at once, like this:

$$\frac{24}{35} \times \frac{28}{36} \to \to \to \frac{\overset{2}{\cancel{24}}}{\underset{5}{\cancel{35}}} \times \frac{\overset{4}{\cancel{28}}}{\underset{3}{\cancel{36}}} = \frac{8}{15}$$

First is the unaltered multiplication. 24 and 36 share a GCF of 12; 35 and 28 share a GCF of 7. After having factored those out, multiply what is left, and the product is already in simplest terms.

Dividing Fractions

If you're suspecting that division works the same way, your suspicion is well founded, up to a point. You would never cancel in division; only in multiplication, but since dividing fractions becomes reciprocal multiplication . . . 'Nuf said! Look at this division:

$$\frac{24}{36} \div \frac{15}{18}$$

I, personally, would never attempt to start solving it the way it looks now. Each fraction can be simplified. Canceling is not restricted to being done across a times sign. It is the way one simplifies a fraction, and within the same fraction, it is always in order before doing anything else:

$$\frac{\overset{2}{\cancel{24}}}{\underset{3}{\cancel{36}}} \div \frac{\overset{5}{\cancel{15}}}{\underset{6}{\cancel{18}}} \to \to \to \frac{2}{3} \div \frac{5}{6}$$

Now you're ready to set up the reciprocal multiplication:

$$\frac{2}{3} \div \frac{5}{6} = \frac{2}{\underset{1}{\cancel{3}}} \times \frac{\overset{2}{\cancel{6}}}{5} = \frac{4}{5}$$

Both 3 and 6 contain a common factor, 3, and that's all the canceling you can do. Next, multiply and get four-fifths—the quotient in lowest terms. Basically, that's all there is to it. Just remember, no canceling between fractions until after it is turned into multiplication.

If some of the exercises that follow look familiar, that's because they were lifted from the previous two lessons so that you could see how much easier they are to do now that you know about canceling. Enjoy them!

Don't dismiss the notion that canceling out common factors is something that your student is going to use to simplify some of the fractions he is multiplying and then never has use for again. While it is introduced into elementary school arithmetic as canceling, the activity's more mature name is factoring, and the ability to recognize factors common to more than one mathematical expression will play a large role in your student's ability to succeed with algebra later on.

Factoring monomials (expressions not containing "+" or "−" signs), binomials (expressions containing one "+" or "−" sign) and polynomials (expressions with two or more "+" and/or "−" signs) is a major technique for the solving of quadratic equations, which both you and your student are destined to encounter in intermediate algebra. That may be high school, but kids grow up very quickly! (A word to the wise . . . , as they say.)

EXERCISES

Multiply or divide as the sign indicates. Make sure to get rid of any common factors before doing your computation.

1. $\frac{4}{6} \times \frac{3}{8} =$ _____

2. $\frac{4}{5} \times \frac{3}{8} =$ _____

3. $\frac{5}{9} \times \frac{6}{10} =$ _____

4. $\frac{12}{15} \times \frac{6}{9} =$ _____

5. $\frac{7}{9} \times \frac{3}{14} =$ _____

6. $\frac{15}{24} \times \frac{12}{30} =$ _____

7. $\frac{9}{16} \div \frac{3}{8} =$ _____

8. $\frac{18}{32} \div \frac{7}{8} =$ _____

9. $\frac{16}{25} \div \frac{14}{20} =$ _____

10. $\frac{15}{42} \div \frac{25}{56} =$ _____

11. $\frac{14}{35} \div \frac{6}{18} =$ _____

12. $\frac{9}{27} \div \frac{7}{21} =$ _____

13. $\frac{36}{42} \div \frac{25}{40} =$ _____

14. $\frac{36}{45} \div \frac{24}{25} =$ _____

15. $\frac{54}{63} \div \frac{36}{42} =$ _____

ANSWERS

1. $\frac{1}{4}$

2. $\frac{3}{10}$

3. $\frac{1}{3}$

4. $\frac{8}{15}$

5. $\frac{1}{6}$

6. $\frac{1}{4}$

7. $\frac{3}{2}$ or $1\frac{1}{2}$

8. $\frac{9}{14}$

9. $\frac{32}{35}$

10. $\frac{4}{5}$

11. $1\frac{1}{5}$

12. 1

13. $\frac{48}{35}$ or $1\frac{13}{35}$

14. $\frac{5}{6}$

15. 1

LESSON 23

Mixed Numbers

Showing up in a few of the answers in the last few lessons were combinations of whole numbers and common fractions. These combinations are generally referred to as **mixed numbers.** Some examples are

$$1\frac{5}{8} \quad 2\frac{3}{5} \quad 3\frac{4}{5} \quad 4\frac{2}{3} \quad 5\frac{6}{7} \quad 6\frac{9}{16}$$

A mixed number is often the result of simplifying a fraction that is larger than one, for example:

$$\frac{21}{16} = 1\frac{5}{16} \qquad \frac{37}{8} = 4\frac{5}{8} \qquad \frac{22}{4} = 5\frac{2}{4} = 5\frac{1}{2}$$

To change a fraction that is larger than one to a mixed number, divide the numerator by the denominator. As many times as it goes in will be the whole-number part of the mixed number. The remainder is put over the denominator to form the fractional part. When appropriate, the fractional part should be expressed in lowest terms.

In the three previous examples, 21 divided by 16 is 1 with a remainder of 5, which was placed over the original denominator. Next, 8 goes into 37 four times to make 32, and there is a remainder of 5, placed over the original denominator. Finally, 22 divided by 4 equals 5 with a remainder of 2, but two-fourths simplifies to one-half.

All four arithmetic operations may be performed with mixed numbers, as we shall see in the lessons that follow this one. In order to perform some of those operations, it is necessary to convert from mixed numbers into common fractions greater than one. The following diagram indicates how this transformation is done:

$$\text{W.N.} \xrightarrow{\;+\;} \frac{\text{Numerator}}{\text{Denominator}} \xrightarrow{\;=\;} \frac{\text{Result}}{\text{Denominator}}$$
$$\overset{\times}{\underset{\text{Start}}{\curvearrowleft}}$$

Start with the denominator and multiply it times the whole number (W.N.). To that product, add the numerator and place the entire result over the original denominator (rewritten, of course).

Here are a couple of examples:

$$3\frac{4}{5} \to \to \frac{(5\times3)+4}{5} = \frac{15+4}{5} = \frac{19}{5}$$

(Just like on the old record jackets . . . .) If you liked that example, you're sure to enjoy:

$$9\frac{11}{12} \to \to \frac{(12\times9)+11}{12} = \frac{108+11}{12} = \frac{119}{12}$$

100

EXERCISES

Express each of the following as a mixed number.

1. $\frac{25}{8}$

2. $\frac{27}{4}$

3. $\frac{45}{7}$

4. $\frac{32}{5}$

5. $\frac{48}{9}$

6. $\frac{32}{3}$

7. $\frac{64}{7}$

8. $\frac{35}{2}$

9. $\frac{72}{10}$

10. $\frac{85}{13}$

Express each of the following as a fraction greater than 1.

11. $2\frac{3}{5}$

12. $5\frac{1}{8}$

13. $13\frac{1}{2}$

14. $8\frac{2}{3}$

15. $7\frac{5}{9}$

16. $4\frac{5}{6}$

17. $5\frac{6}{7}$

18. $7\frac{8}{9}$

19. $8\frac{3}{5}$

20. $9\frac{11}{20}$

ANSWERS

1. $3\frac{1}{8}$

2. $6\frac{3}{4}$

3. $6\frac{3}{7}$

4. $6\frac{2}{5}$

5. $5\frac{1}{3}$

6. $10\frac{2}{3}$

7. $9\frac{1}{7}$

8. $17\frac{1}{2}$

9. $7\frac{1}{5}$

10. $6\frac{7}{13}$

11. $\frac{13}{5}$

12. $\frac{41}{8}$

13. $\frac{27}{2}$

14. $\frac{26}{3}$

15. $\frac{68}{9}$

16. $\frac{29}{6}$

17. $\frac{41}{7}$

18. $\frac{71}{9}$

19. $\frac{43}{5}$

20. $\frac{191}{20}$

Adding Mixed Numbers

Adding mixed numbers can be done either horizontally or vertically. Essentially, the whole numbers are added to the whole numbers and the fractions are added to the fractions.

$$3\frac{1}{4} + 2\frac{1}{4} = 5\frac{2}{4} = 5\frac{1}{2}$$

In the preceding example, in order to express the answer in lowest terms, it is necessary to rename two-fourths as its equivalent, one-half. Additional complexities can develop, however, as is the case with the following addition:

$$3\frac{2}{3} + 4\frac{2}{3} = 7\frac{4}{3} = 7 + 1\frac{1}{3} = 8\frac{1}{3}$$

Adding 3 and two-thirds to 4 and two-thirds adds up to 7 and four-thirds. Four-thirds simplifies to 1 and one-third. 7 + 1 and one-third is certainly not a satisfactory answer. Instead, the whole number portions must be added together to make 8 and one-third.

Following is one more simple addition in vertical format:

$$\begin{array}{r} 3\frac{3}{8} \\ + 2\frac{1}{8} \\ \hline 5\frac{\cancel{4}}{\cancel{8}}\frac{1}{2} \end{array}$$

The sum is five and one-half. Now let's add a wrinkle.

With Unlike Denominators

If we lived in a perfect world, then all fractions we ever needed to add or subtract would have like denominators. I take it that you know where this is leading?

$$\begin{array}{r} 3\frac{1}{3} \\ + 4\frac{1}{4} \\ \hline \end{array}$$

As you know, you can't add fractions with unlike denominators. The least common multiple of 3 and 4 is 12, so I'm going to choose 12ths as the LCD (a), and rename both fractions in terms of 12ths (b):

(a)
$$3\frac{1}{3} \;\Big|\; \overline{12}$$
$$+\,4\frac{1}{4} \;\Big|\; \overline{12}$$

(b)
$$3\frac{1}{3} \;\Big|\; \frac{4}{12}$$
$$+\,4\frac{1}{4} \;\Big|\; \frac{3}{12}$$

(c)
$$3\frac{1}{3} \;\Big|\; \frac{4}{12}$$
$$+\,4\frac{1}{4} \;\Big|\; \frac{3}{12}$$
$$7 \;\Big|\; \frac{7}{12}$$

Finally, in (c), we add the whole numbers together and add the fractions together to get the sum, seven and seven-twelfths.

Three or More

You may recall from whole number addition that it is the one arithmetic operation in which more than two numbers may be involved. Addition of fractions and addition of mixed numbers are no different. That can cause some difficulty—especially in cases like the following:

$$2\frac{3}{5}$$
$$1\frac{3}{4}$$
$$+\,3\frac{2}{3}$$

The most direct way to find a common factor is to multiply $3 \times 4 \times 5 = 60$. Is 60ths the least common denominator? You know that 12ths is the LCD for thirds and fourths. Start counting by 12 until you find a multiple that is divisible by 5: 12, 24, 36, 48, 60. Remember the divisibility tests from Lesson 14? To be divisible by 5, the ones digit must be a 0 or a 5. 60ths it is (a):

(a)
$$2\frac{3}{5} \;\Big|\; \overline{60}$$
$$1\frac{3}{4} \;\Big|\; \overline{60}$$
$$+\,3\frac{2}{3} \;\Big|\; \overline{60}$$

(b)
$$2\frac{3}{5} \;\Big|\; \frac{36}{60}$$
$$1\frac{3}{4} \;\Big|\; \frac{45}{60}$$
$$+\,3\frac{2}{3} \;\Big|\; \frac{40}{60}$$

(c)
$$2\frac{3}{5} \;\Big|\; \frac{36}{60}$$
$$1\frac{3}{4} \;\Big|\; \frac{45}{60}$$
$$+\,3\frac{2}{3} \;\Big|\; \frac{40}{60}$$
$$6 \;\Big|\; \frac{121}{60} \; 8\frac{1}{60}$$

I've converted all fractions to 60ths (b). In (c), the sum one hundred twenty-one 60ths is 2 wholes, which are added to the 6 wholes to make 8 and one-sixtieth.

Whew! I had more than enough mental exercise on that one. Now it's your turn!

EXERCISES

1. $5\frac{3}{8} + 2\frac{7}{8} =$ ____

2. $4\frac{3}{5} + 4\frac{3}{5} =$ ____

3. $3\frac{2}{7} + 2\frac{3}{5} =$ ____

4. $5\frac{3}{8} + 4\frac{1}{4} =$ ____

5. $\begin{array}{r} 7\frac{2}{3} \\ + 6\frac{3}{4} \\ \hline \end{array}$

6. $\begin{array}{r} 8\frac{3}{5} \\ + 6\frac{5}{8} \\ \hline \end{array}$

7. $\begin{array}{r} 9\frac{3}{4} \\ + 8\frac{3}{5} \\ \hline \end{array}$

8. $\begin{array}{r} 6\frac{5}{21} \\ + 8\frac{3}{14} \\ \hline \end{array}$

9. $\begin{array}{r} 9\frac{5}{6} \\ + 7\frac{1}{8} \\ \hline \end{array}$

10. $\begin{array}{r} 5\frac{3}{7} \\ + 4\frac{2}{6} \\ \hline \end{array}$

11. $\begin{array}{r} 3\frac{1}{2} \\ 2\frac{2}{3} \\ + 5\frac{3}{4} \\ \hline \end{array}$

12. $\begin{array}{r} 4\frac{5}{6} \\ 6\frac{3}{8} \\ + 5\frac{3}{4} \\ \hline \end{array}$

13. $\begin{array}{r} 2\frac{3}{5} \\ 1\frac{1}{2} \\ + 3\frac{1}{6} \\ \hline \end{array}$

14. $\begin{array}{r} 3\frac{5}{6} \\ 6\frac{3}{4} \\ + 9\frac{4}{7} \\ \hline \end{array}$

ANSWERS

1. $8\frac{1}{4}$

2. $9\frac{1}{5}$

3. $5\frac{31}{35}$

4. $9\frac{5}{8}$

5. $14\frac{5}{12}$

6. $15\frac{9}{40}$

7. $18\frac{7}{20}$

8. $14\frac{19}{42}$

9. $16\frac{23}{24}$

10. $9\frac{16}{21}$

11. $11\frac{11}{12}$

12. $16\frac{23}{24}$

13. $7\frac{4}{15}$

14. $20\frac{1}{84}$

Subtracting Mixed Numbers

You might reasonably think that subtracting mixed numbers is to adding mixed numbers what subtracting whole numbers and fractions are to adding the same, and to some extent you would be correct. We'll start out with ones that work as expected, before we get to the new wrinkle created by mixed-number subtraction.

Those That Work As Expected

It is perfectly reasonable that when subtracting mixed numbers, the whole number is subtracted from the whole number part and the fraction is subtracted from the fractional part. The following example is from "the best of all possible worlds:"

$$9\frac{7}{8} - 5\frac{1}{8} = 4\frac{6}{8} = 4\frac{3}{4}$$

Subtracting the 5 from the 9 leaves 4. Seven-eighths take away one-eighth leaves six-eighths, which simplifies to three-fourths, so the difference is four and three-fourths.

This next example introduces the solution for subtraction of mixed numbers with differing denominators:

(a)
$$\begin{array}{r|r} 7\frac{3}{4} & \overline{12} \\ -\,4\frac{2}{3} & \overline{12} \end{array}$$

(b)
$$\begin{array}{r|r} 7\frac{3}{4} & \frac{9}{12} \\ -\,4\frac{2}{3} & \frac{8}{12} \end{array}$$

(c)
$$\begin{array}{r|r} 7\frac{3}{4} & \frac{9}{12} \\ -\,4\frac{2}{3} & \frac{8}{12} \\ \hline 3 & \frac{1}{12} \end{array}$$

In (a), I've sized up the situation and decided that the LCD for thirds and fourths is 12ths. In (b), I've made my conversions from fourths and thirds to 12ths. Finally, in (c), the whole numbers have been subtracted, and the fractions have been subtracted, to find a difference of three and one-twelfth.

The Larger Fraction's in the Denominator

Okay, so much for the nitty-gritty. "What makes subtraction any different from addition," you ask, "aside from the obvious fact that you subtract instead of adding?" Fair question! Try this subtraction on for size:

(a)
$$\begin{array}{r} 8\frac{3}{5} \\ -\,3\frac{5}{6} \end{array}$$

(b)
$$\begin{array}{r|r} 8\frac{3}{5} & \overline{30} \\ -\,3\frac{5}{6} & \overline{30} \end{array}$$

(c)
$$\begin{array}{r|r} 8\frac{3}{5} & \frac{18}{30} \\ -\,3\frac{5}{6} & \frac{25}{30} \end{array}$$

"There's nothing very spectacular looking about (a)," you're saying to yourself. You recognize that you're going to need a common denominator, and that the LCD is 30ths, which is reflected in (b). So the next thing is to convert the fractions to 30ths, as in (c), and subtract.

What's the matter? Is something keeping you from subtracting? Oh, I see. 25 is bigger than 18. That is a problem! Do you see the solution?

(d)
$$\overset{7}{\cancel{8}}\,\overset{\frac{30}{30}}{\frac{3}{5}}\,\bigg|\,\frac{18}{30}$$
$$-\,3\frac{5}{6}\,\bigg|\,\frac{25}{30}$$

(e)
$$\overset{7}{\cancel{8}}\,\overset{\frac{30}{30}}{\frac{3}{5}}\,\bigg|\,\frac{18}{30}\,\bigg|\,\frac{48}{30}$$
$$-\,3\frac{5}{6}\,\bigg|\,\frac{25}{30}\,\bigg|\,\frac{25}{30}$$

(f)
$$\overset{7}{\cancel{8}}\,\overset{\frac{30}{30}}{\frac{3}{5}}\,\bigg|\,\frac{18}{30}\,\bigg|\,\frac{48}{30}$$
$$-\,3\frac{5}{6}\,\bigg|\,\frac{25}{30}\,\bigg|\,\frac{25}{30}$$
$$\quad\;\;4\,\bigg|\qquad\;\bigg|\,\frac{23}{30}$$

In (d), I have taken one whole from the 8, leaving 7 behind, have renamed it as thirty-thirtieths, and have placed it above the eighteen-thirtieths that were already in the fractions. Next, I'll combine the renamed one with the eighteen-thirtieths (e). Finally, in (f), I finish the subtraction, and the difference is found to be 4 and twenty-three thirtieths.

Let me give you one piece of reassurance: It doesn't get any more complicated than this. Just to help make sure that you can develop a comfort level with this mechanism, let's do one more that's a little less complex, but still reinforces the main idea:

(a)
$$7\frac{3}{8}$$
$$-\,4\frac{7}{8}$$

(b)
$$\overset{6}{7}\overset{\frac{11}{8}}{\frac{3}{8}}\;\leftarrow\left(1=\frac{8}{8}+\frac{3}{8}=\frac{11}{8}\right)$$
$$-\,4\frac{7}{8}$$

(c)
$$\overset{6}{7}\overset{\frac{11}{8}}{\frac{3}{8}}$$
$$-\,4\frac{7}{8}$$
$$2\overset{4}{\cancel{8}}\frac{1}{2}$$

Because this time, we're subtracting 8ths from 8ths (a), there's no need to find any LCD. Since the fraction being subtracted, however, is greater than what it's being taken from, some renaming is going to be required. In (b), as explained in the parentheses that follow it, 1 is taken from the 7, renamed as eight-eighths, and added to the three-eighths that were already there, to make eleven-eighths. Note that it was all done in one single step, rather than spread out as it was last time. Rest assured, also, that you'll never need to rename anything greater than 1 for purposes of mixed-number subtraction.

Finally, in (c), the subtraction gets completed, and the four-eighths becomes one-half for a total of 2 and a half. Now it's time to get some exercise(s)!

EXERCISES

1. $5\frac{7}{12} - 2\frac{5}{12} = $ ___

2. $14\frac{7}{8} - 9\frac{3}{8} = $ ___

3. $13\frac{8}{9} - 7\frac{1}{3} = $ ___

4. $21\frac{5}{8} - 8\frac{1}{4} = $ ___

5. $\begin{array}{r} 17\frac{3}{4} \\ -15\frac{2}{3} \\ \hline \end{array}$

6. $\begin{array}{r} 18\frac{4}{5} \\ -12\frac{3}{8} \\ \hline \end{array}$

7. $\begin{array}{r} 9\frac{3}{4} \\ -8\frac{3}{5} \\ \hline \end{array}$

8. $\begin{array}{r} 19\frac{11}{21} \\ -14\frac{3}{14} \\ \hline \end{array}$

9. $\begin{array}{r} 9\frac{5}{6} \\ -7\frac{1}{8} \\ \hline \end{array}$

10. $\begin{array}{r} 9\frac{3}{7} \\ -4\frac{2}{3} \\ \hline \end{array}$

11. $\begin{array}{r} 7\frac{3}{5} \\ -6\frac{2}{3} \\ \hline \end{array}$

12. $\begin{array}{r} 8\frac{1}{6} \\ -4\frac{4}{9} \\ \hline \end{array}$

13. $\begin{array}{r} 9\frac{1}{3} \\ -5\frac{3}{4} \\ \hline \end{array}$

14. $\begin{array}{r} 8\frac{3}{5} \\ -3\frac{5}{6} \\ \hline \end{array}$

15. $\begin{array}{r} 17\frac{1}{3} \\ -12\frac{5}{8} \\ \hline \end{array}$

ANSWERS

1. $3\frac{1}{6}$

2. $5\frac{1}{2}$

3. $6\frac{5}{9}$

4. $13\frac{3}{8}$

5. $2\frac{1}{12}$

6. $6\frac{17}{40}$

7. $1\frac{3}{20}$

8. $5\frac{13}{42}$

9. $2\frac{17}{24}$

10. $4\frac{16}{21}$

11. $\frac{14}{15}$

12. $3\frac{13}{18}$

13. $3\frac{7}{12}$

14. $4\frac{23}{30}$

15. $4\frac{17}{24}$

Multiplying and Dividing Mixed Numbers

Certainly you knew when we began dealing with mixed numbers that multiplying them could not be far away. Should you be speculating about multiplying the whole number parts together, and then multiplying the fractional parts together, and then combining all the parts together in the end, banish that thought post haste. I mean, ship that notion to Siberia!

Multiplying Mixed Numbers

$$5\frac{2}{3} \times 3\frac{1}{2} = \underline{\quad}$$

Look at the previous example. If you were to follow the just banished plan, you would have accounted for two-thirds of the half but none of the 3, and then 5 of the threes but none of the halves. If the jumble of what you just read isn't clear to you, let's just say that parts of the multiplication would move on without ever being accounted for in the product.

The solution lies in a method that was examined three lessons ago. You must transform both mixed numbers into fractions, multiply the fractions, and, if appropriate, turn the product back into a mixed number. If you have forgotten how to turn a mixed number into a fraction, I'm perfectly willing to wait while you go back and check Lesson 23. The following is the fractionalization of the preceding multiplication:

$$\frac{17}{3} \times \frac{7}{2} = \underline{\quad}$$

There is no canceling possible here, since all the terms are prime numbers, so:

$$\frac{17}{3} \times \frac{7}{2} = \frac{119}{6}$$

In order to simplify the product, divide 119 by 6 and get the mixed number, $19\frac{5}{6}$.

After you have the idea straight, there is nothing unique about the mechanism for multiplying any particular set of mixed numbers. The routine is always the same:

1. Change the mixed numbers to fractions.
2. Multiply the fractions (canceling first if possible).
3. Simplify the answer.

Here's one more, just so you have an adequate number of models to study:

$$6\frac{2}{5} \times 5\frac{5}{8} = \underline{\quad}$$

1. $\dfrac{32}{5} \times \dfrac{45}{8} = \underline{\quad}$

2. $\dfrac{\overset{4}{\cancel{32}}}{\cancel{5}} \times \dfrac{\overset{9}{\cancel{45}}}{\cancel{8}} = \dfrac{36}{1}$

3. $\qquad \dfrac{36}{1} = 36$

Dividing Mixed Numbers

Dividing mixed numbers is identical to multiplying mixed numbers, except for the step where the division is converted to a multiplication by the reciprocal of the divisor (the invert and multiply part). You can summarize the division routine by amending the previous mantra as follows:

1. Change the mixed numbers to fractions.
2. Invert the divisor and replace the ÷ with an ×.
3. Multiply the fractions (canceling first if possible).
4. Simplify the answer.

Here are two examples of the process, with numbered steps that follow the recipe from before:

I. $\quad 6\frac{2}{5} \div 5\frac{5}{8} = \underline{\quad}$

1. $\dfrac{32}{5} \div \dfrac{45}{8} = \underline{\quad}$ 3. $\dfrac{32}{5} \times \dfrac{8}{45} = \dfrac{256}{225}$

2. $\dfrac{32}{5} \times \dfrac{8}{45} = \underline{\quad}$ 4. $\qquad \dfrac{256}{225} = 1\dfrac{31}{225}$

And (as it was the tradition to find on old record jackets), if you liked that one, you're sure to enjoy this:

II. $\quad 8\frac{3}{4} \div 3\frac{4}{7} = \underline{\quad}$

1. $\dfrac{35}{4} \div \dfrac{25}{7} = \underline{\quad}$ 3. $\dfrac{\overset{7}{\cancel{35}}}{4} \times \dfrac{7}{\underset{5}{\cancel{25}}} = \dfrac{49}{20}$

2. $\dfrac{35}{4} \times \dfrac{7}{25} = \underline{\quad}$ 4. $\qquad \dfrac{49}{20} = 2\dfrac{9}{20}$

There is only one way to fix these procedures in your brain so that you get comfortable enough with them to help your student, and that's the same way you can keep yourself fit and trim—exercise!

EXERCISES

Solve each of the following multiplications and express the product in lowest terms.

1. $5\frac{3}{4} \times 2\frac{7}{8} = $ _____

2. $4\frac{2}{5} \times 4\frac{1}{2} = $ _____

3. $5\frac{1}{3} \times 6\frac{3}{4} = $ _____

4. $7\frac{4}{5} \times 3\frac{5}{6} = $ _____

5. $4\frac{3}{8} \times 7\frac{2}{3} = $ _____

6. $10\frac{2}{7} \times 5\frac{4}{7} = $ _____

7. $3\frac{11}{12} \times 7\frac{7}{11} = $ _____

8. $7\frac{5}{9} \times 5\frac{7}{10} = $ _____

9. $8\frac{1}{6} \times 4\frac{3}{8} = $ _____

10. $6\frac{3}{5} \times 4\frac{5}{6} = $ _____

11. $4\frac{3}{4} \times 3\frac{3}{8} = $ _____

12. $8\frac{4}{5} \times 3\frac{3}{4} = $ _____

Solve each of the following divisions and express the quotient in lowest terms.

13. $4\frac{2}{5} \div 4\frac{1}{2} = $ _____

14. $8\frac{1}{3} \div 5\frac{3}{4} = $ _____

15. $9\frac{3}{8} \div 2\frac{3}{3} = $ _____

16. $7\frac{4}{5} \div 3\frac{5}{6} = $ _____

17. $7\frac{11}{12} \div 3\frac{7}{11} = $ _____

18. $8\frac{4}{5} \div 3\frac{3}{4} = $ _____

19. $7\frac{5}{9} \div 5\frac{7}{10} = $ _____

20. $10\frac{2}{7} \div 5\frac{4}{7} = $ _____

21. $5\frac{3}{4} \div 2\frac{7}{8} = $ _____

22. $10\frac{3}{4} \div 3\frac{3}{8} = $ _____

23. $8\frac{1}{6} \div 4\frac{3}{8} = $ _____

24. $6\frac{3}{4} \div 4\frac{5}{6} = $ _____

ANSWERS

1. $16\frac{17}{32}$

2. $19\frac{4}{5}$

3. 36

4. $29\frac{9}{10}$

5. $33\frac{13}{24}$

6. $57\frac{15}{49}$

7. $29\frac{10}{11}$

8. $43\frac{1}{15}$

9. $35\frac{35}{48}$

10. $31\frac{9}{10}$

11. $16\frac{1}{32}$

12. 33

13. $\frac{44}{45}$

14. $1\frac{31}{69}$

15. $3\frac{33}{64}$

16. $2\frac{4}{115}$

17. $2\frac{17}{96}$

18. $2\frac{26}{75}$

19. $1\frac{167}{513}$

20. $1\frac{11}{13}$

21. 2

22. $3\frac{5}{27}$

23. $1\frac{13}{15}$

24. $1\frac{53}{145}$

Many students agonize over common fractions and mixed numbers and get very frustrated when they have to deal with them. If you were such a person when you originally studied them, then it's going to be doubly difficult for you now. That shouldn't have to be the case, and—toward making you and your student more comfortable—I have the following suggestions.

First of all, make sure that you know the many different meanings that common fractions may have, and decide which of those fits the problem at hand—if it is a problem that you're dealing with. As far as computation with common fraction and mixed numbers goes, the rules are simple:

1. To add or subtract fractions, the denominators must be the same. Do whatever it takes to get them that way. Then add or subtract the numerators, and put the result over that denominator.

2. If the fraction portion of the mixed number being subtracted is greater than that in the number it's being taken from, rename 1 in the latter as a fraction with the same denominator as that in use; then add it to the existing fraction to make a fraction greater than 1. Then go to Rule 1.

3. To multiply mixed numbers, first change them to common fractions greater than 1.

4. To multiply common fractions, multiply the numerators together, then multiply the denominators together.

5. To divide fractions, invert the divisor and change the ÷ to a × then go to Rule 4.

6. To divide mixed numbers, change them to fractions greater than 1 first. Then go to Rule 5.

Decimal Fractions

Much more common these days than common fractions are decimal fractions. You're used to seeing them on calculators, and in representations of the monetary system. Decimal fractions are figured in terms of the place value system that we first looked at way back in the beginning of this book. You'll recall that as we move from right to left in our place value system, each place is worth 10 times as much as the place to its right.

Period	Bil-lions	Millions			Thousands			Ones		
Place to the right x 10	100 millions × 10	Ten millions × 10	Millions × 10	Hundred thousand × 10	Ten thousand × 10	Thousands × 10	Hundreds × 10	Tens × 10	Units × 10	Units
Name of place	Billions	Hundred millions	Ten millions	Millions	Hundred thousands	Ten thousands	Thousands	Hundreds	Tens	Ones

Extending Place Value

But the reverse of that is also true. That is, as we move from left to right, each place is worth $\frac{1}{10}$ as much as the place to its left—*and that situation does not end at the ones place.* Between the whole numbers and the decimal fractions is a sentry that marks the border, and that sentry is known as the **decimal point.**

Place to the left × 1/10	1/10 × hundred thousand	1/10 × thousands	1/10 × hundreds	1/10 × tens	1/10 × ones	1/10 × tenths	1/10 × hundredths	1/10 × thousandths	1/10 × ten thousandths	1/10 × hundred thousandths
Name of place	Thousands	Hundreds	Tens	Ones	Tenths	Hundredths	Thousandths	Ten thousandths	Hundred thousandths	Millionths

0.1 is read "one-tenth."

0.3 is read "three-tenths."

0.35 is read "thirty-five hundredths."

0.478 is read "four hundred seventy-eight thousandths."

Each of the preceding would be read in exactly the same way if there were no "0" in front of the decimal point. The "0" in each case is essentially a convenience, which makes it easier to interpret the fraction than it might be were you to be suddenly confronted by .37 in a sentence.

Decimal fractions do not suddenly stop at the millionths place, but I have chosen to stop there, since your student is not likely to need to deal with smaller ones. Suffice to say, they continue forever.

> Note that to read a decimal fraction, read it as if it were a whole number, followed by the name of the place that holds its least significant digit (the one farthest to the right).
>
> 0.3284 is read "three thousand two hundred eighty-four ten-thousandths."
>
> 0.709487 is read "seven hundred nine thousand, four hundred eighty-seven millionths."

The Place-Holder

Zero serves the same function as a place-holder with decimal fractions as it does with decimal whole numbers. Try interpreting the next four numbers, before reading on:

   (a) 0.04   **(b)** 0.005   **(c)** 0.0063   **(d)** 0.000074

The first (a) is four hundredths, while (b) is five thousandths. Note how the zeroes force the significant digits into those places. Letter (c) has a value of sixty-three-ten thousandths, while (d) represents seventy-four millionths. Notice that commas are not used between periods in decimal fractions.

0.30 is not read as "thirty-tenths," nor is 0.300 read "three hundred-thousandths." Zeroes to the right of the least **significant digit** in a decimal fraction are meaningless. (The same is true of zeroes to the left of the largest significant digit in a whole number.) Therefore, 0.30 and 0.300 are both equivalent to 0.3, or three-tenths.

3.475, 46.07, and 250.5 are decimal equivalents of mixed numbers with values of three and four hundred seventy-five thousandths, forty-six and seven hundredths, and two hundred fifty and five tenths.

No doubt you and your student are going to hear the three decimals here read as "three point four seventy five," "forty-six point oh seven," and "two hundred fifty point five." There is nothing either politically nor mathematically incorrect about that, as long as you both understand what the actual values of those quantities are.

Some Common Decimal Fractions

The title of this section might look like an oxymoron, but the following table lists decimal fractions that are readily interchangeable with common fractions. I've avoided listing tenths, since they should be readily obvious.

Decimal Fraction	Common Equivalent	Decimal Fraction	Common Equivalent
0.125	$\frac{1}{8}$	0.6	$\frac{3}{5}$
0.2	$\frac{1}{5}$	0.625	$\frac{5}{8}$
0.25	$\frac{1}{4}$	0.75	$\frac{3}{4}$
0.375	$\frac{3}{8}$	0.8	$\frac{4}{5}$
0.4	$\frac{2}{5}$	0.875	$\frac{7}{8}$
0.5	$\frac{1}{2}$		

One-third is the never-ending decimal 0.333. . . and two-thirds is the never-ending decimal 0.6666 . . ., usually rounded to 0.6667.

Money

I'm sure that it hasn't been lost on you that our monetary system is based on dollars and cents, with cents being another name for hundredths. Very often, money is a good motivational device for getting your student more than just passingly interested in decimal fractions. This is especially true when it comes to adding dollars and cents. Additionally, you'll want to emphasize the "ths" ending that distinguishes decimal fractions from their similar sounding whole number counterparts. One hundred thousand sounds an awful lot like one hundred-thousandths, a mistake one would not want to make when there's money involved!

EXERCISES

For exercises 1–6, name the place where the specified digit is located within the numeral 0.123456.

1. 6		**4.** 1	
2. 4		**5.** 3	
3. 2		**6.** 5	

For exercises 7–12, name the place where the specified digit is located within the numeral 0.973568.

7. 3		**10.** 5	
8. 6		**11.** 8	
9. 7		**12.** 9	

For exercises 13–18, express the decimal fraction in words.

13. 0.060		**16.** 3.0023	
14. 0.006		**17.** 0.00058	
15. 0.059		**18.** 9.0303	

For exercises 19–24, write the decimal fraction. Warning, 24 is very tricky!

19. forty-five millionths

20. three hundred thousandths

21. eighty-nine thousandths

22. sixty-five hundred thousandths

23. eight thousandths

24. three hundred twenty-four tenths

ANSWERS

1. millionths

2. ten thousandths

3. hundredths

4. tenths

5. thousandths

6. hundred thousandths

7. thousandths

8. hundred thousandths

9. hundredths

10. ten-thousandths

11. millionths

12. tenths

13. six hundredths

14. six thousandths

15. fifty-nine thousandths

16. three and twenty-three ten thousandths

17. fifty-eight hundred thousandths

18. nine and three-hundred-three ten thousandths

19. 0.000045

20. 0.00003

21. 0.089

22. 0.00065

23. 0.008

24. 32.4

LESSON 28

Adding Decimals

Adding decimals is very much like adding any other two numbers. The one catch is that it is difficult to do it horizontally. In cases like the one that follows, there's no real problem.

$$3.2 + 4.3 = 7.5$$

It's when you get to something like the next one that the difficulties begin to creep in.

A Jagged Affair

$$5.67 + 19.324 = \underline{}$$

The secret to successfully adding decimals is to align the decimal points one over the other:

$$5.67 + 19.324 = \underline{} \text{ becomes } \begin{array}{r} 5.67 \\ + 19.324 \\ \hline \end{array}$$

That is now something that you'll be able to add, paying careful attention to columns, of course:

$$\begin{array}{r} {}^{1}5.67 \\ + 19.324 \\ \hline 24.994 \end{array}$$

There is no number above the 4, although, if you like you could put a zero there. Remember, zeroes to the right of the least significant figure *on the right side of the decimal point only* are meaningless. So the rightmost digit in the sum is 4. Next we have 7 + 2, which makes 9; then 6 + 3 which is another 9. Here is where you place the decimal point, to the left of the just found 9 and directly below both other decimal points. Moving right along, 5 + 9 = 14, from which we'll place the 4 beneath the addend 9, and rename the 10 as 1 in the next column. Finally, add 1 + 1 to get 2.

Now try adding the following:

$$524.831 + 9.65 = \underline{} \text{ becomes } \begin{array}{r} 524.831 \\ + 9.65 \\ \hline \end{array}$$

(a) $\begin{array}{r} 524.831 \\ + 9.65 \\ \hline 81 \end{array}$ (b) $\begin{array}{r} {}^{1}524.831 \\ + 9.65 \\ \hline .481 \end{array}$ (c) $\begin{array}{r} {}^{1\ 1}524.831 \\ + 9.65 \\ \hline 4.481 \end{array}$ (d) $\begin{array}{r} {}^{1\ 1}524.831 \\ + 9.65 \\ \hline 534.481 \end{array}$

In (a), the 1 and what's under it total to 1, and 3 + 5 = 8. Moving along to (b), 8 + 6 = 14, write the 4 beneath the 6 and rename the 10 as 1 in the next column; then place the decimal point. Note the fact that carrying or renaming across the decimal point has no effect on anything. That is, it did not change the renaming technique, nor the placing of the decimal. With the exception of lining up decimal points

118

and keeping them lined up, the addition of decimals is not especially different from the addition of whole numbers.

Completing the addition, in (c), we add the 1 + 4 and add that 5 to the 9, writing the 4 from the 14 beneath the 9 and renaming the 10 as 1 in the next column (over the 2). Then we finish it off in (d), adding 1 to 2 and 5 to the air underneath it.

Three and More Numbers

In actuality, we're dealing with three or more numerals, but let's not split hairs. Check out these:

$$0.032 + 2 + .56 + 1.89 = \underline{}$$

You already know what the procedure is, that is lining up the decimal points, but what about that "2?" It doesn't have a decimal point. So who's stopping you from giving it one? 2 = 2.0, so substitute. For that matter, I don't care for the naked ".56," so I'll dress it up as "0.56:"

	(a)		(b)		(c)		(d)
	0.032		0.032		0.032		0.032
	2.0		2.0		2.0		2.0
	0.56		0.56		0.56		0.56
	1.89		1.89		0.89		1.89
			82		.482		4.482

In (a), the numerals have been aligned on the decimal points—the most critical step. Starting on the right of (b), 2 and nothing makes 2, 3 + 6 = 9, and 9 + 9 = 18; put the 8 under the 9 and rename the 10 as a 1 in the next column. On to (c) where the renamed 1 + 5 = 6 and that 6 + 8 = 14; put down the 4 beneath the 8, rename the 10 as 1 in the next column, and place the decimal point. Finally, 1 + 2 = 3, and 3 + 1 = 4, which is placed beneath the 1.

Phew! I'm winded. How about you doing some?!

EXERCISES
Find the sums.

1. 354.26 + 3.8
2. 4.1 + 0.007
3. 10.03 + 2.9
4. 12 + 0.67
5. 71.35 + 342.016
6. 136.9 + 25.68
7. 23.45 + 6.573

8. 5.04 + 0.593 + 23
9. 6.12 + 3 + .035
10. 1.35 + 40.3 + 0.64
11. 0.035 + 0.0063 + .0715 + 4
12. 0.235 + 26 + .008 + 3.1

13. 24.036 + 50.081 + 5.0075 + 3.72
14. 1 + 0.006 + 0.108 + 0.04
15. 31.415 + 26.613 + 7.314 + 8.057
16. 28.36 + 34.52 + 36.28 + 52.34

ANSWERS

1. 358.06
2. 4.107
3. 12.93
4. 12.67

5. 413.366
6. 162.58
7. 30.023
8. 28.633

9. 9.155
10. 42.29
11. 4.1128
12. 29.343

13. 82.8445
14. 1.154
15. 73.399
16. 151.5

Subtracting Decimals

If you are thinking that subtracting decimals is likely to work substantially the same way as subtracting whole numbers, you are absolutely correct—up to a point. We'll deal with the part that you're right about first, and then we'll proceed to tackle the not-so-obvious twist that you probably have not anticipated.

The Obvious Part

To subtract: 12.85 – 9.34, first arrange them with the decimal points one above the other, as in (a):

(a)
$$12.85$$
$$- 9.34$$

(b)
$$12.85$$
$$- 9.34$$
$$\overline{1}$$

(c)
$$12.85$$
$$- 9.34$$
$$\overline{.51}$$

(d)
$$12.85$$
$$- 9.34$$
$$\overline{3.51}$$

In (b), I've done the subtraction in the hundredths place. Subtracting the tenths is shown in (c), as well as placing the decimal point. In (d), I cheated a little by subtracting 9 from 12, and skipping the renaming mumbo-jumbo.

A word of caution, or help, is in order here. If you read the preceding lines, you'll see that I referred to the hundredths and the tenths, but I didn't really pay any attention to the places while subtracting the numbers. In fact, when I first wrote the preceding paragraph, I had to replace the word "ones" with "hundredths" and "tens" with "tenths." All you need to do, after the decimal points are aligned, is to subtract in the usual way. The places will take care of themselves.

Now for something completely different! Well, a little different, anyway. Take 6.68 from 9.35:

(a)
$$9.35$$
$$- 6.68$$

(b)
$$9.\overset{2}{\cancel{3}}{}^{1}5$$
$$- 6.6\ 8$$
$$\overline{7}$$

(c)
$$\overset{8}{\cancel{9}}.\overset{12}{\cancel{3}}{}^{1}5$$
$$- 6.6\ 8$$
$$\overline{.6\ 7}$$

(d)
$$\overset{8}{\cancel{9}}.\overset{12}{\cancel{3}}{}^{1}5$$
$$- 6.6\ 8$$
$$\overline{2\ .6\ 7}$$

Again, I've aligned the decimal points in (a). In (b), since 8 is greater than 5, I renamed one from the column to its left as 10 to turn the 5 into 15. 8 from 15 is 7. Moving on to (c), since 6 is greater than 2, I renamed one from the column to its left as 10 to turn the 2 into 12. 6 from 12 is 6; place the decimal point and move on to (d), where 8 take away 6 is 2. Two and sixty-seven-hundredths, or two point six seven is the difference.

The Less Obvious Part

By now, you should be sufficiently comfortable with the idea of subtracting decimals that you're ready for anything I can throw at you, so try this one: 7.3 – 4.126 = __.

What's the problem? Just kidding! Aligning the decimal points is no trouble, but . . .

$$
\begin{array}{r}
7.3 \\
- 4.126
\end{array}
$$

There are some numbers in need of subtracting, and nothing from which to subtract them, specifically, the "2" and the "6." If you cast your mind back, you'll recall that "0s" placed to the right of the last significant figure on the right side of the decimal point have no value:

$$
\begin{array}{r}
7.3 \\
- 4.126
\end{array}
\quad = \quad
\begin{array}{r}
7.300 \\
- 4.126
\end{array}
$$

The two subtractions shown here are identical in value, but it sure is a heck of a lot easier to solve the one on the right:

(a)
$$
\begin{array}{r}
7.\overset{2}{\cancel{3}}\,\overset{9}{\cancel{0}}\,{}^{1}0 \\
- 4.1\;2\;6
\end{array}
$$

(b)
$$
\begin{array}{r}
7.\overset{2}{\cancel{3}}\,\overset{9}{\cancel{0}}\,{}^{1}0 \\
- 4.1\;2\;6 \\
\hline
3.1\;7\;4
\end{array}
$$

You need to go all the way over to the 3 (a) before you have anything that you can rename. Take 1 from the 3 and make it into 10 in the column to its right. Next, take 1 from that 10, leaving 9, and rename it as 10 in the rightmost column. Now, you're set to subtract everything (b) in one swell foop [yes, I know]!

Do you need to see one more of those? Well if you do, here it is; otherwise, go get some exercise(s).

$$
5 - 2.35 = \underline{}.
$$

(a)
$$
\begin{array}{r}
5.00 \\
- 2.35
\end{array}
$$

(b)
$$
\begin{array}{r}
\overset{4}{\cancel{5}}.{}^{1}0\,0 \\
- 2.\,35
\end{array}
$$

(c)
$$
\begin{array}{r}
\overset{4}{\cancel{5}}.\overset{9}{\cancel{0}}\,{}^{1}0 \\
- 2.\,3\,5
\end{array}
$$

(d)
$$
\begin{array}{r}
\overset{4}{\cancel{5}}.\overset{9}{\cancel{0}}\,{}^{1}0 \\
- 2.\,3\,5 \\
\hline
2.\,6\,5
\end{array}
$$

In (a), the 5 has been accessorized with a couple of zeroes and a decimal point, which not coincidentally, is directly above the decimal point of the number to be subtracted from it. In (b), the renaming process has been started, regrouping 1 from the 5 as 10 in the place to its right. In (c), 1 from the 10 created in (b) is renamed as 10 in the rightmost place, leaving 9 on top in the middle place. All is now ready to subtract, as is done in (d).

EXERCISES

1. 12.06 – 8.03 = __
2. 68.391 – 25.674 = __
3. 8.9 – 3.6 = __
4. 35.059 – 9.246 = __
5. 58.672 – 34.48 = __
6. 6.824 – 2.57 = __
7. 41.6 – 24.58 = __
8. 6.4 – 0.057 = __
9. 8.3 – 3.75 = __
10. 15.8 – 3.648 = __
11. 489 – 0.634 = __
12. 36 – 2.85 = __
13. 64.046 – 28 = __
14. 46.72 – 9.037 = __
15. 34.31 – 18.327 = __
16. 84.1 – .0469 = __

ANSWERS

1. 4.03
2. 42.717
3. 5.3
4. 25.813
5. 24.192
6. 4.254
7. 17.02
8. 6.343
9. 4.55
10. 12.152
11. 488.366
12. 33.15
13. 36.046
14. 37.683
15. 15.983
16. 84.0531

Multiplying Decimals

Multiplication of decimals has its easy parts and its not so easy parts. The problem is, nobody can say for sure which is which. One thing is for sure: If you are completely comfortable with multiplying multiple-digit numbers, then that's the easy part for you. If you're not, then keeping track of the decimal point is your bright spot. To make a long story short, multiplication of decimals begins as if no decimal points are involved. That is:

$$2 \times 2 \equiv 2 \times 0.2 \equiv 0.02 \times 0.02 \equiv 0.2 \times 0.2 \equiv 0.002 \times 0.002$$

The three-line symbol means "is the same as," and, in fact, the result of all of those multiplications is some version of the number 4. In the first case, it's 4; in the second, it's 0.4; the third is 0.0004; the fourth is worth 0.04; last is 0.000004. Can you figure out the formula?

It is a matter of performing the multiplication as usual. Then count up all of the digits to the right of the decimal point in the factors being multiplied. That is how many decimal places there must be in the product. Here are some examples, all of which use the same numbers:

(a)
$$\begin{array}{r} 12 \\ \times\ 0.2 \\ \hline 2.4 \end{array}$$
(b)
$$\begin{array}{r} 1.2 \\ \times\ 0.2 \\ \hline 0.24 \end{array}$$
(c)
$$\begin{array}{r} 0.12 \\ \times\ 0.2 \\ \hline 0.024 \end{array}$$
(d)
$$\begin{array}{r} 0.12 \\ \times\ 0.02 \\ \hline 0.0024 \end{array}$$
(e)
$$\begin{array}{r} 0.012 \\ \times\ 0.02 \\ \hline 0.00024 \end{array}$$

Note that in each case, $2 \times 12 = 24$. By counting up the total number of decimal places (figures to the right of the decimal point) there are in the two factors, you can determine the number of decimal places there will be in the product.

Now let's consider a multiplication involving 2 digits by 2 digits. The following example should serve the purpose:

(a)
$$\begin{array}{r} 0.2\ 4 \\ \times\ 1\ .2 \\ \hline \end{array}$$
(b)
$$\begin{array}{r} 0.2\ 4 \\ \times\ 1\ .2 \\ \hline 4\ 8 \end{array}$$
(c)
$$\begin{array}{r} 0.2\ 4 \\ \times\ 1\ .2 \\ \hline 4\ 8 \\ 2\ 4\ 0 \end{array}$$
(d)
$$\begin{array}{r} 0.2\ 4 \\ \times\ 1\ .2 \\ \hline 4\ 8 \\ 2\ 4\ 0 \\ \hline 2\ 8\ 8 \end{array}$$

The multiplication is stated in (a). In (b), the multiplication by 2 is shown. Next, I multiplied by 1, the result of which is shown in (c). The usual next step is to add the two partial quotients, as is shown in (d). Next, count up all digits to the right of the decimal point in both factors. There's a "2" in the bottom factor and a "24" in the top one. That's a total of three digits to the right of the decimal point. Now go to the product and count from the right three digits: There's an "8" and an "8," and a "2." Place the decimal to the left of the "2," as in (e). Optionally, you might want to place a zero, as in (f).

$$\begin{array}{r} 0.2\ 4 \\ \times\ 1.2 \\ \hline 4\ 8 \\ 2\ 4\ 0 \\ \hline .2\ 8\ 8 \end{array}$$

(e)

$$\begin{array}{r} 0.2\ 4 \\ \times\ 1.2 \\ \hline 4\ 8 \\ 2\ 4\ 0 \\ \hline 0.2\ 8\ 8 \end{array}$$

(f)

If you would like to see that one more time, here's another example:

(a)
$$\begin{array}{r} 0.3\ 6 \\ \times\ .1\ 2 \\ \hline \end{array}$$

(b)
$$\begin{array}{r} 0.3\ 6 \\ \times\ .1\ 2 \\ \hline 7\ 2 \end{array}$$

(c)
$$\begin{array}{r} 0.3\ 6 \\ \times\ .1\ 2 \\ \hline 7\ 2 \\ 3\ 6\ 0 \end{array}$$

(d)
$$\begin{array}{r} 0.3\ 6 \\ \times\ .1\ 2 \\ \hline 7\ 2 \\ 3\ 6\ 0 \\ \hline .0\ 4\ 3\ 2 \end{array}$$

This time, there are four decimal places in the two factors combined, so there must be four digits to the right of the decimal point in the product. In order to accomplish this, it is necessary to add a zero before the "4" in the product.

EXERCISES

1. $3.2 \times 4 =$ __
2. $2.8 \times 2.4 =$ __
3. $5.7 \times 6.9 =$ __
4. $5.02 \times 6 =$ __
5. $8.34 \times 3.6 =$ __
6. $3.18 \times 2.05 =$ __
7. $8.45 \times 3.06 =$ __
8. $4.02 \times 2.06 =$ __

9. $1.25 \times 0.36 =$ __
10. $0.02 \times 0.04 =$ __
11. $0.13 \times 2.08 =$ __
12. $0.04 \times 0.3 =$ __
13. $1.012 \times 0.05 =$ __
14. $0.002 \times 0.026 =$ __
15. $1.032 \times 0.001 =$ __
16. $3.027 \times 2.008 =$ __

ANSWERS

1. 12.8
2. 6.72
3. 39.33
4. 30.12
5. 30.024
6. 6.519
7. 25.857
8. 8.2812

9. 0.45
10. 0.0008
11. 0.2704
12. 0.012
13. 0.0506
14. 0.000052
15. 0.001032
16. 6.078216

LESSON 31

Dividing Decimals

It is not possible to divide by a decimal. Wait! Don't close the book and think you're done with this lesson, because I didn't say decimal division was not doable—just that you can't divide by a decimal. Examples like the following are very real and very solvable:

$$1.27 \div 0.2 = \underline{}$$

Are you totally confused yet? I don't blame you if you are, but the story goes like this:

(a) $0.2\overline{)1.27}$ **(b)** $2\overline{)1.27}$ **(c)** $2\overline{)1\overset{.}{2}.7}$

The division from the fourth line of this page has been rewritten above in (a). Since, as already mentioned, it is not possible to divide by a decimal, the divisor is made into a whole number (b) by moving the decimal point one place to the right. That is the equivalent of having multiplied the divisor by 10. To maintain the integrity of the relationship between divisor and dividend, the decimal point in the dividend must also be moved one place to the right (a multiplication by 10). This has been done in (c), and as a bonus, the decimal point in the quotient has been placed above the decimal point in the dividend. Now the example is ready to be divided, as is done here:

(d) $2\overline{)12.7}^{\,6.}$ **(e)** $2\overline{)12.7}^{\,6.3}$ **(f)** $2\overline{)12.7^{1}0}^{\,6.3}$ **(g)** $2\overline{)12.7^{1}0}^{\,6.3\,5}$

I'm using the short division method here that you looked at earlier (in Lesson 13). In (d), since 2 can't go into 1, you'll group the 1 with the 2 and divide 2 into 12 for a partial quotient of 6, which is written above the ones digit of the 12. In (e), you divide the 7 by 2, and find that it goes in 3 times with 1 leftover, which is accounted for in (f), after tacking a zero onto the dividend (remember, zeroes after the last significant digit on the right of the decimal point do not affect the number's value). Finally, divide 10 by 2 to get 5 (g).

Heck, I'll bet you had as much fun doing that as I did! No? Well, truth be told, I didn't have much fun either, but I hope you get the idea. I'll do another example for you. This time, it'll be one with a 2-digit divisor (see following page):

(a) $0.24\overline{)0.288}$ (b) $24\overline{)28.8}$ (c) $24\overline{)28.8}$ (d) $24\overline{)28.8}$ (e) $24\overline{)28.8}$

(c):
```
      1.
  24 )28.8
     24
```

(d):
```
      1.
  24 )28.8
     24 ↓
      4 8
```

(e):
```
      1.2
  24 )28.8
     24 ↓
      4 8
      4 8
```

You might argue that it's a 3-digit divisor in (a), and you would be right—temporarily. By (b) it's a 2-digit divisor, since the decimal point has been moved two places to the right in order to make the divisor a whole number, and to keep the relationship the same, it was moved the same distance in the dividend, as well as placing it in the quotient above its position in the dividend. In (c), 24 divides into 28 once. So place "1" over the "8," and multiply "1" times "24," writing the product beneath the "28." In (d), subtract "24" from "28" to get "4," and then bring down the "8" to get "48." In (e), "24" divides into "48" 2 times, which is written above the second "8." Then multiply "24 times "2" and get "48," which subtracts from the "48" already there to leave no remainder.

And if you liked that division, you're sure to enjoy these!

EXERCISES

Solve the following divisions. Round off any that do not come out perfectly to 3 decimal places.

1. $33.8 \div 2.6 =$ __
2. $43.2 \div 1.8 =$ __
3. $2.25 \div 0.15 =$ __
4. $4.32 \div 0.24 =$ __
5. $6.46 \div .08 =$ __
6. $72.4 \div 0.4 =$ __
7. $36.3 \div 0.06 =$ __
8. $63.2 \div 0.09 =$ __

9. $96 \div 0.12 =$ __
10. $7.2 \div 0.006 =$ __
11. $9.69 \div 0.012 =$ __
12. $16.2 \div 0.018 =$ __
13. $7.20 \div 0.008 =$ __
14. $5.2 \div 0.004 =$ __
15. $32 \div 0.016 =$ __
16. $84 \div 0.018 =$ __

ANSWERS

1. 13
2. 24
3. 15
4. 18
5. 80.75
6. 181
7. 605
8. 702.222

9. 800
10. 1200
11. 807.5
12. 900
13. 900
14. 1300
15. 2000
16. 4666.667

Percent Fractions

You might not be accustomed to seeing the words at the top of this page together, yet what you and your student know as **percents** are really fractions. They are a unique form of fraction in that they are not based on a whole of one, but rather, on a whole of 100. That is to say, one whole = 100 percent. We write that as 1 = 100%.

Here is 100% of a grapefruit:

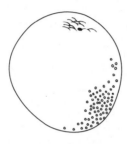

Here is 100% of a book:

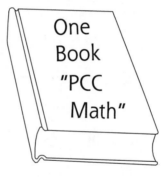

One
Book
"PCC
Math"

This is 50% of an apple:

This plate holds 25% of a cherry pie:

Common Fraction to Percent

I'm pretty sure that you know how to name the four preceding objects in terms other than those that I have used. You would call the first two items 1 grapefruit and 1 book, respectively. You might also name the third figure as half of an apple, and the last as one-fourth of a cherry pie. This is all by way of reinforcing the notion that percents are nothing but a different way to write fractions.

"Percent" literally means "for every hundred." Many common fractions can be readily expressed as percents by finding equivalent fractions with a denominator of 100:

$$\frac{1}{2} = \frac{50}{100} = 50\% \qquad\qquad \frac{3}{5} = \frac{60}{100} = 60\%$$

$$\frac{1}{4} = \frac{25}{100} = 25\% \qquad\qquad \frac{3}{4} = \frac{75}{100} = 75\%$$

$$\frac{9}{10} = \frac{90}{100} = 90\%$$

Other fractions are not so easily expressed as percents. If you absolutely must represent a fraction as a percent, and that fraction is not congenial to such expression, you might set up a special formula. (There's an easy way to do this in algebra, but that's beyond this book's scope.) Just plug the numerator and denominator into the following:

$$\% = \frac{100 \times \text{numerator}}{\text{denominator}}$$

The solution will be that fraction expressed as a percent. For example, to change two-fifths to a percent:

$$\% = \frac{100 \times \text{numerator}}{\text{denominator}}$$
$$\% = \frac{100 \times 2}{5} = \frac{200}{5}$$
$$\% = 40$$
$$\therefore \frac{2}{5} = 40\%$$

Percent to Common Fraction

To express a percent as a common fraction, remove the percent sign, put the number over 100 and express it in lowest terms. Here are two examples:

$$52\% = \frac{52}{100} = \frac{13}{25}$$
$$80\% = \frac{80}{100} = \frac{4}{5}$$

Decimal Fraction to Percent

To express a decimal fraction as a percent, keep in mind that percent means hundredths, and 0.## means hundredths, so 0.34 = 34%, 0.81 = 81%. The rule of thumb is move the decimal point two places to the right and slap a percent sign (%) after it.

$$.09 = 9\%$$
$$3.24 = 324\%$$
$$0.005 = 0.5\%$$
$$42 = 4200\%$$

That's right, you *can* give more than 100 percent, but not of yourself. You can give 300 percent the amount of oranges in one carton. That would be the number of oranges in 3 cartons, but when it comes to trying 110 percent, that's hyperbole—exaggeration. When you've given 100 percent of yourself, you have nothing more left to give.

Percent to Decimal Fraction

In order to convert from a percent to a decimal fraction, you reverse the process that you performed in the last section. That is to say, remove the percent sign and move the decimal point left two places:

26% becomes .26, or 0.26.

48% becomes .48, or 0.48.

212% becomes 2.12.

300% becomes 3.

Decimals, Common Fractions, and Percents

The following table maps out the different ways of expressing the same fraction from one-twentieth to one. Note that all common fractions in the table have been expressed in lowest terms.

Common Fraction	Decimal	Percent	Common Fraction	Decimal	Percent
$\frac{1}{20}$	0.05	5%	$\frac{4}{10}$	0.4	40%
$\frac{1}{10}$	0.10	10%	$\frac{9}{20}$	0.45	45%
$\frac{3}{20}$	0.15	15%	$\frac{1}{2}$	0.5	50%
$\frac{1}{5}$	0.20	20%	$\frac{11}{20}$	0.55	55%
$\frac{1}{4}$	0.25	25%	$\frac{3}{5}$	0.6	60%
$\frac{3}{10}$	0.30	30%	$\frac{5}{8}$	0.625	62.5%
$\frac{7}{20}$	0.35	35%	$\frac{13}{20}$	0.65	65%
$\frac{3}{8}$	.375	37.5%	$\frac{7}{10}$	0.7	70%

Common Fraction	Decimal	Percent	Common Fraction	Decimal	Percent
$\frac{3}{4}$	0.75	75%	$\frac{9}{10}$	0.9	90%
$\frac{4}{5}$	0.8	80%	$\frac{19}{20}$	0.95	95%
$\frac{17}{20}$	0.85	85%	$\frac{1}{1}$	1	100%
$\frac{7}{8}$	0.875	87.5%			

EXERCISES

Express each of the following as a percent:

1. 0.36
2. 0.59
3. $\frac{25}{70}$
4. 2.17
5. 0.08
6. 21.8
7. $\frac{5}{1000}$
8. $3\frac{7}{10}$

Express each of the following as a common fraction or mixed number in lowest terms:

9. 38%
10. 45%
11. 112%
12. 9%
13. 380%
14. $66\frac{2}{3}$%

Express each of the following as a decimal fraction:

15. 87%
16. 500%
17. 48.5%
18. 7%
19. $20\frac{3}{4}$%
20. 38%

Extra Credit

A percent is not a pure number. It is a quantity with an attached label, as much as if it were inches or centimeters. When labeled quantities are multiplied, their labels are also multiplied, so 3 inches times 2 inches produce 6 square inches, and 3 centimeters times 4 centimeters produce 12 square centimeters, abbreviated 6 in.^{2} and 12 cm^2, respectively. Both the aforementioned units are very useful, which you might already know if you deal with goods measured by area, or as you'll see when we deal with area and volume later in this book. %^{2}, or square percent, however, is a meaningless unit, so percents cannot be multiplied together. Before we can find a percent of a number, we must first change that percent to a pure number—its decimal fraction equivalent.

ANSWERS

1. 36%

2. 59%

3. 35.71%

4. 217%

5. 8%

6. 2180%

7. 0.5%

8. 370%

9. $\frac{19}{50}$

10. $\frac{9}{20}$

11. $1\frac{3}{25}$

12. $\frac{9}{100}$

13. $3\frac{4}{5}$

14. $\frac{2}{3}$

15. 0.87

16. 5

17. 0.485

18. 0.07

19. 0.2075

20. 0.38

The Arithmetic of Percents

Percents can be added and subtracted just like any other number, but they rarely are. That's because people are rarely interested in percents as pure fractions. They are, rather, interested in percents *of* some other number, usually a price or a population. Putting that differently:

$$12\% - 5\% = 7\%$$
$$23\% + 21\% = 44\%$$

And that's about as much addition or subtraction of percents you'll ever need to use. You may subtract percents to compare interest rates and/or discounts to see which is a better deal, but by and large you are going to be dealing with multiplication.

Taking a Percent of Something

I mentioned somewhere way back in this book that you should associate the word "of" with multiplication and lock that association away somewhere in your brain. Well, the time has come to unlock the brain and let that association out. A percent of a number is found by multiplying; however, there's one small technical problem. Percents cannot be multiplied. If you're interested in why percents cannot be multiplied, you can check out the sidebar on page 130. Otherwise, take my word for it. They can't be multiplied.

In order to take a percent of a number, we must first change that percent to its decimal fraction equivalent. In order to take 50 percent of 24, change 50% to 0.50, or 0.5, and then multiply:

$$0.5 \times 24 = 12$$

So, 50 percent of 24 is 12, which I trust you already knew.

What is 20 percent of 225? There are two ways to approach the solution to this question. First, let's use the approach shown previously in which 20% is changed to a decimal and you multiply:

(a) $\begin{array}{r} 225 \\ \times\ .2 \\ \hline \end{array}$
(b) $\begin{array}{r} 225 \\ \times\ .2 \\ \hline 45.0 \end{array}$
(c) 20% of 225 = 45

The other approach to this problem is based on the fact that 20 percent is a multiple of 10 percent. Taking 10 percent of a number is the same thing as dividing that number by 10. You don't have to take my word for it. It's that reciprocal operations thing all over again. Try it and see for yourself. Take 10 percent of 225; then divide 225 by 10 and see whether you don't get the same result.

Now, dividing 225 by 10, or any number by 10, for that matter, is accomplished by moving the decimal point one place to the left. I remember mentioning that earlier. In fact, I believe it was in the last lesson. So 225 divided by 10 is 22.5; 20 percent is twice as much as 22.5, or 45. You may be thinking that that was much ado about nothing, but it's really very useful to be able to figure discounts on the fly when you're out shopping. What do you save on an item listing for $300 selling at a 40% discount? Well 10% of $300 is $30, and 40% is 4 times that, or $120. You can save $120 on that item. What would the item then cost you?

Here again, there are two ways to get to the answer: Since the discount is $120, subtract $120 from $300 to get $180.

Alternately, if the product is selling for 40 percent off, you will be paying 100% − 40% = 60% of the list price. Since 10% of the list price is $30, 6 × $30 = $180 (since 6 × 3 = 18). And don't forget sales tax. Where I live, that's 6 percent. How much sales tax will I have to pay on this item? (The item's neither food nor clothing, which in my state are exempt.)

To find 6 percent of $180, multiply $180 by 6%'s decimal equivalent:

(a)
$$\begin{array}{r} 180 \\ \times\ .06 \\ \hline \end{array}$$

(b)
$$\begin{array}{r} 180 \\ \times\ .06 \\ \hline 10.80 \end{array}$$

Sales tax is $10.80. How much will you pay the salesperson? To find the answer to that, add $180 and $10.80 to get the grand total of $190.80.

Consecutive Discounts

Some stores like to use the lure of "Take an additional percent off this Saturday only." How good is an additional discount when compared to a larger one-time discount? There is no hard and fast rule for this, so I'll present you with three sales, all intended to draw customers into the store on Wednesday: Store A is advertising 50 percent off everything. Store B offers 40 percent off everything, plus take an additional 15 percent off. Finally, Mega-Mart is offering 40 percent off everything, with an additional 20 percent off. Which store is offering the biggest savings?

Consider an item that is normally priced at $100. At Store A it will go for 50 percent of that, or $50. That same item at Store B will be discounted 40 percent, which makes it 60 percent of the list price, or $60. The same is true at Mega-Mart, but now the additional discounts kick in. At Store B you get to take off an additional 15 percent, but it's not 15 percent of the $100; it's 15 percent off the already discounted price of $60. 10% of $60 is $6, so 15% of that is $9. Taking off that additional $9 brings the price to $51.00, a dollar more than at Store A. Mega-Mart takes an additional 20 percent off. Again, that's 20 percent of the already discounted $60. That's $12 more, for a final price of $48. That's definitely the lowest of the three prices, so where should I buy that $100 list-price item? The answer will lie in how far I have to drive to get the best price, because gasoline costs money, too.

Most important from the problem just done is to learn that you can't tell whether an initial larger discount is a better or a worse deal than two consecutive smaller discounts, until you've done the math.

Finding the Percentage

Sometimes you have raw numbers and want to know what those numbers mean as a percentage of a total, say the percent of the electorate favoring one position on a political issue rather than another, or a certain group's tastes in ballpark food.

At a certain West Coast ballgame, about 32,000 attendees bought sushi as a snack, but about 28,000 did not. About what percent of the crowd opted to eat sushi?

To answer the question, you first need to know the total number of people at the ballgame. To obtain that number, add 32,000 + 28,000 to get 60,000. Keep in mind that you're dealing with "abouts," so that your answer will, at best, be an approximation. The question can be simplified by getting rid of all those zeroes: It has become "what percent of 60 is 32?" The solution is to turn that into a fraction, representing a division:

$$\frac{32}{60} = 60\overline{)32}$$

The next step is to place a decimal point in the dividend and quotient and add a couple of zeroes. (Remember, percent means "for each hundred.")

$$60\overline{)32.00}$$

Since there are 5 "6s" in 30, it stands to reason that there are 5 "60s" in 320:

(a)
$$\begin{array}{r} 0.5 \\ 60\overline{)32.00} \\ \underline{30\ 0} \end{array}$$

(b)
$$\begin{array}{r} 0.5 \\ 60\overline{)32.00} \\ \underline{30\ 0} \\ 2\ 00 \end{array}$$

(c)
$$\begin{array}{r} 0.53 \\ 60\overline{)32.00} \\ \underline{30\ 0} \\ 2\ 00 \\ \underline{1\ 80} \\ 20 \end{array}$$

In (a), I've placed a zero in the quotient's ones place (a frill, in no way necessary), and placed a "5" over the first "0" in the dividend. Then, multiply the 5 × 60 = 300, which is written below the dividend. In (b), subtract and bring down the 0 to make a new dividend of 200. 60 divides into 200 3 times, as is noted in (c), and 3 × 60 = 180. After subtracting, I can see that were I to add more zeroes, the 3 would continue to repeat in the quotient, so end it here. All there is left to do is to make the quotient into a percent:

> Instead of dividing 32 by 60, as was done in the sushi exercise on this page, you could have divided both numerator and denominator by 10 and then performed the simpler division of 3.2 ÷ 6.

$$0.53 \times 100 = 53\%$$

53% of the crowd ate sushi.

Determining the Original

Suppose that you know a certain amount is a certain percent of a number, and you want to determine what the original number was. Then you would use the following formula:

$$\text{original amount} = \frac{\text{known amount}}{1} \times \frac{100}{\text{percent of original}}$$

That percent of the original is the whole number representation of the percent without the percent sign. Here's an example:

320 is 80% of a number. What is that number? To find it:

$$\text{original} = \frac{320}{1} \times \frac{100}{80}$$

$$\text{original} = \frac{\overset{4}{\cancel{320}}}{1} \times \frac{100}{\cancel{80}} = \frac{400}{1}$$

$$\text{original} = 400$$

> That process is actually dividing by the decimal. Remember, the decimal was 80%. That's worth 80 over 100. Multiplying by 100 over 80 means you're multiplying by the reciprocal of 80%. That, you may recall, is the definition of dividing fractions.

EXERCISES

For 1–6, find the asked-for percents.

1. 25% of 84
2. 30% of 125
3. 34% of 250

4. 8% of 150
5. 120% of 70
6. 300% of 12

For 7–10, tell which is the better buy off a $100 item.

7. (a) 35% off or (b) 25% off and an additional 15% off the already discounted price
8. (a) 45% off or (b) 25% off and an additional 25% off the already discounted price
9. (a) 55% off or (b) 30% off and an additional 30% off the already discounted price
10. (a) 40% off or (b) 30% off and an additional 20% off the already discounted price

For 11–15 find the percentage.

11. blue marbles in a bag with 8 blues, 8 whites, and 4 reds
12. 1700 pizza-eaters versus 3500 hot-dog eaters at a hockey game
13. 25,000 cheering for the home team in an arena holding 40,000 fans
14. 16,000 tickets sold out of 22,000 tickets printed
15. automobile commuters in a city in which 2 million drive to work and 6 million use public transportation

For 16–20, find the original quantity.

16. 52 is 65% of __.
17. 72 is 60% of __.
18. 144 is 48% of __.

19. 75 is 30% of __.
20. 224 is 70% of __.

ANSWERS

1. 21
2. 37.5
3. 85
4. 12
5. 84
6. 36
7. (b)

8. (a)
9. (a)
10. (b)
11. 40%
12. 33%
13. 62.5%
14. 73%

15. 25%
16. 80
17. 120
18. 300
19. 250
20. 320

Part 3
Some Esoteric Stuff

Terms You Should Know

After each word in the Glossary, the lesson where it first appears is cited. Occasionally a second or third appearance is also given if there are additional major references, but not all appearances of each word are necessarily cited.

arithmetic mean (Lesson 34). See mean.

average (Lesson 34). A central tendency, hence normal; mathematically one of three methods for approximating that central tendency; see mean, median, and mode.

base (Lesson 39). A word with several uses in mathematics; in the lesson cited it refers to the number that is being raised to an exponent; it often refers to the number upon which a system of numeration is arranged, as the decimal system is base-10, the binary system base-2, etc.

exponent (Lesson 39). Is a little number written high and following another number, like this: 3^4, wherein 4 is the exponent and 3 is known as the base.

integer (Lessons 35–38). Any whole number, whether positive or negative, and zero.

mean (Lesson 34). An average arrived at by adding a string of values together and then dividing their sum by the number of members in that string; also arithmetic mean (with the stress on the third syllable of "arithmetic").

median (Lesson 34). An average found by arranging a sequence of numbers in ascending or descending order, and choosing the central one in that sequence.

mode (Lesson 34). An average arrived at by taking the single value that appears in a list the most frequently.

negative (Lessons 35–38). Having a value less than zero (designated by a – sign).

origin (Lesson 35). In Cartesian (rectangular) coordinate geometry, the point where the x-axis and the y-axis cross, having coordinates (0, 0).

positive (Lessons 35–38). Having a value greater than zero (indicated by a + sign, or understood when no sign is present).

scientific notation (Lesson 41). A method for representing very large or very small quantities in terms of a number that is 1 or greater and less than 10, multiplied by 10, or raised to a positive (in the case of large ones) or negative (in the case of small ones) power.

Averages

If you're looking for an **average** chapter, you've come to the right place. This chapter is better than some and not as good as others. Its subject is, as the title suggests, averages, or methods of finding central tendencies. Statisticians use three separate methods to find central tendencies: **mean, median,** and **mode.** Each one has advantages, and we will study them separately, beginning with the one with which you're probably most familiar.

Arithmetic Mean

"Arithmetic" in the heading is not pronounced "uh RITH muh tik," but, rather as a short a (as in yak) "-rith MEH tik." It is probably to avoid having to remember to pronounce it that way that statisticians usually just refer to it as "the mean." The arithmetic mean is the method by which we get baseball players' batting averages, students' grade-point averages, and the average length of time it takes to run a mile.

To arrive at the mean of three numbers, add them and divide the sum by three:

$$15 + 20 + 55 = 90$$

$$90 \div 3 = 30$$

That makes 30 the mean value for those three numbers. How do you suppose that you find the mean for four numbers?

$$80 + 75 + 85 + 90 = 330$$

$$330 \div 4 = 82.5$$

Did you see that coming? I think it's time to state a formula for determining the arithmetic mean, no matter how many numbers are involved:

1. Count how many numbers there are.
2. Add all those numbers together to find their sum.
3. Divide the sum by the number you counted to in step 1.

So how come baseball batting averages are always three decimal places long, you ask? Well, for some reason known only to organized baseball, batting averages are figured as decimals to the nearest thousandth with 1.000 being perfect; therefore, if someone bats five times and gets two hits, add his hits together (I already did when I said he got 2 hits), and divide by the number of at-bats (5). Also, round the answer to three decimal places:

$$5\overline{)2.000} \rightarrow 5\overline{)2.000}^{.4} \rightarrow 5\overline{)2.000}^{.40} \rightarrow 5\overline{)2.000}^{.400}$$

If the answer had not worked out evenly, one more division would have been done, so as to know whether to round that thousandths digit up or leave it alone. As of the writing of this book, Ted Williams was the last batter to play a full season and finish up with a .400 batting average, 185 hits in 456 at bats. You figure out his average. The year was 1941.*

Median

Median is the choice of statisticians in situations where the mean would be disproportionately skewed by a small number of subjects with way out of the ordinary representative stuff, either too little or too great. Consider the average income for an American family. How might the Rockefellers', Gates's, Carnegies', and Vanderbilts' incomes being included tip that average? According to the U.S. Census Bureau, the three-year median household income by state for the years 2000–2003 varied from a low of $30,072 in West Virginia to a high of $55,912 in Maryland. Washington, the home of the head of Microsoft, was in 16th place with a median income of $44,252. How is that number arrived at? I'm glad you asked.

Consider 7 people with weekly incomes of $224, $1000, $580, $800, $650, $50, and $40,000.

Put those incomes into order (it doesn't matter whether the order is ascending or descending):

$50, $224, $580, $650, $800, $1000, $40,000

$40,000, $1000, $800, $650, $580, $224, $50

Select the middle figure—the one equidistant from both ends. That's the median. Now if that doesn't strike you as a very good way to determine an average income, consider the alternative. If the arithmetic mean of those weekly incomes were found, you would have gotten an average of $6186! I'm sure you'll agree that that would have been a far less representative figure.

Suppose that there were an even number of figures; could there still be a median? Of course, there could. For the purpose of demonstrating while keeping from cluttering the page, I'll use the same weekly incomes from before and add one at the upper end.

$50, $224, $580, $650, ^ $800, $1000, $40,000, $50,000

$50,000, $40,000, $1000, $800, ^ $650, $580, $224, $50

This time, there are four elements on each side of the center, which falls between $650 and $800. To get the median, take the arithmetic mean of the two central terms:

$$650 + 800 = 1450$$
$$1450 \div 2 = 725$$

The median income is now $725.

> Your student's teacher may require that in order to find the median, the list be arranged in ascending order of values. Even though this is not the only way of doing it, it's not worth taking a stand over and alienating the kid's teacher. A word to the wise. . . Do what the teacher wants.

---

* Ted Williams' batting average in 1941 was .406.

Mode

The mode is the value that appears most frequently in a list of numbers. Consider the group of numbers {3, 6, 5, 6, 7, 6, 9, 6, 10}. The mean is 6.44, the median is 6, and the mode is also 6, since there are more 6s than any other number. For this set of numbers, then, it would have made very little difference how you computed the average.

Ali plays for her school basketball team. She wants to convince the coach that she is a valuable asset. In the 7 games she has played, she scored 1, 3, 7, 6, 15, 4, and 15 points. She could take the mean of her scores and tell the coach that she's averaging 7.3 points per game. The median would not be advantageous to her, since it is just 6 points per game, but look at the mode. The mode shows her averaging 15 points per game. Wow, now she can make a strong argument to the coach. Of course, if the coach has done her homework, she'll bring Ali back to earth by pointing out to her what her mean or median is.

You could argue, persuasively, that the preceding example doesn't convince you of the usefulness of the mode, so consider this situation. You are looking for a job, and you interview at a small company with a total workforce of 10. The interviewer tells you that the average earnings of the company's workforce is $200 per day. Now that's not a bad salary, except that it was arrived at by use of the arithmetic mean. What you don't know is that 9 of the workers receive $100 per week, while the boss gets $1100. Do the math, I'll wait.

Of course, if you had found the median of {100, 100, 100, 100, 100, 100, 100, 100, 100, 1100} It would have told you the same thing as the mode. You are likely to be making the salary of a worker, and not that of the boss. But, the median doesn't always give you the information you're looking for either.

Still on that job hunt, you find an ad for a company advertising the average worker's income as $300 per week. Knowing better than to fall for that mean figure, you call the company and ask what the median income is for the workers at this company. You are told it is $300. Things are looking better—or are they? It turns out that there are a total of 17 persons at the company in question. 8 of them are entry-level salespeople earning $100 per week each. There are 5 assistant managers, each of whom earns $300 per week. Three managers each earn $400 per week, and the owner gets $1600 per week. Check the math. Mean and median incomes are both $300 per week, but the mode—the amount the most workers make—is $100 per week. Caveat somebody!

EXERCISES

For exercises 1–6, find the arithmetic mean.

1. 12, 16, 24, 32, 36

2. 38, 56, 17, 29

3. 15, 25 18, 36, 58, 28

4. 14, 46, 24, 36, 34, 20

5. 800, 400, 200, 700, 900, 300

6. 65, 90, 45, 25, 35, 50, 75, 40

For exercises 7–12, find the median.

7. 15, 25 18, 36, 58, 28, 40

8. 38, 56, 17, 29, 42

9. 42, 16, 94, 32, 36

10. 800, 400, 200, 700, 900, 300

11. 65, 90, 45, 25, 35, 50, 75, 40

12. 14, 46, 24, 36, 34, 20

For exercises 13–15, find the mode.

13. 6, 3, 4, 5, 6, 10, 8   15. 82, 25, 32, 85, 19, 32, 25, 16, 72

14. 25, 67, 38, 49, 89, 38, 14

ANSWERS

1. 24	6. 53.125	11. 47.5
2. 35	7. 28	12. 29
3. 30	8. 38	13. 6
4. 29	9. 36	14. 38
5. 550	10. 550	15. 25, 32 (It's bimodal.)

Integers

Through the early portion of your student's mathematical experience, half of the world of numbers has been completely ignored. You might introduce it with reference to a building such as that in the following figure.*

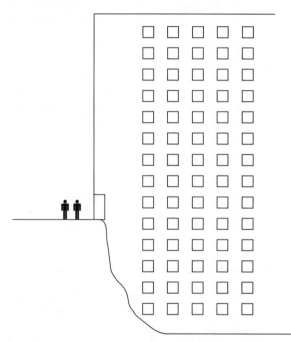

You'll notice that many of the floors in this building are above ground level—the level where the main entrance is. Many other floors are below the entry level. People travel up and down from floor to floor in this building by means of an elevator. The buttons in the elevator have floor numbers on them, and the entry-level floor's button is labeled with a "0," although it could just as easily have been marked "G" for ground, "M" for main, or "L" for lobby. The floors above the entrance level are labeled "1," "2," "3," and so forth. How do you think the floors below the entry level are marked?

Ultimately, you want to elicit or tell her that the solution was to put "negative signs" (indistinguishable from minus signs) on the buttons, and call them "negative 1," "negative 2," and so forth.

This principle can be demonstrated on a number line, which is always drawn with arrow heads at each end, demonstrating that it continues infinitely in the indicated direction.

---

*This building, as well as other examples in the discussion of integers, is derived from the work of the Madison Project, with which I had the honor to be associated—a federally funded math improvement project of the 1960s led by Professor Robert B. Davis of Syracuse University and Webster College.

The first thing your student should notice is that 0 is no longer at the extreme left of the number line, where she is accustomed to seeing it. It should also be clear that numbers are to the left of 0, each of which has an attached "–" preceding it. These are negative numbers. Those numbers to the right of the "0" are positive numbers, whether or not there is a "+" preceding them. The numbers, like the hash marks on the line, are uniformly spaced intervals apart. Have your student identify what numbers should be written at the marks currently occupied by the letters A–H. They should be A = 2, B = 5, C = –5, D = –1, E = –10, F = –7, G = 9, and H = 13. What is the distance from E to G? If you count it out, you'll find it to be 19.

A favorite game for learning and teaching integers is a version of tic-tac-toe, where dots and Xs are placed on the intersections, and the objective of the game is to get four in a row. Markers (dots and crosses) are placed by the player's calling out two coordinates, and the other person marking that point. The first coordinate given is the distance across, and the second is the distance up or down. All positions are counted from the intersection of the heavy lines (also known as the **origin**). As a horizontal coordinate, positive is right and negative is left of the vertical heavy line; vertically, positive is up and negative is down. Check out the partially played game in the following figure.

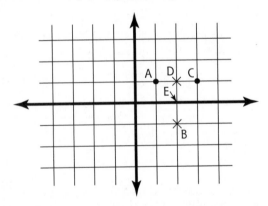

In the preceding game, Player 1 went first, and called out "(1, 1)," causing a dot to be placed at "A." Player 2 called out "(2, –1)" (read "two, negative one"), causing an "X" to be placed at "B." Player 1 next called "(3, 1)" causing the dot at "C." Player 2 realized that this was a trap, since if one player gets three marks in a row not at the edge of the playing field, it is a guaranteed win on the next turn. That realization caused Player 2 to call out "(2, 1)," blocking player 1 with an "X" at D. Where had Player 1 best go next if he wants to save the game?

The answer to that question is (2, 0), E, to prevent Player 2 from establishing a trap of his own. The combination of two coordinates represented within parentheses and separated by a comma is known as an **ordered pair.** The tic-tac-toe exercise is not only a great reinforcement for the concept of integers, it's also a great introduction to **rectangular coordinates** for **graphing.** If your student is reluctant to call out negative coordinates, keep the same size playing board as was used previously, but shrink the portion of that board that is positive.

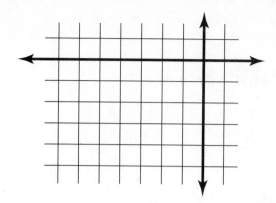

Make a mental note that integers are often referred to as **"signed numbers."** The relevance of this will become clear in Lesson 38.

EXERCISES

Given a horizontal number line, tell the distance and direction of the second number from the first.

1. 0 to 12
2. 0 to –12

3. –3 to +3
4. –9 to 14

5. 12 to –18
6. 15 to –15

Given a pair of crossed axes and an equally spaced grid of lines, tell how one would move in order to get from the origin to the point named by the ordered pair.

7. (7, 11)
8. (5, –6)

9. (–5, 12)
10. (–8, –14)

11. (9, 12)
12. (8, –9)

ANSWERS

1. 12 right
2. 12 left
3. 6 right
4. 23 right

5. 30 left
6. 30 left
7. 7 right, 11 up
8. 5 right, 6 down

9. 5 left, 12 up
10. 8 left, 14 down
11. 9 right, 12 up
12. 8 right, 9 down

Adding Integers

As you have probably surmised, arithmetic of integers has its own set of rules for achieving addition, subtraction, multiplication, and division. In order to help you to visualize what is going on, we'll make extensive reference to the number line, and to another, rather quaint device. But first, something a bit different.

Absolute Value

Every number possesses a quality known as its **absolute value.** Marked on the number line shown here are +5 and –5. Each of those numbers is the same distance from 0. We refer to the distance from zero as the absolute value of the number. Thus, +5 and –5 both have the same absolute values. You can write that as:

$$|+5| = |-5| = 5$$

Read that as "The absolute value of positive 5 equals the absolute value of negative 5, equals 5," or "The absolute values of both positive 5 and negative 5 equal 5." Obviously, those vertical bars (| |) indicate the absolute value of the figure contained within them.

Find two numbers on the given number line such that their absolute values are 8. In other words, $|a|$ and $|b|$ = 8? The answers, of course, are $|+8|$ and $|-8|$. You'll see the relevance of this information in the sections that follow.

Positive Plus Positive

The addition of two positive numbers is something you and your student are accustomed to, since it's what he's been doing all along. He just never stopped to think of it in those terms before.

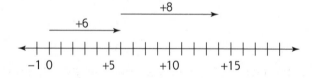

Check out the number line shown here. It shows the addition of positive 6 and positive 8. Note that the tail of the +8 arrow begins at the tip of the +6 arrow. That places the result of the addition at +14 on the number line. It would not be at all out of line to conclude that the addition of two positive quantities results in a positive quantity.

The rule that ties all this together goes like this: In order to add two positive quantities, add their absolute values and tack on a positive sign, or no sign at all. (Remember, no sign preceding a number defaults to positive.)

Negative Plus Negative

If you check out the number line shown here, you'll see an illustration of the meaning of the addition of two negative numbers.

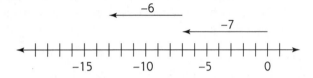

The rightmost arrow, −7, demonstrates the location −7 on the number line. Beginning at the tip of that arrow is the tail of an arrow marked −6, whose tip is at position −13. That is to say:

$$-7 + (-6) = -13$$

The parentheses around the −6 are to keep from getting the plus sign and the negative sign confused. Positive and negative signs identify the positions of integers with respect to zero. Plus and minus signs also signify the operations of addition and subtraction.

The rule that applies here goes this way: In order to add two negative quantities, add their absolute values and tack on a negative sign.

Positive Plus Negative

Now comes the fun part! Above the number line shown here is the addition of −8 + (+7), or, more simply put, −8 + 7. Notice that the −8 comes first, so we follow its arrow from 0 down to its tip at −8 on the number line. At that point, you can find the tail of the +7 arrow, heading in the positive direction. Its tip ends up at the −1 mark on the number line, so −8 + (+7) = −1.

Below the number line is the addition +9 + (−5). Starting with the +9 arrow, we move to its tip, which is, as expected, by +9 on the number line. Even with the tip of the +9 arrow is the tail of the −5 arrow, which moves in the opposite direction, ending at +4 on the number line. You may, therefore, conclude that +9 + (−5) = +4. Do you see the pattern?

The rule for adding two integers with opposite signs works like this: First notice which addend has the larger absolute value and make a mental note of its sign. Next, subtract their absolute values and tack on the sign you made a mental note of before—in other words, that of the addend that had the larger absolute value.

Three or More Addends

In cases with three or more numbers being added together, first combine all like-signed ones. Of course, if all signs are the same, there's no problem. Just add them up and attach the appropriate sign. If there are both positive and negative quantities being added, then note which is larger, because that will determine the sign of your sum. For example:

$$+8 + (-7) + (-9) + (+11) = \underline{\quad}$$

First collect likes with likes: $+8 + (+11) + (-7) + (-9) = \underline{\quad}$

Combine likes with likes: $+19 + (-16) = \underline{\quad}$

Notice the positive is larger and then add: $= +3$

EXERCISES
Find the following sums.

1. $+5 + (+8) = \underline{\quad}$
2. $+7 + (+5) = \underline{\quad}$
3. $-6 + (-9) = \underline{\quad}$
4. $-7 + (-11) = \underline{\quad}$
5. $-8 + (+12) = \underline{\quad}$
6. $-15 + (+9) = \underline{\quad}$
7. $8 + (-13) = \underline{\quad}$
8. $11 + (-15) = \underline{\quad}$
9. $15 + (-7) = \underline{\quad}$
10. $20 + (-17) = \underline{\quad}$

11. $-9 + (-12) = \underline{\quad}$
12. $-15 + (+17) = \underline{\quad}$
13. $-16 + (-12) = \underline{\quad}$
14. $+14 + (+17) = \underline{\quad}$
15. $-18 + 13 = \underline{\quad}$
16. $(-9) + (-8) + (-7) = \underline{\quad}$
17. $(-8) + (-11) + (-13) + (21) = \underline{\quad}$
18. $(-11) + (14) + (-18) + (16) + (-12) = \underline{\quad}$
19. $(15) + (-12) + (11) + (-15) + (10) = \underline{\quad}$
20. $(8) + (-7) + (12) + (-11) + (15) + (-9) = \underline{\quad}$

ANSWERS

1. 13
2. 12
3. −15
4. −18
5. 4
6. −6
7. −5
8. −4
9. 8
10. 3

11. −21
12. 2
13. −28
14. 31
15. −5
16. −24
17. −11
18. −11
19. 9
20. 8

LESSON 37

Subtracting Integers

The Madison Project, mentioned in Lesson 35, modeled adding signed numbers by teaching about an old hermit who lived by himself in a small house at the edge of a cliff. The hermit preferred to be where nobody could disturb him, and even at the edge of a cliff, someone is likely to pass by from time to time. So, to ensure his privacy, the hermit attached some helium balloons to the roof. This made his house float freely above the cliff and helped him to achieve peace and quiet. The balloons that the hermit used were of varying sizes, and each one was marked as to the number of feet above the ground it would cause the house to float, so, as you can see in the accompanying picture, on this particular day, the hermit's house had a +8 and a +7 balloon on it, and so was a balmy 15 feet above the edge of the cliff.

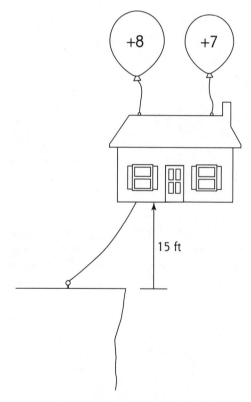

This state of affairs sufficed for days, until one morning the hermit discovered that he was running low on groceries and would have to do some shopping. Realizing that he would have to lower his house in order to go to the store, the resourceful fellow hung a –10 and a –8 sandbag onto the house. He really should have been more careful, since that brought his doorstep to –3, or three feet below the edge of the cliff.

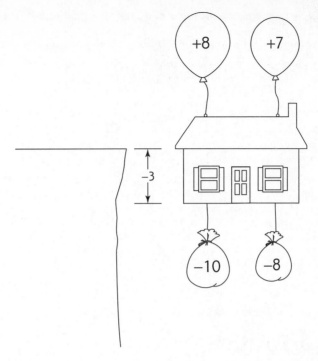

Fortunately, after searching around, the hermit was able to find a board that allowed him to walk out and go to the store.

If your student has difficulty visualizing with the use of the number line, balloons and sandbags just might be the way to get him to relate. Balloons are positive; sandbags are negative; and the hermit is always adding one or the other on to his house—or taking one or the other off, as below.

Subtracting integers requires one step to turn the process into adding integers. That step is to turn the second sign around and turn it into an addition of integers. Think about it in terms of balloons and sandbags, or in terms of the number line. The hermit is sitting there in mid-air with a whole lot of balloons and a whole lot of sandbags on the house. He is no longer adding balloons to the house to make it go up or adding sandbags to the house to make it go down. Rather, he is cutting them off. When the hermit cuts off a balloon, the house will go down.

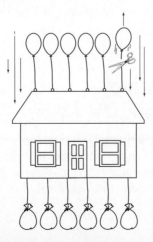

So subtracting a positive is the same as adding a negative. Think about it or look at the house.

When the hermit wishes to go up, he can cut a sandbag off the house. See how that works?

Subtracting a negative has the same effect as adding a positive.

Subtracting a Positive

To subtract +5 from +8, set it up: +8 [– (+]5) = __ The bracket shows where the action will be.

Since subtracting a positive is the same as adding a negative, reverse the two middle signs:

$$+8 \; [– (+]5) \;) \; = \_\_ \; \text{becomes} \; +8 \; [+ \; (–]5) \;) \; = \_\_$$

Finally, follow the rule for adding with two different signs, namely subtract the absolute value and give the sum the sign of the larger addend:

$$+8 + (–5) = +3, \text{or } 3$$

For a second example of subtracting a positive, try this: –6 – (+7) = __.

Once more, reverse the two middle signs: –6 [– (+]7) = __ becomes –6 [+ (–]7) = __.

Finally, follow the rule for adding two numbers with the same sign, that is, add their absolute values and keep the sign:

$$–6 + (–7) = –13$$

Subtracting a Negative

To subtract –4 from +9, write the mathematical sentence: +9 [– (–]4) = __.

The bracketed part of the mathematical sentence should be recognizable from English class as a **double negative.** An example would be "I'm not not going to class." Well, of course, since a double negative is the same as a positive, that sentence is a round-about way of saying "I am going to class." In a nutshell, that is the rule for rewriting our mathematical double negative:

$$+9 \; [– (–]4) \; = \_\_ \; \text{becomes} \; +9 \; [+] \; 4 \; = \_\_$$

Once again, follow the rule for adding two numbers with the same sign—that is, add their absolute values and keep the sign:

$$9 + 4 = +13, \text{ or } 13$$

To subtract –5 from –11, write the mathematical sentence: –11 [– (–]5) = __.

Once more, we have a double negative, which must be corrected by exchanging it for a positive:

$$-11 \; [- \; (-]5) \; = \; \_\_ \text{ becomes } -11 \; [+] \; 5 \; = \; \_\_$$

Following the rule for adding two numbers with different signs, subtract their absolute values, and the answer takes the sign of the larger addend:

$$-11 + 5 = -6$$

EXERCISES

1. +8 – (+9) = __
2. –11 – (+7) = __
3. +13 – (–8) = __
4. –12 – (–10) = __
5. +14 – (+7) = __
6. –15 – (+6) = __

7. +11 – (–12) = __
8. –13 – (–6) = __
9. +10 – (+5) = __
10. –7 – (+12) = __
11. +16 – (–12) = __
12. –24 – (–9) = __

13. +18 – (+15) = __
14. –17 – (+4) = __
15. +21 – (–8) = __
16. –19 – (–11) = __
17. +20 – (+15) = __
18. –9 – (+9) = __

ANSWERS

1. –1
2. –18
3. 21
4. –2
5. 7
6. –21

7. 23
8. –7
9. 5
10. –19
11. 28
12. –15

13. 3
14. –21
15. 29
16. –8
17. 5
18. –18

Multiplying and Dividing Integers

Multiplying and dividing integers follow the same rules, so there is no reason not to handle them together. Multiplying and dividing integers essentially breaks down into two categories according to the relationships of the signs

Like Signs

If both factors have a plus sign, it is equivalent to having no sign at all. A multiplication would yield a product with no sign, also known as a positive, and ditto for a division. If both signs are negative, we again have the situation we encountered in subtraction—that of a double negative, which by now, you should recognize as always forming a positive. The same holds for both multiplication and division, so the rule may be stated simply:

When multiplying, if both factors have the same sign, the product is positive.

When dividing, if divisor and dividend have the same sign, the quotient is positive.

Unlike Signs

Multiplying a positive number by a negative one will result in a negative product. Since multiplication is commutative, you can safely assume that multiplying a negative number by a positive one will yield a negative product.

Positive divisor and negative dividend yield a negative quotient; negative divisor and positive dividend yield a negative quotient. This permits the rule governing multiplication or division of numbers with unlike signs to be rather simply stated:

When multiplying or dividing integers with unlike signs, the result is negative. The Madison Project provided a model for multiplication of signed numbers, which space considerations do not permit including here, but which you'll find in the Appendix.

EXERCISES

1. $+6 \times +8 =$ __
2. $-24 \div -3 =$ __
3. $+9 \times -4 =$ __
4. $+56 \div -7 =$ __
5. $+6 \times -9 =$ __
6. $+144 \div -6 =$ __

7. $+5 \times -8 =$ __
8. $-36 \div +4 =$ __
9. $-35 \div -7 =$ __
10. $+6 \times -7 =$ __
11. $-90 \div -6 =$ __
12. $-8 \times +9 =$ __

13. $-8 \times -8 =$ __
14. $-7 \times +4 =$ __
15. $-121 \div +11 =$ __
16. $-3 \times +9 =$ __
17. $+49 \div -7 =$ __
18. $-81 \div +9 =$ __

The laws governing arithmetic with integers also apply to common and decimal fractions with positive and/or negative signs, hence the designation "signed numbers" mentioned as an afterthought in Lesson 35. When doing any arithmetic with signed fractions or decimals, follow the same rules as you would if there were no signs, but then superimpose the rules for integers over them. That is to say, if you were adding or subtracting two signed common fractions, they would need to have the same denominators. When that's achieved, if it's an addition, add their absolute values if the signs are the same, and assign them that sign. If the signs are different, subtract their absolute values and assign the sum the sign of the larger. Take care to make sure that you know which is larger, for example, one-half outranks three-eighths.

If it's a subtraction, reverse the middle signs (minus-positive becomes plus negative and minus-negative becomes plus), and then follow the rules for signed number addition.

In the case of multiplication or division, like signs will yield a positive product or quotient, respectively, and unlike signs will yield a negative result.

ANSWERS

1. 48
2. 8
3. –36
4. –8
5. –54
6. –24

7. –40
8. –9
9. 5
10. –42
11. 15
12. –72

13. 64
14. –28
15. –11
16. –27
17. –7
18. –9

Introducing Exponents

An **exponent** is a little number written high and following another number, like this: 3^1. That would be read as "three to the first power," and has a value of 3. In fact, any number raised to the first power has a value equal to that of the number itself. "So why would anyone bother raising a number to the first power?" you're probably asking yourself. The answer, I must say, is that they wouldn't—under normal circumstances. There are, occasionally, not-so-normal circumstances in which a math person is trying to make a point. Then, she might raise a number to the first power. I'll show you an example of that before the next lesson is done, but not yet. When raising a number to a power, the number being raised is called the **base.**

Squares and Cubes

Raise a number to the second power, and it is no longer worth itself—that is, unless that number happens to be 1, as is illustrated here:

$$1^2 = 1 \times 1 = 1 \quad \ldots \text{but:}$$
$$2^2 = 2 \times 2 = 4$$
$$3^2 = 3 \times 3 = 9$$
$$4^2 = 4 \times 4 = 16 \quad \ldots \text{and so forth!}$$

I'll leave it to you to figure out what the rest of them are—at least up to 13^2, which is 169.

Whether or not you remember it, the area of a square is computed by multiplying one side of the square by itself, so numbers raised to the second power are known as squared numbers. That is to say the short way for saying "2 raised to the second power" is "2 squared."

Since the volume of a cube is found by multiplying a number by itself and again by itself, raising to the third power has a special name, too. "2 to the third power" is referred to in short-speak as "2 cubed."

Raise a number to the third power, and it is no longer worth itself—unless, of course, that number is 1:

$$1^3 = 1 \times 1 \times 1 = 1 \quad \ldots \text{but:}$$
$$2^3 = 2 \times 2 \times 2 = 8$$
$$3^3 = 3 \times 3 \times 3 = 27$$
$$4^3 = 4 \times 4 \times 4 = 64 \quad \ldots \text{and so on}$$

Extending the Pattern

Without fear of overburdening you with two much information at one time, you should be seeing a pattern, that is not too difficult to decipher. To extend that pattern for the number 2, look at these:

$$2^1 = 2$$
$$2^2 = 2 \times 2 = 4$$
$$2^3 = 2 \times 2 \times 2 = 8$$
$$2^4 = 2 \times 2 \times 2 \times 2 = 16$$

Can you see the pattern now? The exponent tells you the number of times the base is written down for the purpose of multiplying. Since anything to the first power writes only one instance of the number, there is nothing to multiply it by, and so it remains unchanged. If 2 were written to the tenth power, there would be 10 of the 2s, and the result of the multiplication would be 1024.

EXERCISES

Find the value of each:

1. 4^3
2. 5^4
3. 6^5

4. 7^4
5. 2^8
6. 3^7

7. 8^3
8. 2^9
9. 11^3

Express each in terms of its simplest base and exponent form.

10. $5 \times 5 \times 5 \times 5 \times 5$
11. $6 \times 6 \times 6 \times 6$
12. 81

13. 343
14. 256
15. 729

16. 3125
17. 1296
18. 243

ANSWERS

1. 64
2. 625
3. 7776
4. 2401
5. 256
6. 2187

7. 512
8. 512
9. 1331
10. 5^5
11. 6^4
12. 3^4

13. 7^3
14. 2^8
15. 3^6
16. 5^5
17. 6^4
18. 3^5

More About Exponents

Numbers raised to exponents can be added and subtracted, but you're not likely to enjoy knowing what the results will be. For example, adding 5^4 and 2^3 results in the sum $5^4 + 2^3$. See what I meant? Similarly, they can be subtracted with just as unsatisfactory results. Taking 7^2 from 3^4 will get you a difference of $3^4 - 7^2$. If you're looking to resolve either of those into single numbers you're going to have to expand each term and then add or subtract, as appropriate.

What if the bases are the same? $3^4 + 3^4 = 2 \times (3^4)$, but that doesn't help a whole lot, and $5^3 + 5^2 = 5^3 + 5^2$. You can't do much more with those until algebra. The same is true of multiplication and division—*unless the bases are the same*.

Multiplying and Dividing Exponential Terms

When two exponential terms have the same base, it is possible to multiply and divide them according to the following scheme. To multiply them, keep the base the same and add their exponents:

$$2^2 \times 2^3 = 2^{2+3} = 2^5$$

Furthermore, I can prove it. $2^2 = 4$; $2^3 = 8$:

$$4 \times 8 = 32, \text{ which, not coincidentally, happens to be } 2^5.$$

Would you like to see another one? Try $3^2 \times 3^3 =$ __.

By the formula: $3^2 \times 3^3 = 3^{2+3} = 3^5$

To prove it, find that $3^2 = 9$, and $3^3 = 27$.

$$9 \times 27 = 243$$

And, in fact, that does work out to be 3^5.

Have you figured out yet how division of exponential terms with the same base is going to work? I'll bet you have. To divide them, keep the base the same and subtract their exponents:

$$2^6 \div 2^4 = 2^{6-4} = 2^2$$

Let's check that out: $2^6 = 64$; $2^4 = 16$:

$$64 \div 16 = 4, \text{ which also goes by the name of } 2^2, \text{ so that works.}$$

Let's do one more for the road. Let's try $3^6 \div 3^2 =$ __

Using the formula: $3^6 \div 3^2 = 3^{6-2} = 3^4$

To prove that, find that $3^6 = 729$, and $3^2 = 9$:

$$729 \div 9 = 81$$

81, in fact, works out to be 3^4.

Negative Exponents

Rarely in everyday life are you likely to encounter a negative exponent, but this is the world of mathematics, where you are liable to encounter items with highly specialized purposes. The negative exponent's specialized function is to move the number it's part of from above or below the fraction line to the other side. They say that a picture is worth a thousand words, so permit me to cut down on the length of this book by showing you the following:

$$4^{-3} = \frac{1}{4^3} \qquad\qquad \frac{2}{5^{-4}} = \frac{2 \times 5^4}{1} = 2 \times 5^4$$

In the first case, the negative exponent has served to place the number into the denominator of a fraction. In the second, it has brought the number from the denominator to be multiplied by what it was previously dividing. You must admit that's a pretty powerful negative sign.

Check this next one out:

$$\frac{5^{-3} \times 3^{-2} \times 7^{-4}}{4^{-4} \times 11^{-2} \times 13^2}$$

Every figure that has a negative exponent is on the side of the fraction line on which it doesn't belong. Following, the situation is remedied:

$$\frac{4^4 \times 11^2}{5^3 \times 3^2 \times 13^2 \times 7^4}$$

The Zeroth Power

Here is a proof that you could probably live without, but that your student may demand (or desire) you come up with: Suppose that n represents a number—any number (and by the way, you may use any number in place of n to prove this).

Then $n^3 \div n^3 = n^{3-3}$ which in turn equals n^0. (You might have used any exponent with your number, as long as you used the same exponent in both cases, so that following the rules for fractional division would result in an exponent of "0.")

But we already know that any number divided by itself is equal to 1. It is, therefore, safe to conclude that any number raised to the 0 power must be equal to 1.

That is to say $n^0 = 1$, $5^0 = 1$, $35^0 = 1$, and so forth.

Place-Headings as Powers of 10

Now, at last, you are ready to receive the information that I promised you at the beginning of the last lesson, the reason for the exponent one to ever be needed. If you cast your mind back to the very beginning of this book, the discussion centered upon place value and the fact that a digit's value depended upon its face value and the place that it's in, thereby permitting an infinite number of values to be written using only 10 digits, 0–9.

In fact, systems of numeration other than base-10, the decimal system, do exist. Very popular with computer types are the binary system, which contains only 0 and 1 (electronically on and off), and the hexadecimal system based upon the number 16 and containing 16 digits. Both of these are place-value systems, and once, students were required to do some conversions to other, non-decimal place-value systems. For every one of these systems, the template for the column headings is consistent. We'll use b to stand for the base number. Then, for any place-value system, the whole number places are as follows:

...	b^9	b^8	b^7	b^6	b^5	b^4	b^3	b^2	b^1	b^0

Remember, anything to the zero power = 1, so the column on the extreme right is the 1s column, no matter what base you're in. Next is b^1, which is the name of the base. In the decimal system, it's the 10s place. Then comes b^2, which for the decimal system is 100ths, and so on.

I'm sure that by now you've noticed the progression of exponents from right to left of 0, 1, 2, and so on in the exponents in a never-ending procession, but what about the progression from left to right? I arbitrarily stopped where the last whole number stops, but does the pattern really end there? No way! Check this out:

...	b^7	b^6	b^5	b^4	b^3	b^2	b^1	b^0	b^{-1}	b^{-2}	b^{-3}	b^{-4}	b^{-5}	b^{-6}	...

You and your student might have fun playing around with the language in which computers used to talk. Although today's machines talk in hexadecimal, they used to speak binary, as noted previously. Binary numbers are ideal for electronic devices, since the two digits, 0 and 1, correspond to an electrical switch's choices, off and on. Use the place headings given previously to figure what the name of each column is. Then use them to find the values of the binary numbers 11_2, 1001_2, and 110110_2.

Okay, I hope you really tried to do them. We need the first 6 places to the left of the binaral point (that's right, binaral, not decimal). From left to right, $2^5 = 32$, $2^4 = 16$, $2^3 = 8$, $2^2 = 4$, $2^1 = 2$, and $2^0 = 1$. Now drop the numbers into their columns:

32	16	8	4	2	1
				1	1
		1	0	0	1
1	1	0	1	1	0

That means $11_2 = 2 + 1$, or 3; $1001_2 = 8 + 1$, or 9; $110110_2 = 32 + 16 + 4 + 2$, or 54. Working in bases other than the decimal system is helpful to give students an understanding of how the decimal system works without repeatedly drilling and boring them to death. If you enjoyed that little excursion into base-2, try making up a few in base-6 or base-8. I promise I won't tell anyone, either way.

Now remember, a negative exponent puts a 1 over the base raised to that exponent. Look at b^{-1}. In the decimal system: b^1 would be 10, so b^{-1} is 1 over 10, or 0.1 (one-tenth). The progression to the right of the decimal point for our base-10 system goes like this:

...	$\frac{1}{10}$	$\frac{1}{100}$	$\frac{1}{1000}$	$\frac{1}{10,000}$	$\frac{1}{100,000}$	$\frac{1}{1,000,000}$	...

. . . and that's exactly the way that it's supposed to work, only we're more accustomed to seeing those fractions (from the lessons on decimal fractions) as 0.1, 0.01, 0.001, 0.0001, 0.00001, and 0.000001.

EXERCISES

Perform the indicated arithmetic operation and express your answer in simplest terms.

1. $6^2 + 3^2 =$ __
2. $3^5 \times 3^8 =$ __
3. $5^9 \div 5^6 =$ __
4. $3^2 - 2^2 =$ __

5. $6^2 \times 7^2 =$ __
6. $2^3 + 2^3 =$ __
7. $7^2 \times 7^4 =$ __
8. $8^5 - 8^2 =$ __

9. $3^8 \div 3^5 =$ __
10. $9^2 \times 3^2 =$ __
11. $5^2 \div 5^5 =$ __
12. $8^7 \div 8^5 =$ __

Express each of the following with positive exponents only and in simplest terms.

13. $\frac{1}{6^{-3}}$
14. 7^{-5}
15. 6^{-9}

16. $\frac{5^{-3} \times 8^{-4} \times 2^7}{6^3 \times 8^{-3} \times 4^5}$

17. $\frac{8^{-5} \times 5^4 \times 3^{-7}}{7^{-3} \times 8^7 \times 5^{-5}}$

18. $\frac{2^{-3} \times 5^{-6} \times 3^{-7}}{3^{-5} \times 2^{-8} \times 5^6}$

ANSWERS

1. $6^2 + 3^2$
2. 3^{13}
3. 5^3
4. $3^2 - 2^2$
5. $6^2 \times 7^2$
6. $2^3 + 2^3$
7. 7^6

8. $8^5 - 8^2$
9. 3^3
10. $9^2 \times 3^2$
11. 5^{-3} or $\frac{1}{5^3}$
12. 8^2
13. 6^3
14. $\frac{1}{7^5}$

15. $\frac{1}{6^9}$
16. $\frac{2^7}{5^3 \times 6^3 \times 8 \times 4^5}$
17. $\frac{7^3 \times 5^9}{8^{12} \times 3^7}$
18. $\frac{2^5}{3^2 \times 5^{12}}$

Scientific Notation

The last use of exponents that we'll explore in this part of this book is the form that is used to represent very large and very small numbers. Those who ordinarily deal with such figures are primarily scientists dealing with billions and trillions of miles of space, or infinitesimally sized subatomic particles. It is probably for that reason that this form of numerical representation is known as **scientific notation.** In all cases, scientific notation represents figures in terms of a number that is 1 or greater and less than 10, multiplied by 10, and raised to a power.

Numbers Greater than One

Five billion is a nice round number. In standard notation, it looks like this:

$$5,000,000,000$$

In scientific notation it's: $\qquad 5.0 \times 10^9$

It is customary to write the non-powers of 10 part of the numeral with a single digit and a decimal point. In this case, since no significant digit follows the decimal point, a zero is written there just for form. Next count the number of places that decimal point was moved from where it originally was (not showing, but understood to be after the last "0" in five billion). Did you count them? If you did your counting carefully, you should have come up with 9, and so, not by coincidence, that's the exponent of the 10. Five point oh times ten to the ninth is the scientific notation for 5 billion.

Another number just crying out to be represented in scientific notation is 117 million, which in standard notation looks like this: 117,000,000. Take a moment before reading on and use what you already know to express 117 million in scientific notation.

Approximating

The uses we've been putting scientific notation to up until this point have been exact at every turn, and if you can be exact, then you certainly should be, but there are times when it is okay to approximate. For example, 5 hundred 61 trillion, 1 hundred 37 thousand would be written in standard notation as 561,000,000,137,000. Exactly how significant do you think 137,000 is in a number of that magnitude?

Now taken all by itself, without anything to compare it to, 137,000 is a pretty big number, and I wouldn't mind having that many dollars suddenly and mysteriously showing up in my bank account, but stacked up against 561 trillion, it is worth somewhere around a ten-millionth of the total. Therefore, although when written in scientific notation to a sensible amount of accuracy, it is perfectly acceptable to approximate the number as 5.61×10^{14}. The 137,000 is mere chump change! Of course, it must be made clear in either the instructions that you're following, or in your answer, or in both, that the number is about, almost, or approximately the other number.

Finished already? Wow, that was fast! Based upon the fact that the whole-number part of the expression must be a single-digit number, the decimal point is going to be placed between the 1s. That's a movement to the left of 8 places, so the answer is 1.17×10^8.

Try one more of those before moving on. Express 63 trillion in scientific notation. In standard notation, that's 63,000,000,000,000. How far are you going to have to move the decimal point? Count from its current location to where it's going to wind up, and you should get a total of 13 places. So, in scientific notation it is 6.3×10^{13}.

Numbers Less than One

Up until now, we've been dealing with very large to very very large numbers. Now it's time to take a look at the other end of the spectrum. Let's start with something smaller than we've been dealing with, yet larger than we will deal with, and work our way down from there. Consider the number 0.5. To write it in scientific notation, we must move the decimal point one place to the right, so that:

$$0.5 = 5.0 \times 10^{-1}$$

Let's do another one: 0.045. In order to change it from standard notation to scientific notation, the decimal point is going to need to be moved two places to the right, so:

$$0.045 = 4.5 \times 10^{-2}$$

Do you see the pattern? Earlier we saw that moving the decimal point to the left gave a positive exponent equal to the number of places it was moved. By moving the decimal point to the right, we are moving in what is for "the science of decimal point moving" a negative direction, so the exponent equals negative the number of places the decimal point is moved.

Now, you're ready for a giant leap. Try representing 27 millionths in scientific notation.

27 millionths in standard notation: 0.000027

To properly place the decimal point in scientific notation, that point will need to be moved right 5 places:

$$0.000027 = 2.7 \times 10^{-5}$$

That makes 10's exponent a negative 5.

Here comes one more colossal jump, also known as "if you liked that . . . :"

Represent 237 trillionths in scientific notation. Since you already saw that trillions are the fifth period to the left of the decimal point (ones, thousands, millions, billions, trillions), you should be able to figure out where trillionths will go (or check out the figure).

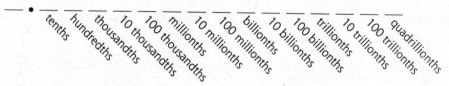

In standard form, that's 0.00000000000237. To properly place the decimal, it's going to have to be moved 12 places: $0.00000000000237 = 2.37 \times 10^{-12}$

Undoing Scientific Notation

You might think that it would be easy to work the reverse of scientific notation, and to a degree it is, but you need to exercise a good deal of care. The first thing you need to make sure you know is the direction in which you are going to move the decimal point. The second is how many places that point is going to have to be moved. Consider the following number:

$$5.35 \times 10^8$$

Since the exponent is positive, this is a larger number when written in standard form. The exponent, 8, tells us to move the decimal point 8 places to the right. A move of 2 places will put the decimal point after the 5, with 6 places remaining to be moved. Those 6 places will get filled in with zeroes:

$$5.35 \times 10^8 = 535000000 = 535,000,000$$

. . . also known as 535 million.

When the exponent is negative, the thinking changes a bit. Think about this number:

$$4.85 \times 10^{-10}$$

Since the exponent is negative, to write it in standard form, the decimal point is going to be moving to the left. A move to the left of the "4" will leave 9 more places to be filled with "0s:"

$$4.85 \times 10^{-10} = .000000000485 = 0.000000000485$$

The zero to the left of the decimal point is placed as a matter of form. That pretty well covers the subject of scientific notation. If you have any uncertainties while working the exercises, look back to the appropriate section of the lesson. It's all in here. Also, check out the Appendix on page 240.

EXERCISES

Express each of the following large numbers in scientific notation.

1. 234,000
2. 53,800,000
3. 647,000,000
4. 59,240,000,000

5. 483,000,000,000
6. 245,700,003,400
7. 89,000,000,000,761

Express each of the following small numbers in scientific notation.

8. 0.000000065
9. 0.0000009
10. 0.00000000463
11. 0.000000000059

12. 0.000000000000324
13. 0.0000000000005064
14. 0.0000000000000001

Change each of the following numbers from scientific notation to standard form.

15. 9.3×10^8

16. 6.2×10^{-9}

17. 3.7×10^{11}

18. 3.21×10^{-12}

19. 6.95×10^{10}

20. 4.2×10^{-14}

ANSWERS

1. 2.34×10^5
2. 5.38×10^7
3. 6.47×10^8
4. 5.924×10^{10}
5. 4.83×10^{11}
*6. $\approx 2.457 \times 10^{11}$
7. $\approx 8.9 \times 10^{13}$
8. 6.5×10^{-8}
9. 9.0×10^{-7}
10. 4.63×10^{-9}

11. 5.9×10^{-11}
12. 3.24×10^{-13}
13. 5.064×10^{-13}
14. 1.0×10^{-16}
15. 930,000,000
16. 0.0000000062
17. 370,000,000,000
18. 0.00000000000321
19. 69,500,000,000
20. 0.000000000000042

---

*The symbol "$\approx$" means " is about equal to. It is used to indicate an approximation. Some refer to it as "the wavy equal sign."

Roots

Sometime after my hair decided it preferred to be gray, I stopped worrying about my roots—my hair-roots, that is. After all, worrying might well be what turned them gray in the first place. But, I had no less concern about my **square roots.** Square root is the term given to the undoing of a number raised to the exponent 2 (we studied squared numbers in Lesson 39). To look at a cause-and-effect relationship, squaring is multiplying a number by itself. Finding the square root of a number is to find the number which, when multiplied by itself, would form the number in question. The square root of a number is indicated by a square root, or **radical** sign, pictured here. The following are inverse relationships:

$$2^2 = 4 \quad \sqrt{4} = 2$$

Read the left side as "Two squared equals four." Read the right side as "The square root of 4 equals 2." See; completely inverse relationships.

Perfect Squares

It's not easy to be perfect, which is why **perfect squares** are so rare. A perfect square is a number that has an integer for a square root. Although it's not necessary for your student to be concerned about the following fact, it wouldn't hurt for him to keep in mind that every number has both a positive and a negative square root. The square root of 4 is ±2 (which means plus or minus 2).

The following line has a list of all perfect squares up to 100, inclusive:

1, 4, 9, 16, 25, 36, 49, 64, 81, 100

That's 10 perfect squares in the first hundred numbers, or 1 in 10. Do you think that ratio will continue to hold at 1:10 through each hundred numbers? Let's look at the perfect squares in the second hundred:

121, 144, 169, 196, and for the third hundred:

225, 256, 289

The higher you go, the fewer perfect squares you will find. The results shown here were not difficult to come by. For those on the line of perfect squares up to 100, we squared, consecutively, each of the numbers 1 through 10. The second hundreds contains the squares of 11 through 14, and the third, 15 through 17. Three more perfect squares exist between 290 and 400, inclusive.

So what about all the other numbers that are not perfect squares? Do you think they have square roots? Every positive integer has a square root (two actually, as noted earlier), and if it is not a perfect square, the way to find its square root is with a calculator. Round the nonending decimal result, or estimate it.

Two of the handiest square roots of nonperfect squares are those of 2 and 3, which come up over and over again in geometric problems, which, of course, you and your student need not worry about for a few years yet, still . . . . There are great historically based mnemonics for remembering those roots, although, again, I wouldn't bother before secondary school. Christopher Columbus's birth year is 1414. George Washington's birth year is 1732. Did you say, "So what!"? Well, I'll tell you so what. So this:

$$\sqrt{2} = 1.414 \qquad \sqrt{3} = 1.732$$

Coincidence? You'd better believe it!

Simplifying under the Radical Sign

Not all radical signs hold either-or situations, that is, either a perfect square or "grab the calculator." In fact, it is often possible to recognize perfect squares within less than perfect radicals: Check this out:

$$\sqrt{50}$$

You may recognize that 50, although not a perfect square, contains the perfect square, 25, so:

$$\sqrt{50} = \sqrt{2 \times 25} = 5\sqrt{2}$$

The square root of 50 may be renamed as the square root of 2 × 25. Then, the square root of 25 may be removed from under the radical sign, leaving 5 times the square root of 2.

Try simplifying the following:

$$\sqrt{80}$$

Sometimes, it's not so easy to figure out what the perfect square is that's under the radical sign. That's when you should start factoring out what you know is there and seeing what's left. 80 is 10 times 8. No help there. Factoring a 4 out of 80 leaves 20. That's a possibility. In fact, that's a good starting point:

$$\sqrt{80} = \sqrt{4 \times 20} = 2\sqrt{20} = 2\sqrt{4 \times 5} = 4\sqrt{5}$$

You don't have to get it all at once. Factoring out 4 left its square root, 2, on the outside, and 20 under the radical sign. Then you realized that 20 is 4 × 5, so another 4 comes out as a 2, which is multiplied by the 2 already in front of the radical sign to make 4 times the square root of 5. You could have gotten there more directly if you had started out by factoring a 5 out of the 80:

$$\sqrt{80} = \sqrt{5 \times 16} = 4\sqrt{5}$$

That would have taken you straight to the solution, since 5 × 16 would have been the result, and the square root of 16 is 4. But it doesn't matter. It just took a couple of extra steps. All roads lead to 4 radical 5. (No, that's not what the doctor means when he or she talks about "a radical procedure.")

Cube Roots

The cube root's relationship to the cube is analogous to the square root's relationship to the square. It's its undoing:

$$\sqrt[3]{8} = 2$$

The preceding line may be read, "2 cubed equals 8; the cube root of 8 is 2." Notice the radical sign that was used for square root, but this time there's a little "3" in the crook. That makes it a cubed root sign.

The next cube is 27, since it is the result of $3 \times 3 \times 3$:

$$3^3 = 27 \quad \sqrt[3]{27} = 3$$

The preceding line is read, "3 cubed (or 3 raised to the third power) equals 27; the cube root of 27 is 3."

The next cube is 64, since it is the result of $4 \times 4 \times 4$:

$$4^3 = 64 \quad \sqrt[3]{64} = 4$$

And, I'm sure that you can figure out that the preceding line is read, "4 cubed (or 4 raised to the third power) equals 64; the cube root of 64 is 4."

Perfect cube comes from the notion of perfect square. It's a number whose cube root is an integer.

The perfect cubes in the first 100 are   1, 8, 27, and 64

In the second hundred: 125, and that's the only one! $\sqrt[3]{125} = 5$

In the third hundred, there is 216, and that also is the only one. $\sqrt[3]{216} = 6$

$$7^3 = 343, \quad \sqrt[3]{343} = 7$$

Note from the spread of the first 10 of them that perfect cubes are much rarer than perfect squares.

nth Roots

From the material that has preceded this section of the lesson, it should have become apparent that there is no limit to the roots of various numbers that you can attempt to find, or actually can find. In fact, a whole branch of mathematics known as **logarithms** exists so that engineers and mathematicians may do just that. Thankfully, we are not going to deal with that in this volume. Suffice it to say that for every exponent that a number may be raised to, there is a corresponding root to undo that raising:

$$2^5 = 32; \quad \sqrt[5]{32} = 2 \qquad\qquad\qquad 2^6 = 64; \quad \sqrt[6]{64} = 2$$

and so forth. We can say that for any number, m, raised to any number, n, then:

$$m^n = p; \quad \sqrt[n]{p} = m$$

When m to the nth equals p, then the nth root of p is m. I hope that didn't confuse you. If you read it over carefully, it really does make sense, despite what you might have thought at first inspection.

> I have tried throughout this book to avoid the use of letters to stand for numbers. There's a whole branch of mathematics devoted to that practice, known as algebra. Algebraic notation permits the making of statements that apply generally to all numbers, without having to give example after example, and at times, with deserved acknowledgement to a certain homemaking diva, it's a good thing.

EXERCISES

Find the square root of each.

1. 81
2. 49
3. 144

4. 256
5. 169
6. 196

Express each in simplest form.

7. $\sqrt{20}$
8. $\sqrt{96}$
9. $\sqrt{125}$

10. $\sqrt{147}$
11. $\sqrt{150}$
12. $\sqrt{405}$

Find the cube root of each.

13. 125
14. 27
15. 64

16. 343
17. 512

Find the specified root of each.

18. $\sqrt[5]{243}$
19. $\sqrt[7]{128}$
20. $\sqrt[4]{625}$

ANSWERS

1. 9
2. 7
3. 12
4. 16
5. 13
6. 14
7. $2\sqrt{5}$

8. $4\sqrt{6}$
9. $5\sqrt{5}$
10. $7\sqrt{3}$
11. $5\sqrt{6}$
12. $9\sqrt{5}$
13. 5
14. 3

15. 4
16. 7
17. 8
18. 3
19. 2
20. 5

Part 4

Geometry and Measurement

Terms You Should Know

After each word in the Glossary, the lesson where it first appears is cited. Occasionally a second or third appearance is also given if there are additional major references, but not all appearances of each word are necessarily cited.

absolute zero (Lesson 47). The freezing point of nitrogen; -273.16°C Celsius), or 0°K (Kelvin).

altitude (Lesson 54). The height of a figure; in a triangle, the segment from any vertex perpendicular to the side opposite it.

area (Lesson 48). The part inside the perimeter of a plane figure; surface; measured in square units, regardless of the shape of the figure.

base (Lesson 48). The side of a rectangle or triangle that is perpendicular to its height; the side of a rectangle that it rests upon; either of the two parallel sides of a trapezoid.

base (Lesson 51). Either of two parallel sides in a geometric solid from which the shape of a right prism takes its name.

capacity (Lesson 52). Volume; the amount of substance, dry or liquid, a container is capable of holding.

Celsius (Lesson 47). The temperature scale that marks water's freezing point at 0° and its boiling point at 100°, named after Swedish astronomer, Anders Celsius (1701–1744).

center (Lesson 49). The point that all points on the circumference of a circle are an equal distance from.

cgs (Lesson 43). Centimeter-grams-second system of S.I. units, favored by scientists working with small things.

chord (Lesson 49). A line segment with endpoints on the circumference of a circle.

circle (Lesson 49). A plane figure formed by an infinite set of points, all of which are an equal distance from a fixed point, the center.

circumference (Lesson 49). The perimeter, or distance around, a circle.

cone (Lesson 54). A solid figure that resembles a pyramid with a circular base.

congruent (Lesson 54). Identical in shape and size.

conversion factor (Lesson 45). The number multiplied by to convert from one system of measure to another; e.g. to convert inches to cm, the conversion factor is 2.48.

cylinder (Lesson 53). A solid figure resembling a right prism, but having circles as bases.

diameter (Lesson 49). The longest chord in a circle, passing through the center's circle and equal in length to two radii.

Fahrenheit (Lesson 47). The temperature scale dividing the distance between water's freezing and boiling points into 180 degrees from 32 to 212°F; named after German physicist Daniel Gabriel Fahrenheit (1686–1736).

hexagon (Lesson 54). A six-sided plane figure.

hexagonal (Lesson 54). Shaped like a hexagon.

hypotenuse (Lesson 48). The largest side of a right triangle; the side opposite the 90° angle.

isosceles (Lesson 54). A figure with two equal sides—especially such a triangle.

Kelvin (Lesson 47). Temperature scale named after British physicist Sir William Thompson (1824–1907) entitled Baron Kelvin. Degrees Kelvin (°K) are the same size as °C, but the scale begins at the freezing point of nitrogen, –273.16°C, also known as "absolute zero."

lateral (Lesson 51). Pertaining to the non-base faces of a solid figure.

line (Lesson 49). An infinite series of points in a plane that goes on forever in two directions, and may be named by a lowercase letter or by two points on it; represented by a line segment with arrowheads at either end symbolizing its continuousness.

line segment (Lesson 49). A portion of a line with two endpoints by which it is named; the shortest distance between two points.

meter (Lesson 43). Unit of length in the S.I. system, equal to about 39.37 inches.

metre (Lesson 43). European spelling of meter.

mks (Lesson 43). Meter-kilogram-second system of S.I. units, favored by scientists working with larger objects.

obtuse triangle (Lesson 48). A triangle containing an angle greater than 90° (named after an obtuse angle, which is one greater than 90° and less than 180°).

parallel (Lesson 48). Lines or segments that are everywhere equal distance apart, and will never meet, no matter how far they are extended.

parallelogram (Lesson 48). A quadrilateral with both pairs of opposite sides parallel.

perimeter (Lesson 45). The distance around a plane figure; think of the perimeter as the fence surrounding the area inside the figure.

perpendicular (Lesson 48). Meeting or intersecting at right angles.

π (Lesson 49). Greek letter "pi," representing the relationship between the diameter of the circle and its circumference, approximated as 3.14, or $\frac{22}{7}$.

plane figure (Lesson 45). A figure drawn on a plane, having length and width, but no depth; a two-dimensional figure; included are parallelograms, quadrilaterals, triangles, circles, pentagons, etc.

point of tangency (Lesson 49). The point where a tangent intersects (touches) the circumference of a circle.

polygon (Lesson 54). A plane closed figure of three or more sides. Also said by a person who has lost a parrot.

probability (Lesson 58). The likelihood that something will happen, usually a fraction, determined by the number of desirable outcomes (or results) divided by the number of possible outcomes; a probability of 1 is certainty; a probability of 0 is an impossibility.

pyramid (Lesson 54). A solid figure with a polygon as its base, each vertex of which is connected to a single point on a plane different from the one containing the base, thereby forming triangular sides.

quadrilateral (Lesson 48). Any closed four-sided plane figure.

radius (Lesson 49). A line segment that connects the center of a circle to the circumference.

rectangle (Lesson 48). A parallelogram containing a right angle.

rhombus (Lesson 48). A parallelogram with all sides of equal length.

right angle (Lesson 48). A 90° angle; one quarter revolution of the radius of a circle.

right triangle (Lesson 48). A triangle containing one right angle.

secant (Lesson 49). A line or line segment that touches the circumference of a circle at two points and then continues outside the circle in either or both directions forever, or terminating at some fixed outside point(s); may be thought of as a chord that continues beyond the confines of the circle.

S.I. units (Lesson 43). Units of System Internationale; units of measurement based on the meter, gram or kilogram, and litre.

sphere (Lesson 54). The location of all points in three-dimensional space equal in distance from a fixed point, that being its center.

square (Lesson 48). A rectangle with all sides of equal length and/or a rhombus with one right angle.

square units (Lessons 48, 49). Units used to express area, such as square inches, square centimeters, etc., usually abbreviated as in.^{2}, cm^2, ft.^{2}, etc.

surface area (Lesson 50). The combined areas of all the surfaces of a solid object.

tangent (Lesson 49). Usually a line or line segment that touches a circle at one and only one point; it is perpendicular to a radius of the circle drawn to the point of tangency; two circles may be internally or externally tangent to one another.

trapezoid (Lesson 48). A quadrilateral with one pair of sides parallel.

vertex (Lesson 48). The point of intersection; the point at which two lines, line segments, sides of a closed figure, or curve and line or line segment meet; (Lesson 54) the point of intersection of the segments from all the vertices in a pyramid's base; the point of a cone.

volume (Lesson 50). The amount of space occupied by a solid, usually expressed in cubic measure, e.g., cm^3, in.^{3}, etc.

Traditional versus SI Units

Geometry comes from two Greek words, *ge*, meaning earth, and *metria*, meaning to measure, hence, to measure the earth. Isn't measurement wonderful? Here in the United States, most of our weights and measures are in the traditional system, which used to be called the English System, until even the English stopped using it. The *System Internationale* (pronounce that with a French accent, if you please) was created by the scientists of Napoleon Bonaparte's France and was known (in fact, still is some places) as the metric system. It is more correct these days to refer to units from the metric system as "SI units," with the SI taken from the initials of the already cited French name, but if your student's teacher prefers "metric system," don't sweat it.

Traditional Units of Measure

Back in the days when Noah was building his ark, the absence of a yardstick didn't matter very much. Measuring was all done by a single craftsman building one thing at a time, rather than a number of assembly-line workers making many copies of something piecemeal to be assembled at a later time. It didn't make much difference how long a mile or an inch was, or how heavy a pound was. Today, however, standard measures are needed so that they mean the same thing to everyone. Noah's unit of length was the cubit, the distance from the tip of his middle finger to his elbow. This was a very handy unit of measure (no pun intended), because he could not misplace it. He always had it with him. Standard, however, it was not—at least not for anyone but him.

Even though the cubit is no longer in regular use, many units of traditional measure got their start in the same way. Our foot ruler started out as the length of a man's foot. An inch was the width of a man's thumb or the length of the forefinger from its tip to the first knuckle. Two cubits made a yard (the tip of a man's nose to his outstretched middle finger) and a fathom was two yards (the distance from middle fingertip to middle fingertip of a man's outstretched arms). Interrelationships were discovered between these measurements. A foot could be divided into 12 inches, while 36 inches, or 3 feet made a yard. A cubit was 18 inches, and half a cubit was a span—the distance between the tips of outstretched pinky and thumb on one hand. Half a span was a hand.

This was the way people measured short distances for thousands of years. Each succeeding civilization added or improved upon measurements. Some added ways to measure weights, and others developed means to measure time. The Babylonians made important improvements on the way the balance was used to measure weights. Whereas earlier people had compared weights of two objects, the Babylonians compared the weight of each object against the weights of a set of stones that were kept for just that purpose. This is believed to be the first use of standardized weights in history. The 14-pound stone is still used as a measure of weight in England. The Egyptians and Greeks established the weight of a grain of wheat as the smallest unit of measure, and the grain is still a measure used in some systems today.

With the disappearance of the Roman Empire, Europe drifted into the so-called Dark Ages, and no additional known steps were taken to try to standardize weights until after the signing of the Magna Carta near the beginning of the thirteenth century. Then King Edward I of England took a step forward by ordering a permanent measuring stick made of iron, to serve as the standard against which all others were to be measured. That stick was to be the yard, one-third of it was the foot, and one-thirty-sixth was the inch.

That's enough history. The point of it all was to demonstrate what disarray measurement was in as the world rapidly approached the Industrial Revolution and the need for standardized measure. In traditional measurements, there was no uniformity in subdivisions either. Consider length, weight, and capacity:

Length	Weight	Capacity (liquid)
1 inch = 1000 mils	[grain and dram omitted]	1 minim = .0038 in.^{3}
1 foot = 12 inches	1 pound = 16 ounces	1 fl. dram = 60 minims
1 yard = 36 inches	1 stone = 14 pounds	1 fl. oz. = 8 fl. drams
1 yard = 3 feet	1 short hundredweight = 100 lbs.	1 gill = 4 fl. oz.
2 yards = 1 fathom	1 ton = 2000 lbs.	1 cup = 2 gills
1 mile = 5280 feet		1 pint = 2 cups
1 mile = 1760 yards		1 quart = 2 pints
		1 gallon = 4 quarts

Mind you, the weights listed above are what are known as avoirdupois weights. Really, that's their official name. There are also Troy weight and apothecaries weight. Additionally, there are nautical length and surveyor's length, dry capacity measures, and some exotic units that I didn't bother to list, because you'll never encounter them. Here come some more, so don't go to the refrigerator just yet.

Dry measure	Area	Cubic measure
1 pint = 33.6 cubic inches	1 square foot = 144 in.^{2}	1 cubic foot = 1728 in.^{3}
1 quart = 2 pints	1 square yard = 9 ft.^{2}	1 cubic yard = 27 ft.^{3}
1 peck = 8 quarts	1 square rod = 30.25 yd.^{2}	
1 bushel = 4 pecks	1 acre = 160 rods^2	
	1 square mile = 640 acres	

If you're wondering about the point of all this, it's to show you that the state of traditional measurement is one of a grand mess. But it didn't just become a grand mess; it has been one for a very long time. I haven't selected these measurements capriciously and then put them out there to torture you. All of these and more are out there and in use. Furthermore, you, and perhaps more relevantly, your student, needs to learn to use these thoroughly inconsistent units on—in some cases—a day-to-day basis. Scary, isn't it?

SI Units (Often Called "the Metric System")

In 1793, during the reign of Napoleon Bonaparte, the French government decided to adopt a new system of standards based on the "metre." The metre was supposed to be one-ten-millionth of the distance from the North Pole to the Equator when measured on a straight line along the surface of the earth, with that line passing through Paris. Having determined the metre as the linear basis of the metric system, all other measures of distance were determined as decimal fractions or multiples of the metre. The metre itself is just a little longer than the yard, measuring 39.37 inches. The most commonly used decimal fractions of the meter (spelling now Anglicized) are the millimeter, or thousandth of a meter, and the centimeter, or hundredth of a meter. The most common multiple of the meter is the kilometer. Check the speedometer of your car. The odds are it has markings in kilometers per hour in an off color or smaller numerals than the mph (miles per hour) reading. (As an aid in finding them, know that 55 mph corresponds to 88 km per hour.)

The metric system also contained units for volume, liquid capacity, and weight measurement. The liter is the basic unit of liquid capacity and is actually a volume of 10 cm by 10 cm by 10 cm. It is a little bit larger than a quart. The basic unit of weight in the metric system was originally the gram, which was the weight of one cubic centimeter of water. I don't want to dwell on cubic measure, since we haven't actually dealt with it yet. Don't worry, though, it's coming later. When SI units were standardized, the unit of weight became the kilogram (or 1000 grams). Bear in mind that the weight of a gram is so small that it takes a thousand of them to equal about 2.2 pounds.

Scientists, depending upon the size of the items with which they work, tend to separate SI units into two separate and distinct groupings: Those working with small things use the **cgs,** or centimeter-grams-second system. Those working with larger things use the **mks,** or meter-kilogram-second system; the word "second" in both systems stands for the standard unit of time.

The Metric Conversion Act

Intriguingly, the United States Congress was first introduced to the metric system of units by John Adams, and Thomas Jefferson fully expected the United States to have adopted the system during the first part of the nineteenth century. In 1975, Congress finally passed the Metric Conversion Act. The major provisions of the bill provided for adaptation of SI as the predominant system of measurement units, but set no specific timetable, and made participation voluntary. At the time of this writing, we have two-liter soda bottles to show how far we've come and precious little else.

Today, the entire world has adopted SI units, except for the United States and a couple of African countries. What that means is that anything built in U.S. factories for export must be built to metric specifications, while those built for domestic use must use traditional measures (think screw heads, wrenches, and so on).

SI provides the expected units for area and cubic measure, with the former expressed in square meters (m²), square centimeters (cm²), and so on, and the latter in cubic centimeters (cm³), or meters (m³), and so on.

We convert between units of measure in the SI system by using specific prefixes, which denote the decimal fraction part or power of ten by which we multiply the unit. We'll get into those in detail in the next lesson. The most important difference between working with traditional units and SI units is consistency. The same relationships exist across the board, whether working with length, weight, liquid capacity, area, dry capacity, or cubic measure. Although the units might seem strange to you at first, the overall uniformity of working with decimal relationships is nothing short of refreshing.

EXERCISES

Fill in the blank to identify the number or unit for each answer.

1. 1 gallon = __ cups
2. 224 ounces = 1 ___
3. 32 quarts = 1 _____
4. 8 gills = __ quarts
5. __ inches = 1 fathom
6. 2 fluid oz. = 16 ___
7. 3 miles = 5280 ___
8. 16 fluid ounces = __ pints

9. 5 yards = ___ inches
10. 1 gill = __ minims
11. 2 feet = __ mils
12. 2 square yards = 18 ___
13. 1 yd.² = ___ in.²
14. 3 bushels = __ pecks
15. 18 inches = 1 __

Answer each question as completely as possible.

16. What was the original unit of weight in the metric system?
17. What is the basic SI unit of weight?
18. What 3-letter SI subsystem is preferred by scientists for measuring small things?
19. What 3-letter SI subsystem is preferred by scientists for measuring large things?
20. What do the letters in your answers to 19 and 20 stand for?

ANSWERS

1. 16
2. stone
3. bushel
4. 1
5. 72
6. fluid drams
7. yards
8. 1
9. 180
10. 1920

11. 24,000
12. square feet
13. 1296
14. 12
15. cubit
16. 1 gram
17. 1 kilogram
18. cgs
19. mks
20. centimeter-gram-second, meter-kilogram-second

SI Prefixes

The traditional system of measures has a special name for each unit going up and down the scale, witness minim, fluid dram, fluid ounce, gill, cup, pint, quart, and gallon for liquid capacity alone. Moreover, the relationships are not uniform or predictable. In running up through the units to get from minims to gallons, we need 60, then 8, 4, 2, 2, 2, and 4. There is nothing rational about it. In SI units, the relationships are always in terms of a power of 10, and the names consist of the unit, be it meter, liter, or gram, preceded by a prefix to indicate what fraction or multiple of the unit is being called for.

Fractional Prefixes

Fractional prefixes exist that allow the user of SI units to express millionths, billionths, and smaller fractions of a unit, but for the time being, the discussion will be confined to the first three: deci-, centi-, and milli-. Deci- means one-tenth, as in decimal; centi- means hundredth, as in the number of cents in a dollar; and milli- means thousandth, all from ancient Latin. That means that 10 decimeters, abbreviated "dm," equal 1 meter; 10 centimeters (10 cm) equal 1 dm; and 10 mm (millimeters) equal 1 cm.

Now, in case you haven't yet started to appreciate the beauty of the simplicity of SI, this means that 10 deciliters, abbreviated "dl," equal 1 liter; 10 centiliters (10 cl) equal 1 dl; and 10 ml (milliliters) equal 1 cl. Furthermore, 10 decigrams, abbreviated "dg," equal 1 gram; 10 centigrams (10 cg) equal 1 dg; and 10 mg (milligrams) equal 1 cg. Also take note of the fact that SI abbreviations are written without periods after them, unless, of course, they come at the ends of sentences. We'll take a closer look at converting from one unit to another in a little bit.

Multiplier Prefixes

Multiplier prefixes exist to name SI units to express millions, billions, and greater multiples of a unit, but for the time being, as with the fractions, the focus is on the first three: Deka- (sometimes spelled "deca-"), hecta-, and kilo-. Deka- means ten, hecta- means hundred, and kilo- means thousand, all from the ancient Greek's fractional prefixes. Just so you don't fall for the bait that makes you want to believe Latin prefixes are for fractions and Greek prefixes are for multiples, be aware that the prefix for millionths is micro-, which is Greek.

As with the fractional prefixes, the multiplier prefixes work with meters, liters, and grams. They are abbreviated as Dm, hm, km, Dl, hl, ml, and Dg, hg, and kg, which in each case stands for Deka-, hecta-, and kilo- whatever the unit happens to be.

---

*I know that technically the unit of weight is the kilogram, but for purposes of illustration, I'm going to use the gram. Heck, if you want to get technical, grams and kilograms aren't units of weight, but rather units of mass. Take my word for it; you don't want to go there. Just let me do my thing.

Converting SI Units

Following is a table of the six SI prefixes you and your student are likely to encounter with any sort of regularity. Notice that the prefixes are arranged in increasing order, with no prefix in the column that holds the unadorned name of the unit (liter, meter, or gram).

←	milli-	centi-	deci-	**Name of Unit**	Deka-	hecta-	kilo-	→

To change 5 kilograms to Dekagrams, since you're moving left on the chart, you are changing from a larger unit to a smaller one. That means that to represent the same amount in Dekagrams, it's going to take more units. You've moved left two places, so you are going to increase the amount by two decimal places: 5 kg = 500 Dg.

To change 5 centimeters to meters, you would move right two places. Since meters are larger than centimeters, it's going to take fewer of the new unit to express the same quantity. Two chart places right is equivalent to moving the decimal point two places to the left: 5 cm = 0.05 m.

No matter what the unit-to-unit conversion, decide whether the new unit is smaller or larger than the old one. If you're moving left on the chart, it's smaller; right on the chart, it's larger. If your new unit is smaller, you're going to need more of them; if it's larger, you're going to need fewer. That will determine whether you move the decimal point to the left or to the right. The number of places left or right you move on the chart will determine the number of places (right or left) the decimal point must move.

EXERCISES

Express each amount of the old quantity in terms of the new unit.

1. 20 g = __ kg
2. 50 Dl = __ cl
3. 500 mm = __ dm
4. 2000 ml = __ hl
5. 58 Dm = __ cm
6. 12 kg = __ dg

7. 45 km = __ dm
8. 400 g = __ kg
9. 5 kl = __ dl
10. 50 Dg = __ dg
11. 80 cm = __ m
12. 500 ml = __ l

13. 400 dl = __ kl
14. 80 cg = __ hg
15. 200 dm = __ mm
16. 500 cm = __ Dm
17. 30 hl = __ cl
18. 500 hg = __ mg

ANSWERS

1. 0.02
2. 50,000
3. 5
4. 0.02
5. 58,000
6. 120,000

7. 450,000
8. 0.4
9. 50,000
10. 5000
11. 0.8
12. 0.5

13. 0.04
14. 0.008
15. 20,000
16. 0.5
17. 300,000
18. 50,000,000

Linear Measure

Linear measure is the basis of all measurement of physical size and distance. Literally, it means measurement in a straight line. In traditional units, distance and length are in inches, feet, yards, and miles. The SI unit of linear measure is the meter. Two generations before yours grew up with wooden foot-rulers, ruled in inches. The one preceding yours, as well as your own, grew up with plastic rulers marked in inches down one side and centimeters up the other.

I'm sure that you remember there being 12 inch marks on that side. Did you notice how many centimeter marks were on the other? If you did, you win plaudits for intellectual curiosity. I'll lay you odds that most never noticed that there were 30.5 centimeters, each of which was subdivided by 10 1-mm marks. The not noticing or not remembering is no reflection upon the individual students. It is, rather, a reflection on how little—if at all—that side of the ruler was ever used.

Although a foot is close to 30.5 cm in length, it is defined as 30.48 cm, based upon the agreed-upon **conversion factor** of 2.54 cm = 1 inch. That results in 1 foot = 12 × 2.54 cm, and the product of those two numbers is 30.48. This relationship permits any SI measurement to be expressed in traditional units of distance, and any traditional distance to be expressed in SI units.

The distance around a closed **plane figure,** like a rectangle or triangle, is known as that figure's **perimeter.** (A plane figure is one drawn on a flat surface. It has length and width, but no depth.)

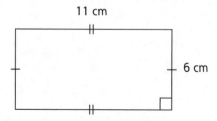

The perimeter of any rectangle is found by adding 2 × length + 2 × width. In the case of the preceding rectangle, that's (2 × 11) + (2 × 6) = 22 + 12 = 34 cm.

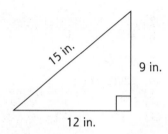

A triangle's perimeter is determined by adding the lengths of its three sides. To find the perimeter of the preceding triangle, add: 15 + 9 + 12.

$$15 + 9 = 24 + 12 = 36 \text{ in.}$$

8 ft.

The preceding figure has two adjacent sides marked as equal, and an angle marked as a 90° (right) angle. We'll see why in a later lesson. That is enough to determine that the figure is a square. To find the perimeter of a square, multiply the length of a side by 4: $4 \times 8 = 32$ ft.

Any plane figure may be considered as a field of various shape and size surrounded by a wire fence that has no thickness of its own. The length of that fence is the perimeter of the figure.

EXERCISES

Questions 1–9 refer to the following figures. Each answer should have a number and unit name.

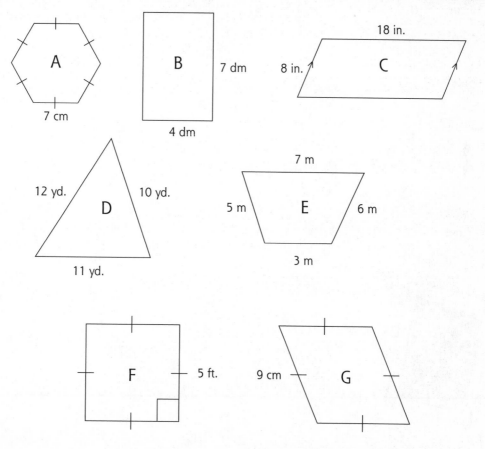

1. Find the perimeter of A.
2. Find the perimeter of B.
3. Find the perimeter of C.
4. Find the perimeter of D.
5. Find the perimeter of E.
6. Find the perimeter of F.
7. Find the perimeter of G.

8. Find the sum of the perimeters of A and C.
9. Find the sum of the perimeters of F and G.
10. Express 3 yards in meters.
11. Express 10 ft. in cm.
12. Express 10 m in inches.
13. Express 15 m in feet.

ANSWERS

1. 42 cm
2. 22 dm
3. 52 in.
4. 33 yd.
5. 21 m
6. 20 ft.
7. 36 cm

8. 174.08 cm or 68.54 in.
9. 21 ft. 2.17 in. or 254.17 in. or 645.6 cm or 6.456 m
10. 2.7432 m
11. 304.8 cm
12. 393.7 in.
13. 49.21 ft.

Mass and Weight

I've alluded to the problem we have when dealing with metric weights before. Grams and kilograms are measures of mass, not weight. The true measure of weight in the SI system is the Newton, abbreviated N. The difference between weight and mass is that weight is related to gravity. It is the force of gravity on something. If you went to the moon, you would weigh about one-ninth what you weigh on Earth, but your mass (the amount of matter you contain) would be the same. Still, since all the weighing we are likely to do is in all probability going to be here on Earth, we'll treat the two units as interchangeable.

There are 454 grams in a pound. 2.2 pounds make 1 kg. In the *avoirdupois scale* (literally French for "to have pounds"), 16 ounces (abbreviated oz.) make one pound (abbreviated lb.). In the United Kingdom, 14 pounds = one stone (we don't use that measure, so you don't have to care), and 2000 lbs. = 1 ton (abbreviated T.). 1 pound is roughly 0.45 kg.

So I have here a small bucket of nails weighing 5 kg. How many pounds is that? Well, there are a number of ways you could go to get the answer to that. Since 2.2 lbs. = 1 kg, multiply 2.2 by 5 (the total number of kilograms) to get 11 lbs. That's certainly the most straightforward, if not necessarily the most accurate.

Another approach is to go with the fact that there are 454 g/lb. (that's grams per pound). 5 kg = 5000 g, so divide 5000 g (the total number of grams) by 454 (the number of grams in one pound) and get 11.01321586. That's pretty darned close to 11 pounds.

Yet a third approach is to rely upon the fact that 1 lb. is about 0.45 kg. Divide 5 kg by 0.45 (the number of kg/lb.) and get 11.11111111 . . . . In case you didn't recognize it, this is really the same division that you did based upon 454 g per pound, except you eliminated the second "4" from the equation. The result is an answer that's less accurate, but is still about 11.

In each of the preceding solutions, the reasoning relied on setting up a proportion (an equating of two ratios) relating pounds to equivalent SI units:

(a) $\dfrac{? \text{ pounds}}{5 \text{ kilograms}} = \dfrac{2.2}{1}$ (b) $\dfrac{? \text{ pounds}}{5000 \text{ grams}} = \dfrac{1}{454}$ (c) $\dfrac{? \text{ pounds}}{5 \text{ kilograms}} = \dfrac{1}{0.45}$

The solution could have been found by cross multiplying, but that thinking is algebra, and we don't want to go there (officially).

Now let's go the other way. Two 4-x-8-ft. sheets of drywall weigh 55 lbs. How many kg is that? The hardest but most accurate way to solve this one is by the 454 g = 1 lb. method:

Multiply: $454 \times 55 = 24{,}970$ g

Change g to kg: $24{,}970 \div 1000 = 24.97 \approx 25$ kg

Of course, there was an easier way, since we just found that 5 kg = 11 lbs. 55 just happens (yeah right!) to be 11 × 5, so we need only multiply 5 kg by 5 and get 25 kg. The first method was more accurate, but the second was way easier.

Finally, for your consideration, is the metric ton, which is 1000 kg. 1 metric ton = 2204.603 avoirdupois pounds. We are not going to deal with Troy weights, which are used by jewelers and others, in this book, since it is very unlikely that your student will encounter them.

EXERCISES

Express each weight in the equivalent number of the asked-for unit. Express your answer to the nearest reasonable decimal place.

1. 12 lbs. = __ oz.
2. 50 g = __ kg
3. 128 oz. = __ lbs.
4. 18 kg = __ g
5. 60 g = __ oz.
6. 200 oz. = __ kg

7. 18 oz. = __ g
8. 2 T. = __ kg
9. 30 lbs = __ kg
10. 180 g = __ kg
11. 20 lbs. = __ g
12. 6000 lbs = __ T.

13. 120 lbs. = __ kg
14. 8 kg = __ oz.
15. 256 oz. = __ lbs.
16. 220 kg = __ lbs.
17. 3T = __ kg
18. 80 kg = __ lbs.

ANSWERS

1. 192
2. 0.05
3. 8
4. 18,000
5. 2.11
6. 5.675

7. 510.75
8. 1816
9. 13.62
10. 0.18
11. 9080
12. 3

13. 54.48
14. 281.9
15. 16
16. 484.58
17. 2724
18. 176 or 176.2

Temperature

Measuring temperature is as much a part of everyday life as getting dressed. Indeed, knowing the temperature helps you to decide what clothing you are going to put on—especially if you're planning on going outdoors. Unlike measures of length and weight, however, the ability to measure temperature has not been around that long.

Fahrenheit

Daniel Gabriel Fahrenheit, German physicist (born Gdansk, Poland, 1686; died The Hague, Netherlands, 1736), invented the alcohol thermometer in 1709 and the mercury thermometer in 1714. The scale that he invented still enjoys widespread use in the United States and practically nowhere else in the world. Fahrenheit divided the distance from the freezing point of water to that of the boiling point of water into 180 parts, or degrees. He set the freezing point at 32°, and the boiling point at 212°. We would normally refer to these temperatures as 32°F and 212°F, the "F" standing for Fahrenheit.

Some other key temperatures on the Fahrenheit scale are 98.6°F, which is considered "normal" body temperature; 101°F, the temperature at which to call the doctor; and 68–70°F, which is generally regarded as comfortable room temperature. 35°F is considered a good temperature for your refrigerator to maintain, and 0° or lower is the preferred temperature for preserving frozen foods in prime condition.

Celsius, Once Called Centigrade

Anders Celsius, Swedish astronomer (born Uppsala, Sweden, 1701; died Uppsala, Sweden, 1744), reported his scale in a paper published in 1742. Because it was divided into 100 parts, it was known for many years as the Centigrade scale. Eventually, however, tradition or conscience dictated that the temperature scale be named for its inventor. Either way, it is expressed in °C. Celsius' scale is most convenient, because it places water's freezing point at 0°C and its boiling point at 100°C.

Some other key temperatures on the Celsius scale are 37°C, which is considered "normal" body temperature; 38.33°C, the temperature at which to call the doctor; and 20–21.1°C, which is generally regarded as comfortable room temperature. 1.67°C is considered a good temperature for your refrigerator to maintain, and –17.6° or lower is the preferred temperature for preserving frozen foods in prime condition.

If those temperatures sound strange to you, you may rest assured, it's those Fahrenheit temperatures in the last section that sound strange to the rest of the world. Degrees Celsius (°C) is the official SI scale for temperature—other than for scientific purposes.

Kelvin a.k.a. Absolute

Sir William Thompson, British mathematician, physicist, and engineer (born 1824, Belfast, Ireland [now Northern Ireland]; died Netherhall, near Largs, Ayrshire, Scotland, 1907), was bestowed with the title Baron Kelvin. He enjoyed the same preeminence in nineteenth-century physics as did Sir Isaac Newton in seventeenth-century physics, or Albert Einstein in the twentieth century.

Kelvin, as history and science have chosen to remember him, determined the freezing point of nitrogen gas (the point at which nitrogen solidifies) and called it **absolute zero** at –273.16°C. He then designed a temperature scale that started at that point, which is now known as = 0°K (0° on the Kelvin scale). Because it is very convenient to have a temperature scale that expresses temperatures as they relate to absolute zero, the Kelvin scale is used by scientists worldwide and is the official SI temperature scale for scientific use.

If you thought the Celsius temperatures sounded strange, check these out. Water's freezing point is 273°K, and its boiling point is 373°K. Some other key temperatures on the Kelvin scale are 310°K, which is considered "normal" body temperature; 311.33°K, the body temperature at which to call the doctor; and 293–294.1°K, which would be considered comfortable room temperature. 274.67°K is considered a good temperature for your refrigerator to maintain, and 255.4° or lower is the preferred temperature for preserving frozen foods in prime condition.

Bear in mind, please, that the last set of temperatures was given more for your information and amusement than for practical value. Nobody takes body temperature or measures room temperature on the Kelvin scale. It is very easy to convert from Celsius to Kelvin and vice versa. Although absolute zero is 273.16°C, that 0.16° is generally disregarded, and absolute zero is referred to as –273°C. Each °C is equal to 1°K, so to change from °C to °K, add 273. To go the other way, subtract 273.

Converting to and from Fahrenheit

The formula for converting from Celsius to Fahrenheit makes perfectly good sense if you think about it. The distance from water's freezing to boiling point takes 180° in Fahrenheit and 100° in Celsius. That means that to find one Fahrenheit degree, use the ratio:

$$\frac{180}{100} = \frac{9}{5}$$

Going the other way, from Celsius to Fahrenheit, turn the relationship over:

$$\frac{100}{180} = \frac{5}{9}$$

Now there's that matter of the 32° difference between the starting points (the freezing point of water). When going from °F to °C, you have to take it off; going from °C to °F, you have to add it on. From all that, we develop the following two formulas:

$$°C = \frac{5}{9}(°F - 32) \qquad\qquad °F = \frac{9}{5} \times °C + 32$$

The temperature at 2 P.M. on a July day in New York City is 86°F. I wish to convey my discomfort to my cousin who lives in Aberdeen, Scotland, U.K., and has no idea what a °F is, but relates only to °C. To let him appreciate my discomfort, I'm going to convert, using the following formula:

$$°C = \frac{5}{9}(°F - 32)$$

$$°C = \frac{5}{9}(86 - 32)$$

$$°C = \frac{5}{9}(54)$$

$$°C = \frac{270}{9}$$

$$30°C = 86°F$$

"Wow; 30°C!" my Scottish cousin remarks, we'll pretend. "Now that's hot!!" You get the idea, I hope.

It's only a matter of time until that same cousin, Daniel, calls me back to complain about the dismal Scottish winter. It is 2°C out on the heath, and he's determined to make me aware of his discomfort, but he knows he's going to have to tell me in Fahrenheit figures, so he gets out the handy, dandy, conversion formula from the right side in the preceding set of numbers and does the work:

$$°F = \frac{9}{5} \times °C + 32$$

$$°F = \frac{9}{5} \times 2 + 32$$

$$°F = \frac{18}{5} + 32$$

$$°F = 3.6 + 32$$

$$35.6°F = 2°C$$

"David," his call goes, "it's so cold out here you can't even feel your toes. It's 35.6°F."

"Are you kidding?" I reply. "Around here, we call that Spring!"

Of course, it could have something to do with the humidity on his island being greater than that on mine.

EXERCISES

Express each temperature to the nearest tenth in terms of the scale specified.

1. 130°F = __°C
2. 30°F = __°C
3. 20°C = __°F
4. 200°F = __°C
5. 85°C = __°F
6. 382°C = __°F
7. −200°C = __°K
8. −20°F = __°C
9. 45°F = __°K

10. 50°C = __°F
11. 200°K = __°C
12. 90°F = __°C
13. 65°F = __°C
14. 47°C = __°K
15. 75°F = __°K
16. 300°K = __°C
17. 140°C = __°F
18. −60°C = __°F

ANSWERS

1. 54.4
2. −1.1
3. 68
4. 93.3
5. 185
6. 719.6
7. 73
8. −28.9
9. 280.2

10. 122
11. −73
12. 32.2
13. 18.3
14. 320
15. 296.9
16. 27
17. 284
18. −76

Area

It is not unusual for **area** and perimeter to be studied together, but we already covered perimeter in Lesson 45. If you think of the perimeter of a plane figure as the fence around a park, you might think of the area as the surface inside the fence. Area is expressed in **square units,** such as square inches, square centimeters, square feet, and so on, usually abbreviated as in.², cm², ft.², and so on.

Quadrilaterals

A four-sided closed figure is known as a quadrilateral. It is likely that in elementary school your student is going to be introduced to two special quadrilaterals, the rectangle and the square, but it couldn't hurt for you to know how they came to be. The diagram that follows takes the quadrilateral from its most general form to its most refined. Beginning with a plain four-sided closed figure, make one pair of opposite sides **parallel** (parallel lines or line segments are always an equal distance apart, and will never meet, no matter how far they are extended), as is indicated by the arrowheads on the pair of parallel sides. Such a figure is known as a **trapezoid.**

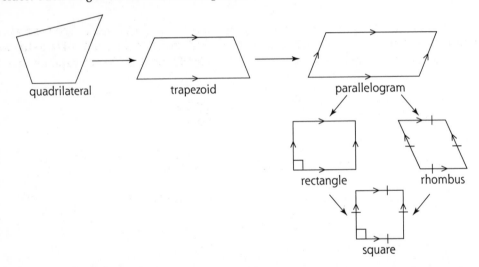

Making the other pair of sides parallel as well turns the trapezoid into a **parallelogram.** Note that both a trapezoid and a parallelogram are still quadrilaterals. From the parallelogram, there are two ways to go. You could add a right (90°) angle and turn it into a **rectangle,** or you could make all sides equal, thereby forming a figure known as a **rhombus.** Whichever of the two you opted to do, the final refinement will bring you to a **square**—a rectangle with all sides of equal length and/or a rhombus with one right angle.

Now that you've seen where a rectangle comes from, let's go about finding its area.

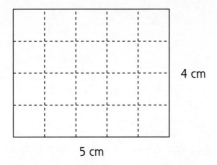

4 cm

5 cm

You could find the area of the preceding rectangle by counting all the square centimeters marked off inside. Did you count them? I get 20. Of course, I hope by now you've stumbled upon the easier way of determining the "area of the rectangular region" (the way some teachers teach this subject). The use of the term "rectangular region" is in use in some circles (no pun intended) to distinguish the region inside the rectangle from the actual four line segments that make up the rectangle itself. The rectangle is 5 cm long and 4 cm high, and 4×5 just happens to make 20. Coincidence? This time, I think not. Some teachers teach the area of a rectangle is found by multiplying its length times its width: $A = l \times w$

My preference, for reasons that will become obvious in a paragraph or two, is for the following formula: $A = b \times h$

In this formula, b stands for base, the side which is horizontal, and h is height, the vertical side. The notion of base times height has one requirement. The height must be **perpendicular** to the base, that is to say, the height and the base must meet at a right angle. By the way, the full expression of the area of the previous rectangle is 20 cm².

Find the area of the square (or square region) in the following.

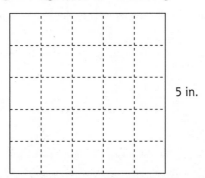

5 in.

Since the base and the height of a square are the same, all that's needed to find its area is the length of one side. The formula for the area of a square is s^2, and the area of the square shown here is 25 in.²— also known as 25 square inches.

The odds are that your student is not going to need to be able to find the areas of any other quadrilaterals, but just for the heck of it, let's check out the parallelogram (see the following).

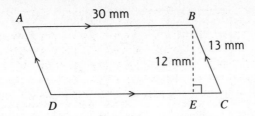

Opposite sides of a parallelogram are always the same length, so the parallelogram has two bases that are each 30 mm long (*AB* and *CD*) and two bases that are each 13 mm long (*AD* and *BC*). What?! Two bases and two bases? What happened to the height? Well, you should recall that the height of a rectangle must be perpendicular to the base. That's true of any figure. The height of parallelogram *ABCD* is *BE*. That happens to be 12 mm long. In case you haven't guessed it yet, the formula for the area of a parallelogram is $A = b \times h$.

I told you that formula would come in handy! So the area of parallelogram *ABCD* is found by multiplying 30 × 12 to get 360 mm². Now you know more than you probably need to.

> If you're hungry for still more knowledge you don't yet need, the area of a rhombus is found by the same formula as that of a parallelogram. That of a trapezoid is found by the following formula:
>
> $$A = \frac{1}{2} h (b_1 + b_2)$$
>
> The parallel sides of a trapezoid are known as its bases, and the non-parallel sides are known as its legs. The preceding formula (Oops! It's algebra.) means that to find the area of a trapezoid, you would multiply half the height times the sum of the two bases.

Triangles

To understand the rationale for finding the area of a triangle, start with a right triangle (a triangle containing one right angle).

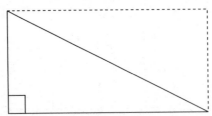

The preceding diagram is designed to lead you to an inescapable and very logical conclusion. A right triangle is half the size of a rectangle with equivalent base and height, so the formula for the area of a right triangle is as follows:

$$A = \frac{1}{2} bh$$

In any closed figure, the point at which two sides meet is known as a **vertex.** The largest angle in any right triangle is the right angle. The two smaller angles of a right triangle total up to 90°, making a total of 180°, which is the total angle measure for any triangle. In any triangle, the largest side is the side opposite the largest angle. Similarly, the shortest side is the side opposite the smallest angle. The largest side in a right triangle is the side opposite the 90° angle and is known as the **hypotenuse.**

But will the same formula work to find the area of a triangle that does not contain a right angle? One such as the triangle pictured here?

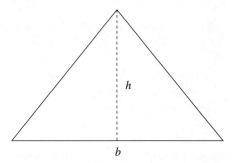

Well, it is not so obvious at first, but if we use each of the oblique sides of the triangle as a diagonal of a small rectangle, the triangle's height being a side common to both rectangles, we have two triangles, I and II, each of which is half of the rectangle of which it is a part.

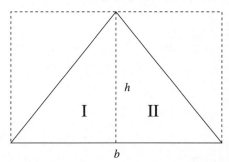

By the process of addition, half of the left rectangle added to half of the right rectangle equals half of the entire rectangle, thereby proving that the area of the original triangle is equal to half the entire rectangle, or

$$A = \frac{1}{2}bh$$

If you think that's true for any triangle, check out the following figure, which takes this proof yet one step further:

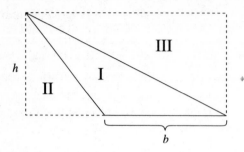

Note that for triangle I, *h* falls outside the **obtuse** triangle (a triangle containing an angle greater than 90°), and *b* is only part of the base of the rectangle. It can be proven, although I'll not bother to here, that the areas of triangles II and III add up to the area of rectangle I. Try to picture picking up triangle II and gluing its left side to the right side of triangle III. It would look like triangle I rotated 180° (half a circle). Hence, the area of triangle I is equal to half the area of the rectangle in which it is inscribed, and the formula holds true. By the way, areas of triangles are also expressed in square units.

EXERCISES

Find the areas of the following figures and express them with the appropriate unit of area.

Rectangles with adjacent (adjacent means touching each other) sides that measure:

1. 3 in. by 6 in.

2. 5 cm by 8 cm

3. 4 ft. by 7 ft.

4. 5 m by 9 m

Squares with adjacent sides that measure:

5. 5 yds.

6. 9 mi.

7. 8 km

8. 15 cm

Parallelograms with bases that measure 20 cm and:

9. sides of 8 cm

10. sides of 12 cm and height of 10 cm

11. height of 30 cm

Right triangles with sides:

12. 5 cm, 12 cm, 13 cm

13. 6 ft., 8 ft., 10 ft.

Non-right triangles with:

14. sides 11, 9, and 12 in. and an 8 in. height drawn from the vertex opposite the 9 in. side.

15. sides 10, 13, and 15 cm, and a 9 cm height drawn from the vertex opposite the 15 cm side.

ANSWERS

1. 18 in.^{2}
2. 40 cm^2
3. 28 ft.^{2}
4. 45 m^2
5. 25 yd.^{2}
6. 81 mi.^{2}
7. 64 km^2
8. 225 cm^2

9. too little info
10. 200 cm^2
11. 600 cm^2
12. 30 cm^2
13. 24 ft.^{2}
14. 36 in.^{2}
15. 67.5 cm^2

LESSON 49

Circles

Circles are different from most other plane figures in that they have no intersecting line segments or sides. On the other hand, circles may be thought of as having an infinite number of sides, each one so small as to appear as only a point in length. A circle might be defined as the location of a set of points, all of which are an equal distance from a single point, known as the **center**. You could say that dealing with circles is easy as pi (pun, and spelling, intended).

Lines and Segments Related to Circles

Although a circle is round, there are many different straight lines and segments that are associated with it, but perhaps we should begin this section by differentiating between lines and segments. A line is a series of points that goes on in the same direction without beginning or end. It may be designated by a single lowercase letter, as in line *l* in the following image, or named by two points on it, as is the case with line *CD*.

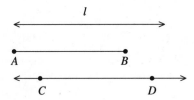

A line segment is a portion of a line with a beginning and an end. The line segment in the diagram may be designated "segment *AB*" or "segment *BA*." Neither line nor line segment occupy space. They are merely locations. When your mother or father told you that "the shortest distance between two points is a straight line," (s)he was in error. The shortest distance between two points is a line segment.

In the following circle, *O* designates the center. That circle contains two segments. The first, labeled *r*, connects the center of the circle to the circle itself. It is known as the **radius** of the circle. Any circle might contain an infinite number of radii (plural of radius). In any circle, all radii are equal in length.

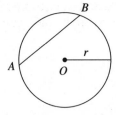

The second segment in the circle, *AB*, is known as a chord. Any segment that connects two points on the circumference of a circle is a chord, and so a circle might contain any number of chords of varying length. The longest chord in a circle is called the circle's diameter, one of which is shown in the following circle, labeled *CD*.

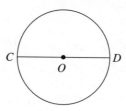

It should be apparent that a diameter is equal in length to twice the radius. Again, there is no limit to how many diameters there might be in a circle, but, in order to be a diameter, a chord must pass through the circle's center.

Line segment *EF* in the following image begins as a chord on the circle at *E* but continues past the circumference to *F*, a point outside the circle.

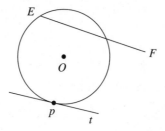

Segment *EF* is known as a **secant**. A secant might continue past *F* as well as ending there and still be a secant. Line *t* is an example of a **tangent**—a line that touches a circle at one point only—in this case, point *P*. Point *P* is known as the **point of tangency**. If a radius were drawn from the center of the circle to *P*, it would form a right angle with the tangent.

Perimeter of a Circle

Like all other plane figures, a circle has a perimeter. That perimeter has a special name, which you've encountered before. It is known as the circumference. The ancient Greeks discovered that there is a relationship between the diameter of a circle and its circumference. By rolling a wheel and measuring very carefully, they discovered that the line made by one rotation of the wheel was three and a little bit more times the diameter of the wheel.

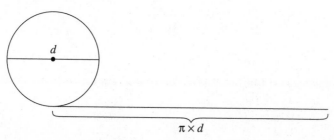

They named this quantity "pi", for the Greek letter (π) of the same name. 3.141592654 is a close approximation of the value of π, which has actually been computed to more than 20 decimal places. It is an example of what is known as a nonterminating nonrepeating decimal. It is usually approximated as $\frac{22}{7}$, or 3.14. To find the circumference of the circle, all you need to know is the circle's radius or diameter. If you think about it for a moment, you'll realize that if you know one, you know both. To find the circumference knowing the diameter, use this formula:

$$C = \pi \times d \quad \text{or, more succinctly,} \quad C = \pi d$$

To find it knowing the radius, the formula is

$$C = 2 \times \pi \times r \quad \text{or, more simply,} \quad C = 2\pi r$$

Since $2 \times r$ is the same as d, there's no reason to choose between them. I recommend, however, that you do the converting, when necessary, in your head, and stick with the first formula, or at least its streamlined form. That will help to prevent the second one being confused with the very similar looking formula for finding a circle's area.

All right, let's find the circumference of a circle whose radius is 7 feet. Since we're abandoning the second set of formulas (if we know what's good for us), double the radius to get the diameter, 14. Next write the formula and substitute:

$$C = \pi d$$
$$C = \pi \times 14$$

Since 14 is a multiple of 7, I would recommend using the $\frac{22}{7}$ approximation of π.

$$C = \frac{22}{7} \times 14$$

$$C = \frac{22}{7} \times \overset{2}{\cancel{14}} = 44$$

That's 44 feet. Usually, the teacher or the book will specify which approximation for π is to be used, and in some cases it is allowable to leave the answer in terms of π, in which case the circumference of the circle would have been expressed as 14π feet. That usually doesn't happen, though, until high school or college.

Here's one more. Find the circumference of a circle with diameter 10 cm. Use 3.14 to approximate the value of π.

$$C = \pi d$$
$$C = 3.14 \times 10$$
$$C = 31.4 \text{ cm}$$

How easy was that?!

I hate to go off on a tangent [sic!] but there's one more topic in this lesson, so let's get to it.

Area of a Circle

Don't ask why (you'll see in a moment anyway), but the area of a circle is expressed in square units. To find a circle's area, you'll need to know its radius, and yes, π is involved. To find the area of a circle, you multiply the radius by itself (or square it), and that's where the square units come from. That is then multiplied by π, so:

$$A = \pi r^2$$

To find the area of a circle of radius 6 in., using 3.14 to approximate π, do the following:

Write the formula: $A = \pi r^2$

Substitute: $A = 3.14 \times (6)^2$

Square the radius: $A = 3.14 \times 36$

Multiply and place unit: $A = 113.04$ in.^{2}

You could safely round your answer to 113 square inches. As a general rule, or unless otherwise specified, it's safe to round answers to the nearest tenth.

Here's another one. To find the area of a circle of radius 8 cm, using 3.14 to approximate π, do the following:

Write the formula: $A = \pi r^2$

Substitute: $A = 3.14 \times (8)^2$

Square the radius: $A = 3.14 \times 64$

Multiply and place unit: $A = 200.96 \approx 201$ cm^2

The "wavy equal sign" means "is about equal to." I have used it here in the interest of accuracy, but your elementary student doesn't need to even know that sign exists.

Both the circumference formula and the area formula are reversible. That is, if you know the circumference or the area of a circle, you can find its diameter, and/or its radius. Given a circle of circumference 12π centimeters, its diameter is found by the following formula:

$$d = \frac{C}{\pi} = \frac{12\pi}{\pi} = 12\text{cm}$$

The radius of that circle would, of course, be half the diameter, or 6 cm.

Now, suppose that the area of a circle is 81π sq. ft. You can find its radius using the following procedure:

$$r = \sqrt{\frac{A}{\pi}} = \sqrt{\frac{81\pi}{\pi}} = \sqrt{81} = 9\text{ft.}$$

The diameter, in this case, would be twice 9, or 18 ft. Of course, in both of the examples just given, I had the convenience of the circumference and the area both being expressed in terms of π, but what the heck—I wrote the book. You don't think I'm going to be that easy on you, do you?! The formulas are there for you to use.

EXERCISES

Approximate π as 3.14. Round each answer to the nearest tenth, if necessary, and use appropriate units of measure in each answer. For 1–6, find the circumference of each circle, given the following information.

1. $r = 7$ cm
2. $d = 12$ in.
3. $r = 15$ m

4. $d = 100$ ft.
5. $r = 9$ yd.
6. $d = 11$ mm

For 7–10, find the area of each circle, given the following information.

7. $d = 16$ cm
8. $r = 11$ yd.

9. $d = 12$ dm
10. $r = 5$ ft.

ANSWERS

1. 44 cm
2. 37.7 in.
3. 94.2 m
4. 314 ft.
5. 56.5 yd.

6. 34.5 mm
7. 201 cm^2
8. 379.9 yd.^{2}
9. 113 dm^2
10. 78.5 ft.^{2}

A Solid Start

So far, all the geometry we have dealt with has pertained to plane figures, but now we're going to depart from that and check out some **cubes.** A cube might be thought of as a three-dimensional square. That is, every edge is the same length, and every surface is a square.

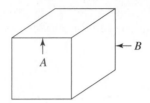

How many edges does a cube have? Remember, edges are shared by more than one face; for example the top front edge, marked "A" in the preceding figure is shared by the top face of the cube and the front. The vertical edge, marked "B" is shared by the right face of the cube and the rear (out-of-sight) face. Have you counted up the edges yet? There are 4 on the bottom, 4 on the top, and 4 vertical ones. That's a total of 12 edges.

Surface Area

Cubes, as well as all other solids, differ from plane figures in that they take up space, called **volume,** and they have many faces, each of which has an area of its own. Assume the cube shown to have edges of 1 cm apiece. That makes the area of one face of this cube 1 cm². How many faces does a cube have? If you look at the diagram, you can see three: front, right, and top. Unseen are left, bottom, and back, so there are six surfaces to a cube. Its total **surface area,** then, is 6 cm², or 6 times the area of a single surface.

The following cube is composed of smaller cubes. How many smaller cubes make up this larger cube?

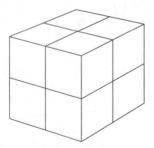

You can see it has 4 cubes in the front and 4 cubes in the rear, or 4 cubes on the bottom and 4 cubes on the top. Either way, there are 8 cubes. Now suppose that those 8 cubes were kept together as in the picture—let's say they were glued together—and then they were painted carefully (so as to have no dripping) all over the outside. After the paint dries, the cubes are separated. How many faces of the unglued cubes would have paint on them? Think about it.

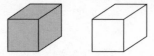

Assuming the original cube had been light in color and the paint was dark, each cube would appear as the two views of the one in the diagram, with three surfaces painted, and three surfaces unpainted. Three painted surfaces times 8 cubes make 24 painted surfaces. What's the surface area of the cube, assuming that each edge of the assembled cube was 2 cm long?

If each edge of the assembled cube (the one in the drawing before the last one) is 2 cm long, then each face of the cube had an area of 2×2, or 4 cm^2, which $\times$ 6 faces makes 24 cm^2. Do you think it's a coincidence that 24 surfaces were painted, and the surface area is 24 cm^2? It's not. Think about it for a minute or so.

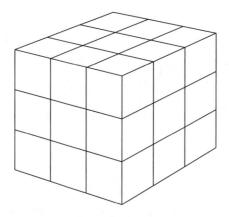

Now it's getting a little more complicated—but only a little. We'll continue using our 1-cm cubes. This stack of cubes is 3 deep by 3 wide by 3 high. How many little cubes make up the big one? Do you need a moment to think about it? Don't read on until you have an answer. Got one? Okay! There are 9 cubes in each layer, and 3 layers; $3 \times 9 = 27$, so 27 cubes it is. What's the surface area? The area of one face is 3 cm $\times$ 3 cm $= 9$ cm^2. There are still six faces, so $9 \times 6 = 54$ cm^2.

Next, let's paint the outside of the glued-together stack, just like we did before, and take them apart. How many 1-cm cube surfaces will have paint on them? Hopefully, you realize that the answer to the last question is 54—the same as the large cube's surface area. Now for the tricky part. How many centimeter cubes have three faces painted? Take a moment to figure that out, and write the number down. How many centimeter cubes will have exactly two faces painted? Write that down, too. Are you having fun yet?

Now figure out the number of cubes with exactly one face painted. Finally, how many cubes will have no faces painted?

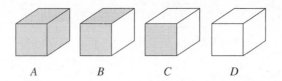

A   *B*   *C*   *D*

In A of the diagram, you see cubes with three painted faces. The only places you'll find those is at the corners. There are 8 corners, so, just as before, there'll be 8 of those. That accounts for 24 ($3 \times 8 = 24$) of the painted faces. B shows a centimeter cube with two faces painted—the two of the three you can see. You'll find one on the top and the bottom rows in the center of the front face of the 3×3 cube, and in the left and right columns in the center of the front face. That takes care of 4; then there are another 4 on the back, in the same positions. Also there are two in the center row, top, and the same in the center row, bottom, for a total of 12.

So far you've accounted for $24 + 24 = 48$ cm cube faces. Centimeter cubes with only one face painted, C, are found dead center in each of the six faces. That's $48 + 6 = 54$ painted faces, which is what we agreed four paragraphs back was the big cube's surface area, but how many of the 27 centimeter cubes have we accounted for? There were 8 with 3 painted sides, 12 with 2 painted sides, and 6 with 1 painted side: $8 + 12 + 6 = 26$. That means there's one cm cube unaccounted for, and that's the one in the interior of the cube. It's the one cube with no paint on it, D.

If you enjoyed that, you're sure to enjoy the 4-by-4-by-4 cube:

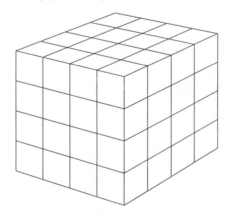

What is its surface area? If we were to paint the entire surface of this cube and then take it apart, how many cm cubes would have paint on 3 sides? How many cm cubes would have paint on 0 sides? The surface area is $16 \times 6 = 96$ cm². As to the other two questions, the answer is 8 for both. I'll leave it to you to figure out the one-face and two-face painted numbers of cm cubes, but you'll find the answers at the bottom of the page.*

By the way, how many centimeter cubes made up that 4-by-4-by-4 cube?

---

*There are 24 apiece with one face and two faces painted.

Volume of a Cube

The answer to the last question is 64 cm³. The volume of any solid is expressed in units of cubic measure. To cube something, you multiply it by itself twice; that is to say, the volume of the cube in the last section is found by performing the operation $4 \times 4 \times 4 = 64$. Because the units being cubed are centimeters, the answer is expressed in terms of cm × cm × cm, which equals cm³. If the cube had been 4 in. by 4 in. by 4 in., the answer would have been 64 in.³.

If it seemed strange to you that the area of a triangle or of a circle is expressed in square units, it should feel even stranger to express the volume of a cone or sphere in cubic units, but that's the way it is done. Cubic units have been demonstrated in this lesson through the use of cubes, yet the cubic unit is actually a purely mathematical situation which the shape of a cube happens to suit.

Find the volume of a cube whose edge measures 6 ft. Did you get an answer of 216 ft.³? The solution is found simply by multiplying 6×6 to get 36, and then 36×6 to get 216. The appropriate unit is then tacked onto the end. Keep in mind that volume does not only represent the amount of space that an object occupies. If the object happens to be hollow, like a carton or a storage container, its volume also lets us know how much the container can hold. Of course, its capacity will be slightly less than the space it occupies.

EXERCISES

Find the surface area of a cube, when one edge of it is the specified dimension.

1. 5 cm		**6.** 11 mm	
2. 8 yd.		**7.** 15 in.	
3. 9 in.		**8.** 20 cm	
4. 12 m		**9.** 25 dm	
5. 7 ft.			

Find the volume of a cube with each edge having the specified dimension.

10. 5 cm		**15.** 11 mm	
11. 8 yd.		**16.** 15 in.	
12. 9 in.		**17.** 20 cm	
13. 12 m		**18.** 25 dm	
14. 7 ft.			

ANSWERS

1. 150 cm^2
2. 384 yd.^{2}
3. 486 in.^{2}
4. 864 m^2
5. 294 ft.^{2}
6. 726 mm^2
7. 1350 in.^{2}
8. 2400 cm^2
9. 3750 cm^2

10. 125 cm^3
11. 512 yd.^{3}
12. 729 in.^{3}
13. 1728 m^3
14. 343 ft.^{3}
15. 1331 mm^3
16. 3375 in.^{3}
17. 8000 cm^3
18. 15,625 dm^3

Prisms

Your student might study **prisms** without ever hearing that word used. It is more likely that she will learn the terms "rectangular solid" and "triangular solids," not to mention "cylinders." All of these, and many more solids, fit into the category of prisms. There are two types of prisms, oblique prisms and right prisms. A quick glance at the following diagram will help you to differentiate.

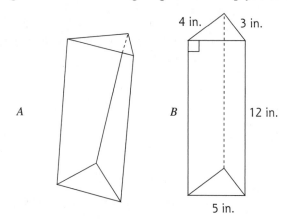

The nominally vertical sides of the prism, A, meet the nominally horizontal base at an oblique angle (non-right). In B, the sides and the bases are perpendicular to one another. That makes A an oblique prism, and B a right one. Schools and teachers do not deal with oblique prisms at a level lower than university, so don't worry about oblique prisms.

Surface Areas of Right Prisms

If you glance back at the right prism, B, you'll notice that its **lateral** faces are rectangles, and its **bases** (top and bottom) are triangles. The surface area of any prism might be found by finding the areas of all of the lateral faces (which may or may not be equal in area to one another) and adding that to twice the area of the base (since those are always equal in area in a right prism).

In the right triangular right prism, B, the 3-inch side of the base is perpendicular to the 4-inch side. That makes the combined areas of the two bases:

$$A = 2\left(\frac{1}{2} \times b \times h\right) = b \times h$$

That means the area of the two bases together is $3 \times 4 = 12$ in.². The areas of the lateral faces are found by adding $(3 \times 12) + (4 \times 12) + (5 \times 12)$.

That's: $\qquad\qquad\qquad\qquad\qquad$ $36 + 48 + 60 = 144$

To that, add the sum of the base areas: $A = 144 + 12 = 156$

And place the units: $\qquad\qquad\qquad$ $A = 156 \text{ in.}^2$

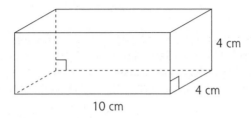

4 cm

4 cm

10 cm

The preceding figure is a square prism, named as the triangular prism is by its ends, or bases. (Note that in any prism, there are exactly two faces—the bases—after which the prism is named.) To find its surface area, find the area of each base:

$$A_{base} = 4 \times 4 = 16 \text{cm}^2$$

Since there are 2 bases, the total base area $= 16 \times 2 = 32 \text{ cm}^2$.

Each side of the prism has an area of $A_{side} = 4 \times 10 = 40 \text{cm}^2$

Since there are 4 lateral faces, the total lateral face area is $4 \times 40 = 160 \text{ cm}^2$.

To get the total surface area: $A_{total} = A_{bases} + A_{faces} = 32 + 160 = 192 \text{cm}^2$.

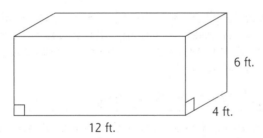

6 ft.

4 ft.

12 ft.

The final surface area we'll explore is that of a rectangular prism. Can you tell why this figure is known as a rectangular prism? Even though you can see only one of the two bases, you have enough information to be able to tell that those bases are rectangles. We're going to have to do three separate computations in this case, since there are two bases with dimensions of 4 ft. by 6 ft., two faces with dimensions 6 ft. by 12 ft., and two faces with dimensions 4 ft. by 12 ft. The prism is unfolded for you in the following figure.

12 ft.

6 ft.

4 ft.

6 ft.   6 ft.

6 ft.

4 ft.

The easiest way to solve this is to multiply each pair of figures once and then to double the solution to get the total:

$$4 \times 6 = 24; \quad 6 \times 12 = 72; \quad 4 \times 12 = 48$$

Add the products: $24 + 72 = 96; \quad 96 + 48 = 144$

Next double the sum: $2 \times 144 = 288$

Finally, place the units: $A_{total} = 288 \text{ft.}^2$

Volume of a Prism

We already encountered volume in the last lesson, dealing exclusively there with volumes of cubes and various cubic spatial relations. When finding the volume of a right prism, the procedure generally is to find the area of a base and multiply it by the height (the distance between the bases).

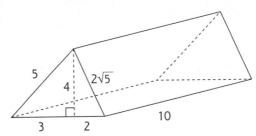

The triangular prism in the preceding figure has bases triangular in shape, measuring 5 cm, 5 cm, and $2\sqrt{5}$ cm. This could get confusing if we're not really careful here, because the same terms need to be applied in two different senses. We refer to the base and height of the prism for the purpose of finding its volume, but we also need to refer to the base and height of the triangular-shaped base. Whew! Make sure you keep that sorted out.

First things first. Isolate the triangle with the measurements as described in the preceding paragraph. That triangle has a base of $3 + 2 = 5$ cm and a height of 4 cm. The formula for the area of a triangle is

$$A_{\triangle} = \frac{1}{2}(b \times h)$$

Substitute: $\qquad A_\triangle = \frac{1}{2}(5 \times 4)$

Compute inside parentheses: $\qquad A_\triangle = \frac{1}{2}(20)$

Finally, multiply and place units: $\quad A_\triangle = 10 \text{ cm}^2$

That's the area of the triangular base of the prism. The next thing to do is to multiply that by the prism's height (not the triangle's height, but the distance between the two bases).

$$V_{prism} = A_{base} \times h_{prism}$$

Substitute: $\quad V_{prism} = 10 \times 10$

Multiply: $\quad V_{prism} = 100$

Place units: $\quad V_{prism} = 100 \text{ cm}^3$

The volume of the triangular prism is 100 cubic cm.

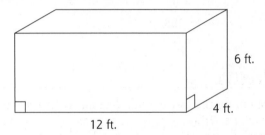

6 ft.

12 ft.

4 ft.

Here we have a rectangular prism of 6 ft. by 4 ft. base and 12 ft. height. You could probably do this one in your sleep. Since there's no fancy maneuvering to be done, you can just straight out attack it as: Volume = length × width × height.

When multiplying length × width, you are finding the area of the prism's base. Then multiplying that by the height gets you the volume of the solid:

$$V_{rect.\ prism} = l \times w \times h$$

Substitute: $\quad V_{rect.\ prism} = 4 \times 6 \times 12$

Multiply once: $\quad V_{rect.\ prism} = 4 \times 72$

. . . and again: $\quad V_{rect.\ prism} = 288 \text{ ft.}^3$

I'll bet that you never dreamed when starting this lesson that by its end you would be speaking volumes!

EXERCISES

Find the surface area of each right prism.

1. square with base edge of 8 cm and lateral edge of 6 cm
2. right triangular with base edges of 5, 12, and 13 in. and lateral edge of 10 in.
3. rectangular with base edges of 6 and 8 m and lateral edge of 12 m
4. triangular with base edges of 7, 8, and 9 mm, a segment from one vertex perpendicular to the 8 mm side of 6 mm, and lateral edge of 10 mm
5. square with base edge of 9 cm and lateral edge of 11 cm
6. right triangular with base edges of 9, 12, and 15 in. and lateral edge of 20 in.
7. rectangular with base edges of 7 and 9 m and lateral edge of 13 m
8. triangular with base edges of 9, 10, and 11 dm, a segment from one vertex perpendicular to the 10 dm side of 8 dm, and lateral edge of 8 dm
9. right triangular with base edges of 10, 24, and 26 in. and lateral edge of 14 in.
10. rectangular with base edges of 5 and 7 ft. and lateral edge 9 ft.

Find the volume of each prism.

11. square with base edge of 6 cm and lateral edge of 9 cm
12. right triangular with base edges of 6, 8, and 10 in. and lateral edge of 10 in.
13. rectangular with base edges of 8 and 10 m and lateral edge of 9 m
14. triangular with base edges of 7, 8, and 9 mm, a segment from one vertex perpendicular to the 8 mm side of 6 mm, and lateral edge of 10 mm
15. square with base edge of 10 cm and lateral edge of 10 cm
16. right triangular with base edges of 9, 12, and 15 in. and lateral edge of 20 in.
17. rectangular with base edges of 4 and 9 m and lateral edge of 12 m
18. triangular with base edges of 9, 10, and 11 dm, a segment from one vertex perpendicular to the 10 dm side of 8 dm, and lateral edge of 10 dm
19. right triangular with base edges of 10, 24, and 26 in. and lateral edge of 14 in.
20. rectangular with base edges of 8 and 7 ft. and lateral edge of 5 ft.

ANSWERS

1. 320 cm^2
2. 360 in.^{2}
3. 432 m^2
4. 288 mm^2
5. 558 cm^2
6. 828 in.^{2}
7. 542 m^2
8. 320 dm^2
9. 1080 in.^{2}
10. 286 ft.^{2}

11. 324 cm^3
12. 240 in.^{3}
13. 720 m^3
14. 240 mm^3
15. 1000 cm^3
16. 1080 in.^{3}
17. 432 m^3
18. 400 dm^3
19. 1680 in.^{3}
20. 280 ft.^{3}

Solid Capacity

Capacity and **volume** are two words that are often used interchangeably. Many of the same units are involved, although there are some differences in the meaning of traditional dry measure units and liquid measure units with the same names. Specifically, the dry pint is defined as 33.6 cubic inches, whereas the liquid pint is 29.184 cubic inches. Beyond the pint, two of them make a quart, whether dry or liquid, 8 dry quarts make a peck, and 4 pecks make a bushel. Four liquid quarts make a gallon, but we're not going to worry about that in this lesson. Fortunately for all of us, the dry pint, quart, peck, and bushel have just about disappeared as units of measure in everyday usage.

The difference between volume and capacity, if there is any difference at all, is in perception. Volume is usually conceived as the amount of space that something occupies, but capacity is perceived as a space in which to place things. For example, a storage shed might have a capacity of 1000 cubic feet, so that it's possible to store a total volume of 1000 cubic feet in that shed. I call that difference a semantic one.

Traditional Measures of Capacity

Much more useful than the measures compared in the preceding paragraph are the cubic inch, foot, and yard of the traditional system, and the cubic millimeter, centimeter, and meter of the SI system. Conversion among these units is often necessary, and it's a good idea to become familiar with how to do it. A cubic foot contains quite a few cubic inches, as you can see in the following figure.

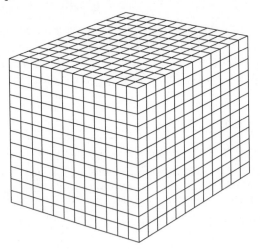

It is 1 foot by 1 foot by 1 foot in volume. Since each foot is 12 inches long, a cubic foot (or ft.³) is 12 inches × 12 inches × 12 inches, or 1728 in.³

Since a yard contains 3 feet, a cubic yard contains 3 × 3× 3 cubic feet. You can see that in the following figure.

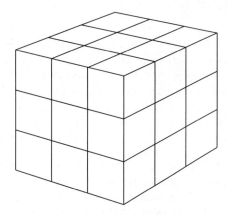

That's three layers of 9 cubic feet each, or 27 cubic feet. How many cubic inches are there in a cubic yard? To get that, you'll need to multiply 1728 in.³, the number of cubic inches in 1 ft.³, by 27. 27 × 1728 = 46,656 in.³

What if you need to express a cubic foot or yard in cubic centimeters, which, by the way, are known as cc(s) as well as cm³? You might, I hope, recall that 2.54 cm = 1 inch. Scared yet? 2.54 × 2.54 × 2.54 = 16.387064 cm³ make 1 cubic inch. That's a rather unwieldy number to work with to find the number of cm³ in a cubic foot, so consider the number of centimeters in a foot (12 × 2.54). That's 30.48, so the number of cm³ in a ft.³ might be found by 30.48 × 30.48 × 30.48 = 28,316.847.

That's a whole bunch of ccs. Without actually doing it, how could you find the number of cubic centimeters in a cubic yard? There are really a number of ways to do it, but the simplest would be to take the figure you just got for the number of cubic centimeters in a cubic foot and multiply it by the number of cubic feet in a cubic yard. That is, 28,316.847 × 27. (I dragged that out so that you would have a chance to figure out the answer for yourself.)

SI Units of Capacity

We've looked at converting from cubic centimeters to cubic feet and yards, but how about from cubic centimeters to cubic decimeters and cubic meters? Remember, the beauty of the SI units is how readily they can be converted from one to another by moving the decimal place. Well, that certainly applies when dealing with capacity, but care must be taken as to how many places that decimal point is moved.

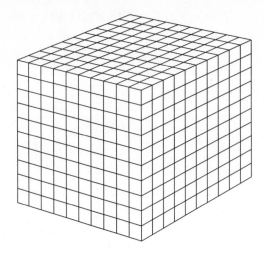

Here we have a cubic decimeter. It is 10 cm by 10 cm by 10 cm, or 1000 cm³. To picture a cubic meter, look at the cubic decimeter and imagine each little cube to be the same size as the whole cube. That is to say each little cube in a cubic meter would be 10 cm by 10 cm by 10 cm. That's 100 cm × 100 cm × 100 cm, or 1,000,000 cm³. That's right, one million cubic centimeters make one cubic meter.

Converting SI measures of capacity to traditional ones is not as neat as the other way around. That's because division is usually required. You can base the division on the ratio of cm³ to in.³ that we found in the earlier part of this lesson, or on the number of cm³ in a ft.³, also developed earlier. Either way, the conversion is quite messy.

We found that about 16.387 cm³ make 1 in.³ So, to find the number of cubic inches in a dm³, you should divide the number of cm³ per dm³. That's 1000 ÷ 16.387 = 61.02 in.³ Doesn't that seem weird?

A cubic meter would be 1,000,000 cm³ ÷ 16.387 = 61,024 in.³ Divide that by 1728 (the number of cubic inches in a cubic foot), and you'll get 35.3 ft.³, as compared with 27 ft.³ per yd.³

Alternately, we could have divided 1,000,000 cm³ by the number of cm³ in a ft.³, which is 28,316.847: 1,000,000 ÷ 28,316.847 = 35.3 ft.³.

Hmm! Not bad at all! It works out to the same thing. Sometimes, it really does pay to be just plain lucky.

EXERCISES

Express each quantity in terms of the unit specified to the nearest whole number.

1. 5 ft.³ = __ in.³

2. 12 m³ = __ cm³

3. 8 dm³ = __ cm³

4. 12 Dm³ = __ cm³

5. 3 yd.³ = __ in.³

6. 12 yd.³ = __ ft.³

7. 25,920 in.³ = __ ft.³

8. 18,000,000 cm³ = __ m³

9. 9 m³ = __ dm³

10. 10 ft.³ = __ cm³

11. 162 ft.³ = __ yd ³

12. 20,736 in.³ = __ ft.³

13. 9 yd³ = __ ft³

14. 6000 dm³ = __ in.³

15. 28 m³ = __ cm³

16. 6 ft.³ = __ cm³

17. 765,932 cm³ = __ yd³

18. 5 m³ = __ ft.³

ANSWERS

1. 8640
2. 12,000,000
3. 8000
4. 12,000,000,000
5. 139,968
6. 324
7. 15
8. 18
9. 9,000

10. 283,168
11. 6
12. 12
13. 243
14. 366
15. 28,000,000
16. 169,901
17. 1
18. 177

Cylinders

The shape of an ordinary food can or oil drum is in the shape of the solid known as a cylinder. The only differences between a can and a cylinder are that a cylinder's top and bottom are at the exact ends of the sides, and it contains no grooves. The cylinder resembles two other figures we have already studied, the prism and the circle. In fact, the cylinder might be thought of as a prism with circular bases.

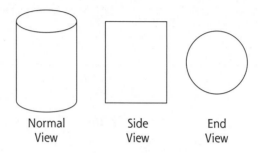

Normal Side End
View   View View

Three Views of a Cylinder

Surface Area of a Cylinder

Unlike any prism we have studied, a cylinder has no lateral edges. It does, however, have a circle-shaped edge at each base. The length of that circular edge is determined by the formula you learned for the circumference of a circle, πd, where d is the diameter of the circle. If you picture the cylinder as being hollow (just for the sake of this exercise), you can unroll it.

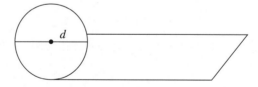

Unrolling a Cylinder

This unrolling results in the two circular lids of diameter d and a rectangular sheet of length πd and height h.

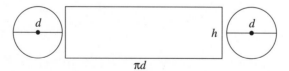

The Cylinder's Surface Is a Rectangle and Two Circles

To find the surface area of the cylinder, then, we must find the area of one circular end, double it to account for the other end, and add it to the area of the rectangle of base πd and height, h.

Let's say we have a cylinder of diameter 6 cm and height 10 cm. To find its total surface area, use 3.14 for π and remember that the radius is half the diameter, so:

Lateral	Bases
$A_{rectangle} = b \times h$	$A_{circle} = \pi \times r^2$
$A_{rectangle} = 6\pi \times 10$	$A_{circle} = \pi \times 3^2$
$A_{rectangle} = 60 \times 3.14$	$A_{circle} = 3.14 \times 9$
$A_{rectangle} = 188.4$	$A_{circle} = 28.26$

To get the total surface area, add the area of the rectangle to twice that of the circle:

$$A_{total} = 188.4 + 28.26 + 28.26$$
$$A_{total} = 244.92 \text{ cm}^2$$

And that's all there is to that.

Volume of a Cylinder

The volume of a cylinder is determined in exactly the same way that we determined the volume of any right prism. It is the area of the base multiplied by the lateral height.

Using the same 6-cm-diameter, 10-cm-high cylinder of which we just found the surface area, take the area of the base, which we found to be 28.6 cm², and multiply it by the height, 10 cm:

$$V = 28.6 \times 10 = 286 \text{ cm}^3$$

Let's do one from scratch. Suppose that we have a cylinder of radius 5 inches and height of 12 inches. Here's how we'd find its volume:

$$V_{cylinder} = \pi \times r^2 \times h$$
$$V_{cylinder} = \pi \times 5^2 \times 12$$
$$V_{cylinder} = \pi \times 25 \times 12$$
$$V_{cylinder} = 3.14 \times 300$$
$$V_{cylinder} = 942 \text{ in.}^3$$

EXERCISES

Find the surface area of the following cylinders to the nearest whole unit. Use 3.14 as π.

1. $h = 6$ cm; $d = 6$ cm
2. $h = 9$ ft.; $r = 5$ ft.
3. $h = 12$ dm; $d = 8$ dm
4. $h = 10$ in.; $r = 7$ in.
5. $h = 7$ m; $d = 12$ m

6. $h = 8$ yd.; $r = 9$ yd.
7. $h = 14$ cm; $d = 10$ cm
8. $h = 20$ in.; $r = 11$ in.
9. $h = 4$ Dm; $d = 6$ Dm

Find the volume of the following cylinders. Leave your answer in terms of π.

10. $h = 5$ ft.; $r = 6$ ft.
11. $h = 7$ cm; $d = 8$ cm
12. $h = 10$ in.; $r = 3$ in.
13. $h = 15$ dm; $d = 10$ dm
14. $h = 9$ yd.; $r = 3$ yd.

15. $h = 2$ m; $d = 12$m
16. $h = 8$ ft.; $r = 11$ft.
17. $h = 20$ mm; $d = 20$ mm
18. $h = 4$ in.; $r = 7$ in.

ANSWERS

1. 170 cm^2
2. 440 ft.^{2}
3. 402 dm^2
4. 747 in.^{2}
5. 490 m^2
6. 961 yd.^{2}
7. 597 cm^2
8. 2141 in.^{2}
9. 132 Dm^2

10. 180 π ft.^{3}
11. 112 π cm^3
12. 90 π in.^{3}
13. 375 π dm^3
14. 81 π yd.^{3}
15. 72 π m^3
16. 968 π ft.^{3}
17. 2000 π mm^3
18. 196 π in.^{3}

Pyramids, Cones, and Spheres

The odds are very great that your student is not going to need to learn, and by extension you won't need to know, the material in this lesson. Some teachers, however, might go into this topic—and your student might be curious enough to ask you even if the teacher doesn't touch it—so here's the skinny on pyramids, cones, and spheres. Feel free to decide whether or not to check it out.

Pyramids

A **pyramid** is a solid figure that has its base in the shape of a **polygon.** A polygon is a many-sided, closed figure, with three being the minimum number of sides and there being no limit to the maximum number of sides except practicality. Actually, the limit to the number of sides comes about when a polygon has so many sides that it is indistinguishable from a circle. Each vertex in the base of a pyramid is connected to a single point in a plane other than the one the base is in. That point is known as the vertex of the pyramid. A pyramid's sides are known as its lateral faces and are triangular in shape. When the base of a pyramid is regular (all sides the same length) then it is known as a **regular pyramid,** and the triangles formed are all **isosceles** (two sides the same length). In fact, in a regular pyramid, all of the triangles formed are also **congruent.**

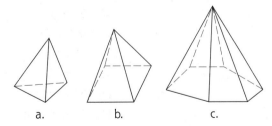

a.   b.   c.

The figure shows three pyramids and serves to demonstrate how a pyramid is named by the shape of its base. The left pyramid is a triangular pyramid. In the center is a square pyramid, and on the right is a regular **hexagonal** pyramid (since hexagon is the name given to a six-sided polygon).

A word we have not used before in this book, but which is very common in geometry, is "**altitude.**" It means the height of a figure, and in a triangle, it is the segment from any vertex perpendicular to the side opposite it. The altitude of any of the triangular faces of the pyramid from its vertex to the base is known as the slant height of the pyramid, but please be extra careful to not confuse it with the altitude of the pyramid, which goes from its vertex perpendicular to the plane of the base (h in the following picture).

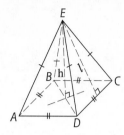

In the square pyramid, square *ABCD* is the base, and the lateral faces are triangles *ABE*, *BCE*, *CDE*, and *ADE*. The slant height of the pyramid is given by the segment *l*. *E* is the vertex of the pyramid, and *h* is the pyramid's altitude. We could find the surface area of the pyramid by finding the individual area of each triangular face and adding those to the area of the base, but there's an easier way. The area of any triangle is always half the base times the height, but the heights of all these triangles are the same, *l*, and the bases add up to the perimeter of the pyramid's base, which we'll call *p*. So, to find the lateral area (the area of the triangular faces) of a pyramid, rather than doing each one separately, use this formula:

$$A_{\text{lateral}} = \frac{1}{2}\,pl \text{ units}^2$$

The total surface area of a pyramid is found by adding the lateral area to the area of the base, or

$$A_{\text{total}} = \frac{1}{2}\,pl + B \text{ units}^2$$

where *B* is the area of the base. I know, it's algebraic notation, but you have to admit it's a neat way of mapping out the steps that need to be followed.

Let's say that each base of that square pyramid is 6 cm long, and the slant height of each triangular face is 7 cm. Find the total surface area of the pyramid.

First the formula: $\quad A_{\text{total}} = \frac{1}{2}\big(p \times l\big) + B$

$4 \times 6 = 24$, the perimeter of the base; $6 \times 6 = 36$, the area of the base.

Substitute: $\quad A_{\text{total}} = \frac{1}{2}\big(24 \times 7\big) + 36$

Multiply: $\quad A_{\text{total}} = \big(12 \times 7\big) + 36 = 84 + 36$

Add and place the units: $\quad A_{\text{total}} = 120 \text{ cm}^3$

To find the volume of a pyramid, we follow the same idea as we used when we found the volume of a prism or cylinder, except you'll notice that in the case of a pyramid compared to a prism of the same base, most of the prism is missing.

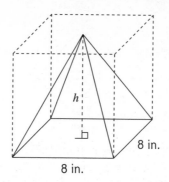

8 in.

8 in.

Where B is the area of the base of the prism, and h is the prism's altitude (the perpendicular distance from the vertex to the base), the formula for the volume is one-third the altitude times the area of the base:

$$V_{pyramid} = \frac{1}{3}(B \times h) \text{ units}^3$$

Now look at the preceding pyramid. Its base area is $8 \times 8 = 64$. Let's call the height 6 in. To find its volume

$$V_{pyramid} = \frac{1}{3}(B \times h)$$

$$V_{pyramid} = \frac{1}{3}(64 \times 6)$$

$$V_{pyramid} = 64 \times 2 = 128 \text{ in.}^3$$

Don't ask me who figured out that with a pyramid two-thirds of the prism with the same footprint is missing, because I have no idea, but that was the conclusion, and if you wanted to, you could prove that it works. Get yourself a prism and a pyramid with the same base and height (you can make them out of two blocks of wood if you're handy). Find a jar with a mouth wide enough for each figure to fit in it and place it in a pot. Fill the jar with water and carefully put the prism in until it is just submerged. Take the jar out of the pot and pour off the water that was displaced into a measuring cup. Repeat the same procedure with the pyramid, and you'll find the volume of water displaced by the pyramid is one-third that displaced by the prism. Hey, you can't make this stuff up.

Cones

A right circular cone is to a pyramid what a right cylinder is to a right prism. It looks like a pyramid with a circle for a base.

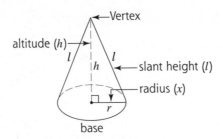

Notice the names attached to the relevant parts of the cone. The formulas for finding the lateral and total areas, as well as the volume of a cone, should be very familiar to you, since they are the same as for a pyramid, except that the formulas for circumference and areas of a circle have been incorporated in place of the perimeter and area accommodations for a plane figure with lateral edges. The lateral area of a cone is found by multiplying half the circumference of the circle by the slant height. Pardon the algebraic notation, but it's worth hundreds of words:

Where d is the base's diameter, $\quad A_{\text{lateral}} = \frac{1}{2}(\pi \times d \times l)$ units^2

or, substituting r, $\quad A_{\text{lateral}} = \frac{1}{2}(\pi \times 2 \times r \times l)$ units^2

or, simplifying, $\quad A_{\text{lateral}} = \pi \times r \times l$ units^2

Do you see how πd became $2\pi r$, and then one-half and 2 make 1, so they just drop out of the formula?

To find the total area, add the area of the circular base to the lateral area. That can be represented in three different ways:

$$A_{\text{total}} = A_{\text{lateral}} + B \text{ units}^2, \text{ or}$$
$$A_{\text{total}} = (\pi \times r \times l) + \pi \times r^2 \text{ units}^2, \text{ or}$$
$$A_{\text{total}} = \pi r(l + r) \text{ units}^2$$

I've been throwing a lot of × signs at you, but, you might recall that in algebraic notation, placing two symbols next to each other is all you need to indicate multiplication. Of course, your student doesn't need to know that yet, but for your sake, the last formula has the π and the radius multiplied together, and the result is multiplied by the sum of l and r. I'll use that last formula to find the total surface area of a right circular cone with a slant height of 8 cm and a radius of 6 cm.

First the formula: $\quad A_{\text{total}} = \pi r(l + r)$

Substitute: $\quad A_{\text{total}} = \pi \times 6(8 + 6)$

Sub for π and add: $\quad A_{\text{total}} = 3.14 \times 6(14)$

Multiply twice: $\quad A_{\text{total}} = 3.14 \times 84 = 263.76$

Round and place units: $\quad A_{\text{total}} = 264 \text{ cm}^2$

Finding the volume of a cone is the same as finding the volume of a prism in the first formula. The second formula allows for the fact that a cone's base is a circle.

$$V_{cone} = \frac{1}{3}(B \times h) \text{ units}^3, \text{ or}$$

$$V_{cone} = \frac{1}{3}(\pi)(r^2)(h) \text{ units}^3$$

Find the volume of a cone with a radius of 10 inches and a height (synonymous with altitude) of 9 inches. Leave the answer in terms of π.

First the formula: $V_{cone} = \frac{1}{3}(\pi)(r^2)(h)$

Substitute: $V_{cone} = \frac{1}{3}(\pi)(10^2)(9)$

Simplify: $V_{cone} = (\pi)(100)(3)$

Multiply and place units: $V_{cone} = 300\pi \text{ in.}^3$

I could write volumes and volumes!

Spheres

To fully round out this lesson's discussion (pun intended), we'll look at the **sphere,** sometimes referred to as the three-dimensional rendition of the circle. A sphere is the location of all points in three-dimensional space equal in distance from a fixed point, that being the sphere's center. That distance, of course, is the sphere's radius.

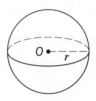

Since a sphere has no base and no sides, it has neither base area nor lateral area, but it does have surface area—that of its skin, and since it's a solid, it also has volume. The surface area of a sphere with radius length r may be found by the formula:

$$A_{sphere} = 4\pi r^2 \text{ units}^2$$

Let's find the surface area of a sphere with radius 8 ft.

The formula: $A_{sphere} = 4\pi r^2$

Substitute: $A_{sphere} = 4(3.14)(8^2)$

Multiply: $A_{sphere} = (12.56)(64)$

Complete and place units: $A_{sphere} = 803.84 = 804 \text{ ft.}^2$

Hey, that wasn't too bad. Finally, for this lesson at least, the formula for the volume of a sphere of radius r is:

$$V_{sphere} = \frac{4}{3} \pi r^3 \text{ units}^3$$

Let's use it to find the volume of a sphere with a radius of 12 dm.

Start with the formula: $V_{sphere} = \frac{4}{3} \pi r^3$

Substitute: $V_{sphere} = \frac{4}{3}(\pi)(12^3)$

Simplify: $V_{sphere} = \frac{4}{\cancel{3}_1}(3.14)\left(\cancel{576}^{192}\right)$

Multiply: $V_{sphere} = 12.56(192)$

Complete and place units: $V_{sphere} = 2411.52 = 2412 \text{ dm}^3$

Now you have a well-rounded geometric education.

EXERCISES

Find the lateral area of each of the following to the nearest whole unit.

1. a triangular pyramid with base 6 cm by 6 cm by 6 cm and slant height 8 cm
2. a square pyramid with base 8 in. on each edge and slant height 9 in.
3. a rectangular pyramid with base 9 dm by 6 dm and slant height 7 dm
4. a right circular cone with radius 9 ft. and slant height 12 ft.

Find the total surface area of each of the following to the nearest whole unit.

5. a square pyramid with base 12 in. on each edge and slant height 15 in.
6. a right circular cone with radius 8 m and slant height 9 m
7. a sphere of radius 15 cm
8. a rectangular pyramid with base 5 dm by 8 dm and slant height 6 dm
9. a right circular cone with radius 4 ft. and slant height 7 ft.
10. a sphere of radius 24 mm
11. a rectangular pyramid with base 8 cm by 12 cm and slant height 9 cm
12. a right circular cone with radius 10 in. and slant height 9 in.

Find the volume of each of the following to the nearest whole unit. Answers, where appropriate, may be left in terms of π.

13. a square pyramid with base 9 in. on each edge and altitude 12 in.
14. a right circular cone with radius 9 m and altitude 10 m
15. a sphere of radius 9 cm
16. a rectangular pyramid with base 7 dm by 6 dm and altitude 9 dm

17. a right circular cone with radius 6 in. and altitude 7 in.
18. a sphere of radius 12 mm
19. a rectangular pyramid with base 7 cm by 12 cm and altitude 10 cm
20. a right circular cone with radius 12 in. and altitude 8 in.

ANSWERS

1. 72 cm²
2. 144 in.²
3. 105 dm²
4. 339 ft.²
5. 504 in.²
6. 427 m²
7. 2826 cm²
8. 118 dm²
9. 138 ft.²
10. 7235 mm²

11. 276 cm²
12. 597 in.²
13. 324 in.³
14. 270π m³
15. 972π cm³
16. 126 dm³
17. 84π in.³
18. 2304π mm³
19. 280 cm³
20. 384π in.³

Minding One's Ps and Qs

The title of this lesson comes from the days when saloons used to dispense beer into customer-provided containers. Of course, that doesn't mean you have to tell that to your student. It was meant as a warning to tavern employees to make sure they dispensed **q**uarts only to customers who paid for quarts and dispensed **p**ints to those who had paid the lesser amount. All of this serves as the introduction to the chaotic state of our traditional liquid capacity measuring.

As mentioned earlier, liquid measure in the traditional units begins with the **minim**, which is about as **minim**um as you can get, being equal to half a drop, if you can conceive of such a thing. It is also equivalent to 0.0038 in.³, or 0.061612 ml. Happily, the use of this unit, as well as the next, is minimal these days. 60 min-

> The dram, although not the fluid one, is also quite popular in Armenia, where it is the basic monetary unit. Come to think of it, most Armenians hope and pray for the dram's liquidity, if not its fluidity.

ims make a fluid dram, which is another archaic unit with all but apothecaries, perfume makers, and some bartenders, who specialize in exotic and very expensive liquors or liqueurs.

Eight fluid drams will get you a fluid ounce, and that's the smallest unit of liquid capacity that most of us are used to dealing with, unless you happen to do a lot of baking. Then you're likely to be familiar with the tablespoon, abbreviated Tbs., and equal to about half a fluid ounce, or 3 teaspoons (tsp.). Did you notice how I snuck that in?!

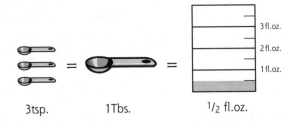

| 3tsp. | 1Tbs. | ¹/₂ fl.oz. |

The next measure that nobody ever uses any more, with the exception of fish or mushrooms, is the gill. Actually, that feeble attempt at humor was a play on the fact that you've probably never heard of the unit of measure, since, although it's spelled with a "g," it's actually pronounced "jill." A gill is equal to four fluid ounces, or a half a cup.

Now the fun really starts, as is alluded to in the following figure.

| Mug | Coffee cup | Soda cup | Milkshake | 8 fl. oz. measure |

You and your student are accustomed to referring to all of the preceding as cups, and they are, in the sense that a cup is a container. As a measure of liquid capacity, however, only the 8 fluid ounce measure is a cup. Strangely, odd units of measure are associated with drinking cups of various things. Coffee instructions direct the maker to use one or two tablespoons of grounds "per 5- or 6-ounce cup." There are two problems with that direction. First of all, there are no ounces of liquid measure. An ounce is a measure of weight; cups are figured in fluid ounces, and it takes eight of them to make a cup. I think you're getting the idea that our system of liquid measure makes as much sense to the outsider as does our language, with so many different ways of saying the same thing. In the case of the language, it has a richness to it that others lack. In the case of our units of liquid capacity, the bounds of logic are not in much evidence.

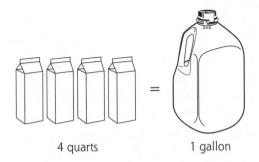

| 1 c. | 1 c. | 1 pt. | 1 pt. | 1 pt. | 1 qt. |

Put together two cups (of the 8 fl. oz. variety), and you will have the unit of measure known as a pint. Two pints make a quart. Have you been following this? All right, then, how many fluid ounces are there in a quart? How many in a pint and a half? How many in a half-pint? The easy way to answer those questions is to answer them from last to first. A half-pint is the same as a glass, so it contains 8 fluid ounces. By the way, a half-pint container is one your student should be very familiar with, since her school lunch probably comes with a half-pint of milk, and that's also the way milk is dispensed at fast-food establishments. A pint and a half is 3 cups, or 24 fluid ounces, and a quart is 4 cups, or 32 fluid ounces.

4 quarts = 1 gallon

Four quarts make a gallon, although your student might be much more familiar with the half-gallon milk container, unless you have a large family, or have refrigerator room to spare.

It is unfortunate that containers are not all proportionate, although you usually can place a pint and half-pint dairy-product container together, along with a quart milk container and see their relative sizes. The difference between the 1-quart milk container and the gallon one is also relatively easy to see. Less easy to see are the relations of the quart to the half gallon or the latter to the gallon. A trip to the paint department of a hardware store might also make an interesting field trip for the purpose of comparing pint, quart, and gallon containers.

The following abbreviations are standard for traditional units of liquid capacity:

fl. oz. = fluid ounce   c. = cup   pt. = pint   qt. = quart   gal. = gallon

EXERCISES

Express each given quantity in terms of the units following the equals sign.

1. 3 gal. = __ qt.
2. 10 pt. = __ qt.
3. 2 gal. = __ fl. oz.
4. 3 qt. = __ pt.
5. 48 fl. oz. = __ c.
6. 5 qt. = __ gal.

7. 5 gal. = __ pt.
8. 160 fl. oz. = __ qt.
9. 5 pt. = __ fl. oz.
10. 3 qt. = __ c.
11. 64 fl. oz. = __ gal.
12. 6 gal. = __ qt.

13. 7 pt. = __ qt.
14. 5 fl. oz. = __ minim
15. 7 qt. = __ c.
16. 40 fl. oz. = __ pt.
17. 7 qt. = __ pt.
18. 3 c. = __ gill

ANSWERS

1. 12
2. 5
3. 256
4. 6
5. 6
6. 1.25

7. 40
8. 5
9. 80
10. 12
11. 0.5
12. 24

13. 3.5
14. 2800
15. 28
16. 2.5
17. 14
18. 6

Liter, Not Litter

As noted in an earlier lesson, the soft drink industry seems to be the only American industry to have somewhat embraced SI units, having created the universally available one- and two-liter bottles of soda. There are also half-liter bottles available to go with the still ubiquitous 12 fl. oz. can. Beer, an unfit subject for your student but still noteworthy, remains available in pints, quarts, and those 12 ouncers again.

Wine comes in SI bottles, generally 750 ml and 1.5 l, which I trust you recognize as milliliters and liters, respectively. Of course, that tradition was created by the Europeans, Australians, and Chileans, with the Californians, for the most part, hopping on board (I must not slight the New York, Pennsylvania, Oregon, or Washington vintners, either). There are some hard liquor purveyors who have embraced liters, but most of the American ones remain keyed in on the "fifth," that amazing liquor bottle containing 25.6 fluid ounces of booze. Thank heavens this is a book intended for adults! Who but an industrious entrepreneur would come up with that idiotic unit? Of course, when whoever it was realized that he could squeeze five bottles out of a single gallon of distilled spirits instead of only 4 quart-sized ones, . . . Well, I'll drink to that!

Unlike traditional units of liquid capacity, liters and milliliters are directly translatable to measures of solid volume. That's because a liter is actually a cubic decimeter, 10 cm by 10 cm by 10 cm. That's part of the beauty of the SI units. One-thousandth of a liter, 1 milliliter, is identical to 1 cm³.

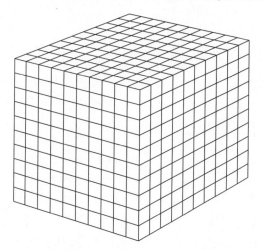

Unfortunately, converting between SI and traditional units of liquid capacity is not very convenient. 1l, also written 1 L, is equivalent to 1.0567 fluid quarts. 1 fluid quart = 0.9464 L. Those are not very user-friendly conversion factors. Based upon the first, we can calculate that since there are 32 fl. oz. in one fluid quart, one liter contains $32 \times 1.0567 = 33.8144$ fl. oz. We might summarize that by saying that one liter is a little bit larger than a fluid quart.

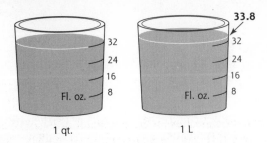

The relative sizes of the quart and the liter are easier to see by looking at the measuring cups in the diagram. As noted, they are close. Since it is rare to need to convert precisely from liters to quarts, or vice versa, we'll settle for approximating a cup to be a bit less than 250 ml and a pint to be a bit less than a half liter (500 ml). Your student might be required by his teacher to do actual conversions, so you're going to get a bit of practice with that in the exercises.

Although the pun might be obvious, when one is asked to work with SI units of liquid capacity, it is best to think literally!

EXERCISES

Use the relationships stated in the last lesson to convert from the given units to the asked for ones.

1. 10 fl. oz. = __ ml
2. 10 ml = __ fl. oz.
3. 0.5 L = __ fl. oz.
4. 12 fl. oz. = __ ml
5. 3 cups = __ ml
6. 200 ml = __ fl. oz.
7. 0.25 L = __ fl. oz.
8. 1 fl. oz. = __ ml
9. 800 ml = __ fl. oz.

10. 1 pt. = __ ml
11. 400 ml = __ fl. oz.
12. 6 fl. oz. = __ ml
13. 600 ml = __ fl. oz.
14. 25 fl. oz. = __ ml
15. 1 c. = __ ml
16. 18 fl. oz. = __ ml
17. 300 ml = __ fl. oz.
18. 0.75 L = __ fl. oz.

ANSWERS

1. 295.75
2. 0.338
3. 16.9
4. 354.9
5. 709.8
6. 6.76
7. 8.5
8. 29.575
9. 27.05

10. 473.2
11. 13.53
12. 177.45
13. 20.3
14. 739.375
15. 236.6
16. 532.35
17. 10.14
18. 25.4

FOO

That's right, **FOO**! It's an acronym standing for **f**undamental **o**rder of **o**perations. It might not have occurred to you, but the order in which numbers are combined matters. Consider the following string of numerals and operating signs:

$$24 \div 3 + 9 \times 2 - 5 \times 6 - 15 \div 3 + 8 = \underline{\quad}$$

I'll solve it from left to right, beginning with $24 \div 3$ and working my way across. $24 \div 3 = 8$. To that I'll add 9, to make 17, and multiply that by 2 to get 34. From the 34, if you're still with me, I'll subtract 5; that's 29. $29 \times 6 = 174$, from which I'll subtract 15 to get 159. Next, I'll divide 159 by 3 to get 53. Adding 8 to that, I get 61, which is the answer, right?

Well, yes and no. 61 is the correct result for the procedure that I followed, but it is certainly not the solution to the sequence of operations called for. To actually solve the project—I call it that for lack of a better term—I'll need to do some grouping. I'm going to use parentheses to do the grouping, just to make it easier for you to see what the solution is about:

$$(24 \div 3) + (9 \times 2) - (5 \times 6) - (15 \div 3) + 8 = \underline{\quad}$$

Those operations that I have grouped together need to be performed ahead of any others. By so doing, we're left with this:

$$8 + 18 - 30 - 5 + 8 = \underline{\quad}$$

$8 + 18 = 26$; $26 - 30 = -4$. To that add -5 to get -9. [I know there's no plus sign between them, but if you're at negative 4, going 5 more in the negative direction is tantamount to having $-4 + (-5)$, which equal -9.] Now add 8 to that, and the total is -1. It wasn't my intention at the start to come out with a negative result, yet there is a lesson here. How can the same group of numbers and signs total to 61 when combined one way, and -1 when done in a different order?

The answer is, there are a few right ways to combine them and a few wrong ways. You might recall that way back in Part I, when we were dealing with whole numbers, I mentioned that certain operations were commutative and certain others were not. Addition and multiplication are commutative. It doesn't matter whether you do them forward or backward, the answer will be the same. $3 \times 4 = 4 \times 3 = 12$. $4 + 5 = 5 + 4 = 9$. But the commutative properties for addition and multiplication do not apply to subtraction or division. $9 - 4 \neq 4 - 9$, and $4 \div 2 \neq 2 \div 4$. Furthermore, they don't apply across mixed addition and multiplication, either.

The fundamental order of operations requires that they be performed in the following sequence: Parentheses, Exponents, Multiplication, Division, Addition, Subtraction, thus giving rise to the mnemonic "PEMDAS," or "Please Excuse My Dear Aunt Sally." Multiplication and division carry equal weight, so you may do whichever you encounter first. The same rule applies to addition and subtraction.

I introduced the parentheses into the preceding mélange just for the purpose of grouping. The parentheses referred to in the FOO are not being used until algebra, where you are likely to come across a construction such as $2(3x + 5)$, indicating that those terms inside the parentheses must both be multiplied by the 2 on the outside before moving on. Neither parentheses nor exponents are likely to apply to your elementary math student, but I'll leave the exponents in and go with a mnemonic device encompassing only the final five, like, "Even My Dog Acts Stupid."

Let's try applying those orders of operation to the following:

$$13 \times 3 - 36 \div 6 + 72 \div 8 + 6 - 9 \times 3 + 11 = \_\_$$

There are no exponents, so first do all the multiplications and divisions: $13 \times 3 = 39$. $36 \div 6 = 6$, $72 \div 8 = 9$ and $9 \times 3 = 27$, so that brings us to this:

$$39 - 6 + 9 + 6 - 27 + 11 = \_\_$$

Next, add and subtract as you move from left to right.

$$39 - 6 = 33;\ 33 + 9 = 42;\ 42 + 6 = 48;\ 48 - 27 = 21;\ 21 + 11 = 32$$

See, it's easy when you know how. I'll slip a few exponents into the exercises for you, just to keep you on your toes.

EXERCISES

Solve each of the following.

1. $12 \div 4 - 3^3 \div 9 + 64 \div 8 + 6 - 6 \times 3^2 + 16 = \_\_$
2. $9^2 + 5 \times 8 - 72 \div 6^2 + 15 \times 4 - 7^2 + 75 \div 5^2 - 8 = \_\_$
3. $90 - 8^2 \div 16 + 2^5 \times 3^2 - 4^3 \times 3 + 3^4 - 60 \div 5 + 9 = \_\_$
4. $12 \times 8 - 21 \div 3 + 54 \div 6 + 6 \times 9 - 3 \times 11 = \_\_$
5. $6 \times 7 \times 2 - 24 \times 6 + 96 \div 12 - 51 \div 17 + 9 - 28 \div 4 = \_\_$
6. $5^3 + 8 \times 7 + 15 \times 8 - 84 \div 12 - 76 \div 4 + 3 \times 18$
7. $11^2 + 7 \times 9 - 90 \div 3^2 + 8 \times 5^2 - 17 + 125 \div 5^2 - 18 = \_\_$
8. $8 \times 7 - 56 \div 2^3 + 9 \times 3^2 + 216 \div 6^2 - 18 \times 7 + 5 \times 3^3 - 75 \div 3 + 6 \times 5^2 + 343 \div 7^2 = \_\_$
9. $5 \times 9 - 4^2 \div 2^3 + 9 \times 7 + 108 \div 6^2 - 12 \times 9 + 4 \times 3^2 - 48 \div 3 + 5 \times 8 + 243 \div 9^2 = \_\_$
10. $6^3 \div 3 + 7^2 \times 3 - 8 \div 4 - 8 \times 16 + 27 \div 3 - 5 \times 4^3 + 17 \times 3 - 72 \div 8 + 3^3 \times 5 = \_\_$

ANSWERS

1. −24
2. 125
3. 260
4. 119
5. −53

6. 329
7. 344
8. 277
9. 64
10. −45

Probability

Probability is part of a branch of mathematics known as statistics. Statistics has gotten a bad reputation over the years with non-mathematicians, such as the Victorian era British Prime Minister Benjamin Disraeli, who is reputed to have said "There are three types of lies: Lies, damned lies, and statistics." The probability of an event is the likelihood it will happen, usually expressed as a fraction, and is determined by the number of desirable outcomes (or results) divided by the number of possible outcomes. A probability of 1 is a certainty. A probability of 0 is an impossibility.

Tossing a Coin

What is the **probability** that when you throw a coin up into the air spinning, it will land with the heads side facing up? Remember:

$$\text{Probability} = \frac{\text{\# of desirable outcomes}}{\text{\# of possible outcomes}}$$

When tossing a coin, there are two possible outcomes, heads or tails. The coin's landing on its edge is not a possible outcome. Of those, one is desirable, heads. So, the probability of throwing one head when flipping one coin is

$$P_{\text{heads}} = \frac{1}{2}$$

What is the probability of throwing a tail? If you have any doubt as to that answer, look back at the formula. There are two possible outcomes, one of which, tails, is desirable:

$$P_{\text{tails}} = \frac{1}{2}$$

Each flip of a coin is an independent event, and has no influence on, nor is it influenced by, any other flip.

Suppose Ian has flipped a coin five times and all five have been heads. What is the probability that the next flip will be a head? Well he's all ready had five heads in a row. So he shouldn't have much of a chance for another one, should he? If you answered "no" to my last question, then you haven't been paying attention. The probability that Ian will throw another head is one-half—the same as it was every other time he tossed the coin.

Suppose I had asked you what the probability was that he would have thrown 5 heads in a row? Well, each of the five times he threw the coin, his probability of a head would be one-half, but the probability of his throwing five in a row would be the probability of the product of those individual probabilities. That is

$$P_{5 \text{ heads in a row}} = \frac{1}{2} \times \frac{1}{2} \times \frac{1}{2} \times \frac{1}{2} \times \frac{1}{2} = \frac{1}{32}$$

An **independent event** is one whose outcome has no effect on any other outcomes. Remember, the probability of a number of independent events is found by multiplying together the probabilities of each of those events together.

Spinners

A spinner is a device that we've all seen, associated as it is with many board games. Of course, depending upon the age of your student, he might never have played a board game, what with the near universal availability of video games. If that's the case, you might actually have to show him what a spinner is.

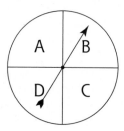

The spinner shown here is a fair one, as must be true of every probability model. Computing probability always assumes that the model is a fair one, with no room for cheating (as within head-heavy coins or tilted spinner with weighted arrow-head).

That being the case, what is the probability of spinning an A on one spin? Since there are four possible outcomes, A, B, C, and D, and one desirable outcome, A, the probability is one-fourth.

What is the probability of spinning an A, B, or a C? This time, three of the four possible outcomes are desirable, so the probability is three-fourths.

What do you suppose the probability is of spinning A, B, C, or D, on the spinner? You probably know this already, but it is better to make sure than to leave you hanging. Four possible outcomes and four correct outcomes. That's four-fourths, which simplifies to 1—the highest possible probability, known as certainty. Now, what do you think the probability is of spinning an E on that spinner? Since there is no E on the spinner, there are no desirable outcomes out of four possible ones. Zero-fourths = 0—impossibility.

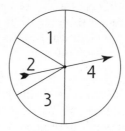

What is the probability of spinning a 2 on the spinner pictured here? Give this one some thought before you respond. The spinner has four sections on it, numbered 1 to 4, but it is *NOT* a fair spinner, in the sense that all numbers are not weighted the same. The answer to the question above is

$$P_{spinning\ 2} = \frac{1}{6}$$

Whether or not that makes sense to you, I'm not going to explain it—yet. Before getting around to that, take a stab at the probability of spinning a 4 on the same spinner. Did you get an answer to that? The probability of spinning a 4 on that spinner is one-half. Now, if you haven't figured it out yet, or even if you have, check out the following figure.

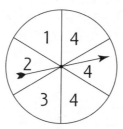

The figure is exactly the same as the one preceding it, except for the fact that the field previously occupied by one 4 has been evenly divided into three parts, each of which contains a 4. It might look different from the previous diagram, but it is mathematically the same. The area occupied by (or in which you might spin a) 4 is 3 times the size of the area in which you might spin any other number. Another way of saying that is you're three times as likely to spin a 4 as you are to spin any other number.

Now let's go back to the reason why one-sixth was the probability of spinning a 2. On the new spinner, which is mathematically identical to the older one (even though it looks a little different), there are 6 possible outcomes (3 of which happen to be 4s), and only 1 way to spin a 2, so

$$P_{spinning\ 2} = \frac{1}{6}$$

When it comes to spinning a 4, there are 3 ways to do it out of the six possible outcomes:

$$P_{spinning\ 4} = \frac{3}{6} = \frac{1}{2}$$

That comes down to one-half. I hope that clears it up for you.

Dependent Probabilities

Not all probability situations concern independent events. If, for example, a card is drawn from a poker deck, and you would like to know the probability of its being a jack, the answer would be

$$P_{jack} = \frac{4}{52} = \frac{1}{13}$$

That's because there are 52 cards in a standard deck, and 4 of them are jacks. The probability of drawing a jack on the next pick, assuming the first card had not been replaced, would depend upon whether the drawn card had been a jack or not. If a jack had not been drawn the first time, the probability of drawing one the second time would be

$$P_{jack} = \frac{4}{51}$$

That's because there are only 51 cards left in the deck, but there are still 4 jacks. If, however, a jack had been picked on the first try, the probability of picking a second one would have significantly decreased as follows:

$$P_{2nd\ jack} = \frac{3}{51} = \frac{1}{17}$$

If a jack had been picked on the first try, there would still have been 51 cards left to pick from, but only 3 of them would have been jacks, since the fourth one would have already been selected.

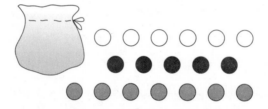

Consider a bag that contains 5 black, 6 white, and 7 gray marbles. You reach into the bag and blindly pick a marble. What is the probability of its being a white one? Since there are a total of 18 marbles in the bag, and 6 of them are white, there are 6 desirable outcomes from 18 total possible:

$$P_{white} = \frac{6}{18} = \frac{1}{3}$$

So, the probability is one-third. Now, keeping that marble out and picking again, what is the probability that the next marble picked will be a black one? Well, do you have an answer yet? The answer is that there is not enough information to answer that question. You know that there are 17 marbles left in the bag, but without knowing the color of the marble that was drawn, you can't compute the probability of the next draw.

Something tells me that you'll probably enjoy the exercises that are coming up right now.

EXERCISES

What is the probability of

1. tossing a coin 6 times and getting 6 tails?
2. tossing 2 coins and getting 2 heads?
3. tossing 2 coins and getting 2 tails?

For 4–5, consider a spinner with 5 equally sized fields marked I, II, III, IV, V. What is the probability of

4. spinning an even number (II or IV)?
5. spinning a number other than III?

For 6–7, consider a spinner with 6 equally sized fields marked 1–6, respectively, and a 7th field marked 7 that is twice the size of each of the other 6. What is the probability of

6. spinning a 5?
7. spinning a 7?

Questions 8–9 refer to a cloth bag containing 7 red and 6 blue marbles of equal size and weight. What is the probability of blindly drawing

8. a red marble?
9. two red marbles in sequence?

ANSWERS

1. $\frac{1}{64}$

2. $\frac{1}{4}$

3. $\frac{1}{4}$

4. $\frac{2}{5}$

5. $\frac{4}{5}$

6. $\frac{1}{8}$

7. $\frac{1}{4}$

8. $\frac{7}{13}$

9. $\frac{7}{13} \times \frac{1}{2} = \frac{7}{26}$

Appendix

More Help for Your Student

Postman Stories

The Madison Project dealt with the multiplication of integers through the device of a crazy postal worker (who ever heard of one of those?), to whom we'll refer as "the postman," and a flaky housewife (blondeness not required). Each morning, the postman would bring the housewife a passel of checks or bills, paying no attention to whose name was on the envelopes. The housewife also paid no attention to the names, which made her the perfect confederate for the postman character. When she received bills, she concluded those were funds that she needed to pay out, and so she would have to reduce her household finances by that amount. When she received checks, the opposite was true. Let's see how that worked:

On Monday morning, the postman brought the housewife 4 bills for $12 apiece. Was she better or worse off than she was before his visit? Well, he brought bills: brought is positive and bills are negative. That translates to: $+4 \times -12 = -48$

She considered herself to be $48 poorer.

The next day, the postman returns and tells the housewife that three of the bills were not for her, and he takes them back. That's: $-3 \times -12 = +36$

She's $36 richer.

On Wednesday, the postman brings the housewife 5 checks for $15 apiece. That translates to $+5 \times +15 = 75$

She believes she's $75 richer.

Remember, brings is $+$ and takes is $-$; checks are $+$, and bills are $-$. So, when on Thursday the postman comes and tells the housewife that 4 of those $15 checks weren't for her, and he'll have to take them back, she considers herself to be: Hmm . . . $-4 \times +15 = -60$. She feels $60 poorer from this visit. And there you have the model for "Postman Stories."

Avogadro's Number

Amedeo Avogadro was an Italian scientist who lived from 1776 to 1856. He discovered that equal volumes of different gases under the identical conditions of temperature and pressure contain equal numbers of molecules. This as known as Avogadro's law. He went on to propose that in one mole (what chemists call one molecular gram weight) of a substance, the number of molecules that it contained was 6.022137×10^{23}. That figure is known to chemists, physicists, and mathematicians of today as **"Avogadro's constant"** or **"Avogadro's number."**

I was just thinking that it must be pretty cool to have a number named after you. Not even Sir Isaac Newton has one of those. All he has are Newton's laws of this and that, and of course, the ever popular filled cookie. I guess most of us will have to settle for grandchildren.

Flash Card Templates for Multiplication and Division

On the following pages are templates for the fronts of flash cards for multiplication and division. I say the fronts because the answers, which would normally go on the back, are omitted. You can supply the answers for the backs on your own, or go find them in Lessons 4 and 5, respectively. These templates are not meant to be cut out because if they were, you would lose half of them (the ones on the other side of each page). Rather, you may photocopy these pages and then cut up those copies and glue or tape them to 3-x-5-inch index cards, either whole or cut in half. Or, if you prefer, feel free to draw your own with a felt marker. I hope this proves useful to you.

$1 \times 1 =$ ___

$1 \times 9 =$ ___

$2 \times 7 =$ ___

$1 \times 2 =$ ___

$1 \times 10 =$ ___

$2 \times 8 =$ ___

$1 \times 3 =$ ___

$2 \times 1 =$ ___

$2 \times 9 =$ ___

$1 \times 4 =$ ___

$2 \times 2 =$ ___

$2 \times 10 =$ ___

$1 \times 5 =$ ___

$2 \times 3 =$ ___

$3 \times 1 =$ ___

$1 \times 6 =$ ___

$2 \times 4 =$ ___

$3 \times 2 =$ ___

$1 \times 7 =$ ___

$2 \times 5 =$ ___

$3 \times 3 =$ ___

$1 \times 8 =$ ___

$2 \times 6 =$ ___

$3 \times 4 =$ ___

$3 \times 5 = \underline{}$

$4 \times 3 = \underline{}$

$5 \times 1 = \underline{}$

$3 \times 6 = \underline{}$

$4 \times 4 = \underline{}$

$5 \times 2 = \underline{}$

$3 \times 7 = \underline{}$

$4 \times 5 = \underline{}$

$5 \times 3 = \underline{}$

$3 \times 8 = \underline{}$

$4 \times 6 = \underline{}$

$5 \times 4 = \underline{}$

$3 \times 9 = \underline{}$

$4 \times 7 = \underline{}$

$5 \times 5 = \underline{}$

$3 \times 10 = \underline{}$

$4 \times 8 = \underline{}$

$5 \times 6 = \underline{}$

$4 \times 1 = \underline{}$

$4 \times 9 = \underline{}$

$5 \times 7 = \underline{}$

$4 \times 2 = \underline{}$

$4 \times 10 = \underline{}$

$5 \times 8 = \underline{}$

$5 \times 9 =$ __

$6 \times 7 =$ __

$7 \times 5 =$ __

$5 \times 10 =$ __

$6 \times 8 =$ __

$7 \times 6 =$ __

$6 \times 1 =$ __

$6 \times 9 =$ __

$7 \times 7 =$ __

$6 \times 2 =$ __

$6 \times 10 =$ __

$7 \times 8 =$ __

$6 \times 3 =$ __

$7 \times 1 =$ __

$7 \times 9 =$ __

$6 \times 4 =$ __

$7 \times 2 =$ __

$7 \times 10 =$ __

$6 \times 5 =$ __

$7 \times 3 =$ __

$8 \times 1 =$ __

$6 \times 6 =$ __

$7 \times 4 =$ __

$8 \times 2 =$ __

$8 \times 3 =$ ___

$9 \times 1 =$ ___

$9 \times 9 =$ ___

$8 \times 4 =$ ___

$9 \times 2 =$ ___

$9 \times 10 =$ ___

$8 \times 5 =$ ___

$9 \times 3 =$ ___

$10 \times 1 =$ ___

$8 \times 6 =$ ___

$9 \times 4 =$ ___

$10 \times 2 =$ ___

$8 \times 7 =$ ___

$9 \times 5 =$ ___

$10 \times 3 =$ ___

$8 \times 8 =$ ___

$9 \times 6 =$ ___

$10 \times 4 =$ ___

$8 \times 9 =$ ___

$9 \times 7 =$ ___

$10 \times 5 =$ ___

$8 \times 10 =$ ___

$9 \times 8 =$ ___

$10 \times 6 =$ ___

$10 \times 7 = \underline{\quad}$	$5 \div 1 = \underline{\quad}$	$6 \div 2 = \underline{\quad}$
$10 \times 8 = \underline{\quad}$	$6 \div 1 = \underline{\quad}$	$8 \div 2 = \underline{\quad}$
$10 \times 9 = \underline{\quad}$	$7 \div 1 = \underline{\quad}$	$10 \div 2 = \underline{\quad}$
$10 \times 10 = \underline{\quad}$	$8 \div 1 = \underline{\quad}$	$12 \div 2 = \underline{\quad}$
$1 \div 1 = \underline{\quad}$	$9 \div 1 = \underline{\quad}$	$14 \div 2 = \underline{\quad}$
$2 \div 1 = \underline{\quad}$	$10 \div 1 = \underline{\quad}$	$16 \div 2 = \underline{\quad}$
$3 \div 1 = \underline{\quad}$	$2 \div 2 = \underline{\quad}$	$18 \div 2 = \underline{\quad}$
$4 \div 1 = \underline{\quad}$	$4 \div 2 = \underline{\quad}$	$20 \div 2 = \underline{\quad}$

3 ÷ 3 = __

27 ÷ 3 = __

28 ÷ 4 = __

6 ÷ 3 = __

30 ÷ 3 = __

32 ÷ 4 = __

9 ÷ 3 = __

4 ÷ 4 = __

36 ÷ 4 = __

12 ÷ 3 = __

8 ÷ 4 = __

40 ÷ 4 = __

15 ÷ 3 = __

12 ÷ 4 = __

5 ÷ 5 = __

18 ÷ 3 = __

16 ÷ 4 = __

10 ÷ 5 = __

21 ÷ 3 = __

20 ÷ 4 = __

15 ÷ 5 = __

24 ÷ 3 = __

24 ÷ 4 = __

20 ÷ 5 = __

$25 \div 5 =$ ___

$18 \div 6 =$ ___

$7 \div 7 =$ ___

$30 \div 5 =$ ___

$24 \div 6 =$ ___

$14 \div 7 =$ ___

$35 \div 5 =$ ___

$30 \div 6 =$ ___

$21 \div 7 =$ ___

$40 \div 5 =$ ___

$36 \div 6 =$ ___

$28 \div 7 =$ ___

$45 \div 5 =$ ___

$42 \div 6 =$ ___

$35 \div 7 =$ ___

$50 \div 5 =$ ___

$48 \div 6 =$ ___

$42 \div 7 =$ ___

$6 \div 6 =$ ___

$54 \div 6 =$ ___

$49 \div 7 =$ ___

$12 \div 6 =$ ___

$60 \div 6 =$ ___

$56 \div 7 =$ ___

63 ÷ 7 = __

56 ÷ 8 = __

45 ÷ 9 = __

70 ÷ 7 = __

64 ÷ 8 = __

54 ÷ 9 = __

8 ÷ 8 = __

72 ÷ 8 = __

63 ÷ 9 = __

16 ÷ 8 = __

80 ÷ 8 = __

72 ÷ 9 = __

24 ÷ 8 = __

9 ÷ 9 = __

81 ÷ 9 = __

32 ÷ 8 = __

18 ÷ 9 = __

10 ÷ 9 = __

40 ÷ 8 = __

27 ÷ 9 = __

10 ÷ 10 = __

48 ÷ 8 = __

36 ÷ 9 = __

20 ÷ 10 = __

30 ÷ 10 = __

60 ÷ 10 = __

90 ÷ 10 = __

40 ÷ 10 = __

70 ÷ 10 = __

100 ÷ 10 = __

50 ÷ 10 = __

80 ÷ 10 = __